AN
L. Francis
Herreshoff
READER

AN
L. Francis
Herreshoff
READER

BY

L. Francis
Herreshoff

INTERNATIONAL MARINE PUBLISHING CO.

Published by International Marine Publishing Company
21 Elm Street, Camden, Maine 04843

Contents

Publisher's Preface

It is indeed a great pleasure to publish another book by the late L. Francis Herreshoff.

Mr. Herreshoff was an articulate spokesman for using the best from man's maritime heritage. In his yacht designs, he always applied to that best his own prodigious imagination to produce boats that are at once innovative and yet that are based on craft that have proven themselves over a long period of time. Because he was an artist, his boats are always sweet to the eye.

This book contains Francis Herreshoff's thoughts and experiences relating to a wide variety of things and people maritime. Fascinating material in itself, Mr. Herreshoff's writing also provides background to an understanding of him as a designer and as a person. We find L. Francis Herreshoff's writing ever interesting and instructive, sometimes prejudiced, often truly wise, rarely overtaken by events, and never boring. He always provides us with "a good read." We trust he will so provide you too.

Of the 30 chapters in the book, 20 appeared during the Forties and Fifties in *The Rudder* magazine. Of these, seven were gathered in that fine little book published by *The Rudder* in 1946, *The Writings of L. Francis Herreshoff.* Nine of the chapters have not before been published.

It was Muriel Vaughn, Mr. Herreshoff's secretary who has stayed on at The Castle in Marblehead to minister to a continuing interest in Herreshoff designs, who located and provided original manuscripts and illustrations for the book. Without her continuing interest and efforts, such a book would have been impossible, and its readers owe her a debt of thanks.

The artwork that forms the background for the dust jacket was drawn by Mr. Herreshoff for a different purpose. Its use on the jacket was suggested by Mrs. Vaughn's daughter, Elizabeth, and Guy Fleming skillfully worked the Herreshoff sea horses, dolphins, and mermaids into his jacket design.

Roger C. Taylor
International Marine

The *America*

Queen Victoria was one of the most beloved sovereigns ever to wield the scepter, and when the time came around to celebrate her jubilee the whole British nation entered wholeheartedly into the arrangements to make this an occasion never to be forgotten. The queen's consort, Prince Albert, was particularly active in arranging an international exhibition of the mechanical arts of the world, and the first large building of glass and metal, the Crystal Palace, was erected for the exhibition. Altogether the year of 1851 was a most notable one in England.

People from every quarter of the globe visited the exhibition, but while the Yankee notions and mechanical contrivances of the young United States were rather laughed at, that year we did make quite an impression on the water. This was rather a surprise and shock to Britannia (who had indisputably ruled the waves for some time), but much of the world saw no reason why Britannia's young daughter should not be fleeter than she had become in the years of her maturity, although it must be admitted that Britannia was not outfooted much this first time, or for that matter at any time after.

This surprise came about somewhat as follows: In 1850 when the Crystal Palace was being built and invitations sent to manufacturers throughout the world to exhibit their products, a London merchant wrote to a New York business man and suggested that this country send over one of its pilot schooners which had become famous for their speed. This was thought to be a good way to represent young America in nautical matters during the coming jubilee, and the letter was brought to the notice of John Cox Stevens, then commodore of the New York Yacht Club, who together with the vice commodore, Hamilton Wilkes, formed a syndicate to build a yacht to send over. One of the most prominent members of this syndicate was George L. Schuyler and he seems to have made the contract with William H. Brown to build the yacht for $30,000. Perhaps Mr. Schuyler was acting as secretary or treasurer for the syndicate, but the existing letters in connection with the building of this yacht are between George L. Schuyler and William H. Brown.

Although W. H. Brown had not built yachts previously, he did have at that time for his superintendent one George Steers who, before being employed by Mr. Brown, had produced several of the yachts in the first fleet of the New York Yacht Club. Mr. Steers had also designed the famous pilot schooner *Mary Taylor*, which is considered the first American vessel built under the wave-line theory developed by the eminent Scottish steamship designer John Scott Russell, and it is most likely that Brown obtained this contract because Commodore Stevens had known Steers and his work for several years. In fact, Steers designed or modeled the early yachts *Una, Ray, Julia, Widgeon, L'Esperance, Cygnet, Cornelia,* and *Haze.*

George Steers was a truly remarkable man. He was the son of an English shipyard superintendent who had served an apprenticeship of seven years and worked in several British dockyards before he came to this country in 1819. George was born in 1820 in Washington, where his father was first employed in this country, and he had twelve brothers and sisters. His father and family later moved to New York and there at the age of only sixteen George built the sixteen-foot sailboat *Martin Vanburen*, which in 1836 won a prize given for small sailboats by John C. Stevens. So it might be concluded that Stevens and Steers were acquainted from that date. George Steers must have been a very active man, for in a short life he designed many boats and ships, which ranged from early sandbaggers to the frigate *Niagara.*

The fast brig of his design, *Sunny South* (which afterward became a Cuban slaver), is said by some to be the handsomest sailing vessel built in America. In the latter part of his life George Steers formed a partnership with his brother, and under the name of James R. and George Steers the firm leased a yard at the foot of 11th Street on the East River in New York, right next to W. H. Brown's yard, and were building the ocean steamer *Adriatic* for the Collins Line when unfortunately George Steers met his death driving a pair of spirited horses. He was only thirty-six years old and if he had lived longer might have become the greatest yacht designer of all time and eclipsed George L. Watson and N. G. Herreshoff, for there is no doubt he was a great artist. But we must get back to the building of *America*.

William H. Brown's yard was at the foot of 12th Street on the East River, which location for the last seventy-five years or more has been a much-populated part of New York City, but a hundred years ago there seem to have been several boat and shipyards in that region. The *America* was contracted for on November 15, 1850, and was supposed to be ready for trials in April 1851, but delays, which always seem unavoidable in shipyards, held back her launching until May 3. By this time her owners were quite annoyed and worried at the delays, where-upon G. L. Schuyler made an offer on behalf of the owners to take her over when completed, but without trials, for $20,000, to which the builders consented. Even this was a high price for the times, for I have heard that General Paine's *Puritan* and *Mayflower* both cost less.

No ceremonies were held at the launching and apparently none of the owners was present, which may have been because of friction between them and the builders caused by the delays. However, the credit for naming her *America* is given to W. H. Brown. The construction of *America* had been followed with much public interest and the *New York Illustrated News* published a woodcut of her on the stocks. This cut shows a model with very fine and sharp ends and no parallel lines amidships, which was unusual in those days. It is said that one of her owners, Vice Commodore Hamilton Wilkes, followed and watched her construction so constantly through the winter that exposure from sitting about in the builders' yard contributed to his death from consumption the following year, although he had been a large, strong man used to all forms of outdoor sport.

Although there are no original drawings or models of the *America*, there is no doubt that she was entirely a product of George Steers as far as design is concerned, but after her success some people hinted that Commodore Stevens, who had designed several fast yachts, had been influential in her design, and W. H. Brown claimed some of the credit. In answer to these reports, Commodore Stevens on his return from England made the following statement to the *New York Herald:* "As I have no wish to appropriate to myself the property of another, I will take this occasion to repeat—what I have over and over stated, both in England and this country—that the model and construction of the yacht *America* were due, and due alone, to Mr. George Steers."

America is conceded to be Steers' attempt at an improvement on the pilot schooner *Mary Taylor,* which he had designed in 1849, and whose long fine bow had created such a sensation that Commodore Stevens had his large sloop *Maria* lengthened forward so that her waterline length was increased from ninety-two to 110 feet. Several smaller yachts, including *Una,* were also given longer, sharper bows in 1850. It is interesting that the *Mary Taylor* was built for the New York pilot Captain Richard Brown, the same Dick Brown who took *America* across and handled her in her races, and no doubt after his experience in sailing the *Mary Taylor,* he was the best possible choice.

In sail plan and general looks, *America* was not dissimilar to the pilot schooners or to the packets that had been used since colonial times to carry passengers and freight before the steamer took the place of this class of vessel along our Atlantic coast. She may have had more rake to the masts than was customary in New England, but still less rake than the notably fast vessels built at Baltimore. It seems evident that in the *America* Steers was trying to produce an example of a good American schooner, and although her entrance (or bow) was much finer than usual, still *America* was not notably different in appearance from the pilot schooners often shown in the background of ship paintings between 1800 and 1850. I also must note, and it will surprise some people, that the French in their Mediterranean ports had developed a type of sailing vessel called a ballahou, which differed little in model and sail plan from the clipper-bowed American schooners in the first half of the nineteenth century. The ballahou, though, did not have a spring stay between the mastheads, but instead, like our modern staysail schooners, they had a mainstay that supported the head of the mainmast. So altogether *America* was not as original a craft as many think.

She might be described in a few words as a typical American schooner of the period, designed by the son of an Englishman on the wave-line theory originated by a Scotsman.

In her trial races before going abroad, *America* was beaten by Commodore Stevens' *Maria*, which is not surprising, for *Maria* not only was a sloop but I believe an all-around larger vessel. During these races *America* also sprung her foremast head and broke her main gaff, all of which might be expected on a new vessel hurriedly rigged.

America sailed for abroad on June 21, 1851. She had a crew all told of thirteen, which would seem unlucky, but *America* was a strange craft. She arrived in England on a Friday and won the famous cup on a Friday, defeating thirteen yachts. Perhaps the unlucky part of it was for the British sailors. While thirteen nowadays seems a small crew for a yacht of that size (170 tons), *America* undoubtedly was a comparatively snug-rigged vessel that could leave her three lower sails set in most weather.

Among the men who crossed on her were George Steers, his brother James R. Steers, and James' son George Steers II, seventeen years of age. She made the crossing in twenty days in moderate summer weather carrying a suit of sails belonging to the *Mary Taylor*, with her own racing sails belowdeck. The only known log of this crossing was kept by James Steers and tells mostly what they had to eat and drink each day. They seemed to fare remarkably well. Speeds of ten, eleven, and twelve knots are spoken of at times, and day's runs of 284 and 272 knots recorded. *America* picked up a channel pilot at the Scillys and proceeded to LeHavre, her time from East 12th Street, New York, to LeHavre being twenty days and six hours. Her time from sight-of-land to sight-of-land was eighteen days and fifteen hours, and as she was becalmed five days and four hours (or 124 hours), her speed at times must have been considerable.

Commodore Stevens was in Paris, and on receiving word of *America*'s arrival, hastened to LeHavre and made arrangements to have her fitted out at the government dockyard, where she was placed in drydock and had her bottom scrubbed, topsides painted, trailboards and stem decorations regilded. This work was not completed until July 31 and then she proceeded to Cowes, sailing the last few miles of the way in company of the English yacht *Lavrock*, and seemed to foot just as fast and out-point this yacht. *America* was given a warm welcome at Cowes.

The waterfront buildings were decorated, and soon after she came to anchor, she was boarded by the commodore of the Royal Yacht Squadron, the Earl of Wilton, and the Marquis of Anglesey, a prominent yachtsman of that time, who gave *America* the official greetings of the Royal Yacht Squadron.

Cowes Roads, where *America* was anchored, had been a favorite yachting locality for some 200 years, as it has been ever since then. At this point there is an indentation in the Isle of Wight formed by the River Madena as it enters The Solent, and while Cowes Roads is a rather exposed anchorage for small yachts, the Madena makes a safe refuge for the small fry. The Madena runs inland about four miles to the town of Newport, near the remains of the ancient castle of Carisbrook, which was garrisoned up to the seventeenth century, and as a matter of interest, Charles I was imprisoned here shortly before he was beheaded.

It is my opinion the Madena has always been such a favorable place to lay yachts up in the winter that this has contributed to the fact that Cowes has been for centuries the yachting center of the world. Almost opposite the mouth of the Madena is a similar but larger inlet known as Southampton Water, and this also for centuries has been a favorite yachting, boating, and fishing locality that has produced some remarkably good types of sailboats, as well as good sailormen and pilots. Altogether within twenty miles of Cowes there are a dozen very interesting anchorages, not to mention Southampton and Portsmouth, the former causing many interesting merchant ships to pass Cowes and the latter generally furnishing a fleet of naval vessels within sight of the city. So all in all The Solent, that sheet of water that separates the Isle of Wight from the mainland, is a yachtsman's paradise, and from a hundred to two hundred years ago must have been quite romantic, for then all vessels were propelled by sail or oar and the small towns were quite unspoiled.

The clubhouse of the Royal Yacht Squadron is located on the west bank of the Madena at the mouth where it enters The Solent. A little to the eastward of the Madena on high land is Osborne House, the favorite summer residence of Queen Victoria at the time her children were young, around 1850. The view out over The Solent is a charming one for those who enjoy the ever-changing colors of water, as with the tide rips, sandy shoals, and deeper parts of blue water, the scene is always changing—here yellow from the sands, there transparent green, with the white-caps beyond giving contrast to the dark blue. The Solent is a choppy sheet of water, which in breezy weather makes a yacht race quite a thrilling spectacle as seen from shore. On account of the strong tides and choppy sea, the yachts seem almost like living beings struggling to pass one another, and in a race often change places so that one may have a good lead at times but still not be first at the finish.

From Osborne House the Queen and her family could over-look most of the usual race courses of the Royal Yacht Squadron, and for some years Queen Victoria had given the principal trophy for the races during Cowes Race Week, as had sovereigns before and since, from King William IV in 1839 to the present time. But the cup that the *America* was to race for was not a royal trophy or, as it is erroneously spoken of, a Queen's Cup, but was instead a special trophy offered for a race without time allowance and open to foreign yachts, I assume to encourage international interest in the Jubilee celebration. I believe all of the royal cups have been raced for under some handicap arrangement giving the smaller yachts a chance.

The Queen's Cup for 1851 was raced for on August 25 and *America* did not start with the other yachts but joined the fleet of racers after a good breeze had sprung up. It is said she passed every yacht in this race, and the general opinion was that if she had started in the race she might have won, but I imagine she would have had to give an enormous handicap to the yachts built under the tonnage rule, and probably Commodore Stevens realized that. It also may have been a race open only to members of the Royal Yacht Squadron.

On August 28 *America* had a match race with the new British schooner *Titania*, which was owned by the famous Stephenson family who were eminent British steam engineers of the time. *Titania* was a heavy, seagoing yacht of approximately two-thirds the tonnage of *America*. Their comparative waterline lengths were: *Titania*, eighty-one feet; *America*, ninety feet four inches. The race was in open water, starting off the east end of the Isle of Wight, to and around a mark boat, southeast by south, a distance of about twenty miles. There was a strong breeze and on the run out, *America* beat *Titania* some four minutes, but on the beat back, probably because *America* took a somewhat different course, she beat *Titania* forty-seven minutes, and while this was a great victory for *America*, still there was a considerable difference in the size of the yachts. But this, like the squadron run that I will tell of, was a race without handicap.

These two races took place on August 25 and 28, while the squadron run of the Royal Yacht Squadron was held on Friday, August 22. This was the day chosen to put up for competition the hundred-guinea cup that was offered for a race open to all foreign yachts and to be run without time allowance. This cup, which afterward came to be called the *America*'s Cup, was of the strange and ornate style of the period. Strangest of all, it is a British vessel without a bottom, which was discovered several years later when the owners of one of the successful defenders tried to fill it with champagne.

This notable race was around the Isle of Wight, inside some buoys and outside others, which was later to cause confusion. The yachts entered for the race were as follows:

Beatrice	Schooner	161 tons	Sir W.P. Carew
Volante	Cutter	48 tons	J.L. Craigie
Arrow	Cutter	84 tons	T. Chamberlayne
Wyvern	Schooner	205 tons	Duke of Marlborough
Ione	Schooner	75 tons	Almon Hill
Constance	Schooner	218 tons	Marquis of Conyngham
Titania	Schooner	100 tons	R. Stephenson
Gipsy Queen	Schooner	160 tons	Sir H. B. Boghton
Alarm	Cutter	192 tons	J. Weld
Mona	Cutter	82 tons	Lord Alfred Paget
America	Schooner	170 tons	J.C. Stevens
Brilliant	3-mast Schooner	392 tons	G.H. Ackers
Bacchante	Cutter	80 tons	B.H. Jones
Freak	Cutter	60 tons	W. Curling
Stella	Cutter	65 tons	R. Frankland
Eclipse	Cutter	50 tons	H.S. Fearson
Fernande	Schooner	127 tons	Major M. Martyn
Aurora	Cutter	47 tons	LeMerchant

One of the reasons there was such a difference in tonnage was that the cutters were mostly built to evade or cheat the tonnage rule then in use for obtaining rating. The schooners, or topsail schooners, were mostly clumsy craft used for cruising. Figure 1 shows *America* before the race, with some of the others in the background.

We shall see now how *America*, through luck or coincidences, eliminated most of her fastest competitors. In the first place *Titania, Fernande*, and *Stella* did not start, and two of these were considered fast. The start was made at 10:00 a.m. among a large flotilla of spectator yachts, boats, and steamers. The first leg was toward the east, and some of the smaller yachts took the lead in the light weather soon after the start. As they passed Osborne House, The Solent was said to have been crowded with yachts from shore to shore, and the sight of the dark-hulled naval ships off Spithead, the green hills of Hampshire, and the white batteries off Portsmouth combined to make a picture never before equaled in the history of yachting.

The breeze was increasing and *America* seemed to have left most of the larger yachts behind, some of the smaller and racier craft only being ahead of her. Just after 11:00 they reached the east end of the island and began to feel the channel swells. By this time *America* was only led by *Volante, Freak, Aurora*, and *Gipsy Queen*. Soon after this in the hardening wind, the schooner *Gipsy Queen* carried away her foresail sheets, and then *Arrow, Bacchante, Constance*, and *Gipsy Queen* stood away to the eastward to round the Nab light vessel, which usually had been a rounding mark in races around the Wight. However *America* and the remaining part of the fleet took the much

Figure 1. A lithograph by Thomas G. Dutton of the yacht America.

shorter course inshore, thus cutting several miles from the length of the course. As they turned to the westward and were tacking up the south side of the island, *America* went in the lead. There must have been a pretty good breeze at the time, for off Shanklin, *America* carried away her jib boom, or temporary extension to her bowsprit, which was used to set an outer racing jib.

There was a head tide along the south side of the island and the cutter *Arrow*, when tacking inshore, struck a rock, whereupon the large cutter *Alarm* gave up the race to stand by *Arrow*. *Alarm*, being a cutter of even larger tonnage than *America*, was of course a dangerous contender and it is interesting how fate seemed to have eliminated *America*'s most dangerous contenders one after the other. But it was Friday. Next *Freak* and *Volante* (which were the leading English yachts) had a collision when tacking inshore, leaving heavy topsail schooners or small cutters of one-half or one-third her tonnage as the only remaining competitors of *America*. It might be said that *America* was the only large racing yacht in the latter part of the race. However, as the wind became lighter toward the end of the day, the smaller cutters began to pick up on her so that, after rounding The Needles and again standing to the eastward, the little cutter *Aurora* of forty-seven tons (as compared to *America*'s 170) finished eight minutes after her, and as the wind was very light at the finish, we can imagine *Aurora* was very close behind, as far as distance was concerned.

Although the victory of *America* has been exaggerated by such expressions as "a hawk among pigeons," "there was no second," etc., the little *Aurora* would have beaten her easily if there had been time allowance based on tonnage, or any other rule, for that matter. It is most likely that *Volante* (shown in Figure 2) would have beaten *America* boat to boat if *Volante* had not been eliminated by collision. I say this only because *Volante* was a crack racer, larger than *Aurora*, held a commanding position up to the time of the collision, and probably would have done well in the light weather of the latter part of the race.

However there is no doubt that a model like *America* is fast in boat-to-boat racing if there is a good beam breeze, and ever since my youth this model (I call it an "American packet schooner model") has so fascinated me that whenever I have had

Figure 2. Volante.

a chance to design a yacht that was to fit no measurement rule, I have chosen it. Now that I have designed six or eight of them, and have seen them sail, I am under the impression this is the fastest and all-around most satisfactory model for a cruising yacht. They are good sea boats, cheap to build, and so easily driven that they can have a moderate sail plan. They also drive well in a head sea under power. But these yachts, nearly a hundred years later than *America*, also do not rate low under the existing rating rules. Consequently, one or two of them have come in first in many races, only to lose out on time allowance to yachts far out of sight astern. Occasionally they have been so far ahead that they have won in spite of a large handicap. Figure 3 shows the lines of the fifty-foot-waterline *Tioga*, now named *Paradise Bird*, which has won the Jeffries Ledge ocean race several times. The *Ticonderoga* won the Lipton Cup in 1950, ninety-nine years after *America*. This yacht holds the record over several ocean race courses as well as the record for a sailing yacht between several ports. Twice she has sailed 180 miles in eighteen hours, and on other occasions logged 100 knots in ten hours. These yachts in some ways have been the forerunners of the light-displacement ocean racers that we hear so much about today, and so far as I know have less comparative displacement for the waterline length than others, either British or American.

But we must get back to *America*, for she had a long and interesting life. Some writers have said that *America* had a profound effect on British yacht design, but I fail to see this effect and believe she had no feature of model that was beneficial under the tonnage measurement rules used for the next twenty-five years in Great Britain. However, after *America*'s visit, the English yachts used flatter sails, and the racing yachts gave up loose-footed mainsails in favor of the foot being laced to the boom as on *America*.

The principal effect of *America*'s visit was to create a spirit of cordiality between British and American yachtsmen, and when Queen Victoria intimated that she would be glad to visit the yacht if *America* dropped down abreast Osborne House, a brotherly spirit of the children of John and Sam was created that has proved of lasting benefit to the two nations. On her visit the Queen was received aboard *America* by Commodore J. C. Stevens, his brother Edwin A. Stevens, and Colonel James A. Hamilton, the son of Alexander Hamilton. These were polished gentlemen of the world and no doubt the effect of this visit caused Queen Victoria to entertain a more friendly feeling for Americans. She came out in a barge accompanied by the prince consort and four or five ladies and gentlemen and apparently gave *America* a sort of military inspection. She showed great interest in the below-deck arrangements, particularly the galley, and congratulated Commodore Stevens on the neatness and cleanliness of the yacht. Captain Dick Brown, the professional captain of *America*, behaved well on the whole, but when the party went below he told the prince consort to wipe his feet on the mat at the companionway. The Queen seemed to take this in good part, for soon after returning ashore, she sent out to Captain Brown a gold pocket compass with a note stating that she hoped that he would keep it as bright as he kept *America*. In his memoirs, Colonel Hamilton said, "The whole thing went off very well."

America had many distinguished visitors during her visit at Cowes, but perhaps none more picturesque than the venerable Marquis of Anglesey, who had been one of England's leading yachtsmen. He was then eighty years old and had a wooden leg,

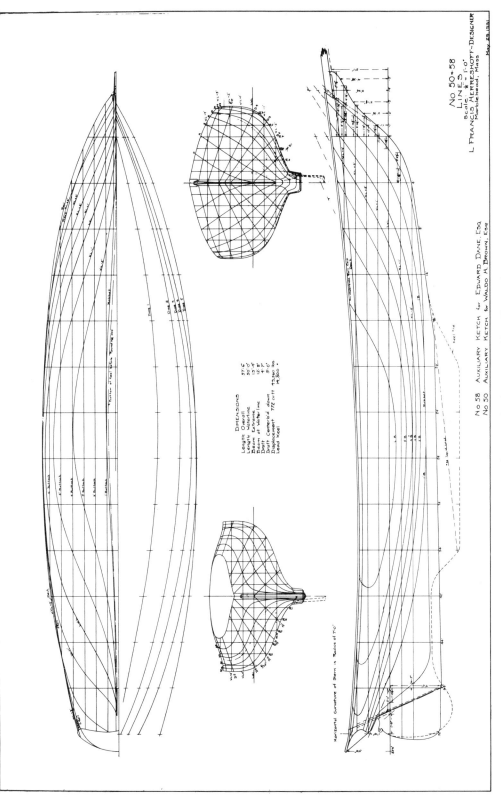

Figure 3. The fifty-foot-waterline Tioga.

having lost the original member while leading Wellington's cavalry at Waterloo. He studied *America* very carefully, and amused himself by telling people that *America* was equipped with an engine.

America was sold in England on September 1 for 5,000 pounds. What with the stakes won in the race with *Titania*, all expenses of building and sailing over were more than covered. In fact, each of her six owners received $1,750 profit from the venture, which to me does not sound like modern yachting and shows that her afterguard, besides being polished gentlemen, had some Yankee blood in them.

America was purchased by Lord de Blaquière, who fitted her out for a cruise in the Mediterranean the next winter. She left England on November 27, 1851, and, as might be expected at that season, met with rather rough weather but proved herself a remarkably good sea boat. During the winter she made a run from Malta to Albania on which she averaged more than ten knots, and the next spring she returned to England to be refitted in time to compete in the Queen's Cup Race on July 22. This course was practically the same as the one when she won *America*'s Cup, but it started off Ryde about five miles east of Cowes Roads. This time it was a remarkably close and exciting race, and the cutters *Arrow* and *Mosquito* beat her only about two minutes.

				H	M	S
Arrow	Cutter	102 tons	finished at	6	59	30
Mosquito	Cutter	50 tons	finished at	6	59	31
America	Schooner	170 tons	finished at	7	1	20
Zephyretta	Schooner	180 tons	finished at	7	39	00

In this race all the yachts went around the Nab lightship, making the course around the Isle of Wight fifty-six miles, which took them about eight and one-half hours to complete. Although this was the same *Arrow* that *America* had beaten the previous year, she had been rebuilt in the meantime and her bow lengthened so that she now rated at 102 tons instead of 84. *Mosquito* was sailed by Jack Nichols, reputed to be the best helmsman in England.

In the meantime a Swedish-built schooner named *Sverige* had arrived in England. She was a larger vessel than *America* and very much a copy in which her builders had exaggerated most of the peculiarities of *America*. She had a longer and sharper bow, a similar sail plan with gaffs peaked up even less than *America*, and she was intended to prove that Sweden could best England and America on the water. After two failures to start a match race because of lack of wind, they started on October 12 in a fifty-five mile race, the course being around the east end of the Isle of Wight, to and around a stake boat in the English Channel, and return. The run to the stake boat was before the wind, and *Sverige* went very well, rounding the mark some eight minutes ahead of *America*, but on the return to windward, *America* overtook and passed *Sverige* and succeeded in beating her twenty-six minutes. Thus *America* seems to have won a hundred pounds, and *Sverige* returned to Sweden.

America was laid up for the next several years and changed ownership twice, in the meantime showing signs of rot. In 1859 she was rebuilt by George Pitcher and Son of Northfleet, which is near Gravesend, and was now named *Camilla*. In rebuilding, her frames were renewed with English oak and her bottom planking of elm and oak, the topsides of teak. In 1860 she was purchased by Henry E. Decie, who later used her as a blockade runner between England and the Confederate states, although she occasionally entered English regattas to keep up her standing as a yacht. *Camilla* apparently made two or three trips across as a blockade runner, but the next we know of her was that she was found by Federal naval officers sunk seventy miles up the St. John's River above Jacksonville, Florida. After the Federal naval forces floated and repaired her, she was used in blockade duty and as a despatch boat off the city of Charleston, performing active and important service. It was written of her, "No vessel of her size was ever held in higher esteem by naval officers." After the Civil War, *America* was used at Annapolis to give the cadets sea training. About this time, Brady took two or three fine photographs of her, one of which (Figure 4) shows her off the Charleston Navy Yard in 1863. There was another showing her hove-down to have her bottom cleaned or repaired, which photograph shows her lines clearly.

During the next few years *America*'s history was about as follows:

1864. Naval school ship at Newport, R.I.

1865. Took a cruise in company with frigate *Constitution*.

1868. Commanded by Lt. George Dewey, later admiral.

1870. Refitted at Brooklyn Navy Yard at cost of about $20,000 to represent the Navy in the races against James Ash-

Figure 4. The America *off Charleston Navy Yard during the Civil War.*
*(*The Rudder*)*

bury's *Cambria*, in which she came in fourth, much to the surprise of the Navy.

1873. The Navy Department decided she was too expensive to keep up (having spent some $30,000 on her in four years), so she was put up at public auction. There was only one bidder, representing General B. F. Butler, who obtained her for $5,000. It is generally considered that this transaction was a political frame-up. General Butler used *America* for the next twenty years and made several long cruises in her. During this time she is credited with making several long runs at over ten knots average speed, but by this time she was beaten quite regularly by the newer schooners.

1886. Redesigned by Edward Burgess, rebuilt at McKee's Yard, including twenty-five tons outside ballast, different-shaped bow and stern, and whole new sail plan. After this she competed with fair success against other yachts of that time.

1887. On August 6 she raced with the New York Yacht Club from Newport to Vineyard Haven. It is interesting that most of the yachts in her class were ex-Cup defenders—*Magic, Madeline, Mischief, Puritan, Mayflower,* and *Volunteer. America* finished third, which was remarkable for her age, but she was considerably longer on the waterline than some of the others.

1893. General Butler died in Washington, and after 1897 she was used by Butler Ames and his family for several years and entered many runs of the New York Yacht Club. I remember her well on the N.Y.Y.C. cruise of 1901, when she looked like Figure 5. That year she took Lipton and George Watson for a sail in the lower bay of New York. That must have been one of her last sails, for in October of 1901 she went out of commission and was stored at Chelsea for several years.

1917. C. H. W. Foster of Marblehead purchased her. Some of her lead was removed and sold for war purposes.

1921. U. S. Navy purchased *America* from the Eastern Yacht Club for one dollar, the money being passed by Rear Admiral Henry B. Wilson to Charles Francis Adams in the presence of a cadet regiment and thirty yachtsmen who represented several yacht clubs. *America* was then permanently berthed in Dewey Basin as a naval museum piece. It is fitting that her final resting place was named after her one-time commanding officer. [Ed. note: In 1945, too rotten to restore, she was broken up.]

Before closing, it is interesting to note that one of the original owners of *America* lived a long time. This was George L. Schuyler, born in 1811, who died aboard Commodore Elbridge T. Gerry's steam yacht *Electra* in New London Harbor, July 31, 1890, on the first day of the New York Yacht Club cruise of that year. Mr. Schuyler seems to have written or received the only existing letters that had to do with the building of *America*, and if I remember correctly, he wrote the original deed of gift of *America*'s Cup and helped with later amendments to the deed.

This August (1951) the King of England is giving a cup to commemorate the 100th anniversary of the race when *America* won the original cup. I understand the course is from Cowes across the Channel and back, and will be for ocean cruisers. It is too bad that *Ticonderoga* will not be one of the competitors, for with a beam wind she might very well duplicate the *America*'s victory, in spite of the handicap.

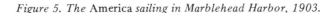

Figure 5. The America *sailing in Marblehead Harbor, 1903.*

Yachting in the 1900s

During the last several years *The Rudder* at times has given us stories of youthful boating experiences, and to me at least these early adventures have been very pleasant reading. Perhaps the reminiscences of others have taken me back to my childhood, the time when sailing was the most thrilling, or perhaps I am entering my second childhood, when some of these childish antics appear more amusing than they would have twenty years ago—at any rate, in return for the pleasure others have given me with their yarns, I will try to relate some of my early impressions.

My earliest experiences in yachting took place on small steam yachts, of which my father had had several, but as I was so young at the time, these experiences all seem hazy now. About all I can remember is a succession of awfully good meals, for which youthfulness and the salt air had prepared a surprising appetite. I was very lucky in having some sort of a valve in my throat that let things go down but prevented them from coming up again, and I cannot now remember a time when it was not a pleasant sensation to be swallowing something. We young ones often munched hardtack in the middle of the afternoon, although only a few hours before, we had stowed a meal that would now cause prostration.

About all I learned in this nautical life was how to tie a few useful knots, how to keep my balance on a vessel that was rolling, and the use of nautical terms. However, as all forms of yachting etiquette were carefully adhered to on these yachts, I had become as accustomed to them as most people are to the civilities on shore, and I could see much more sense to dipping the ensign when passing the stern of a government vessel than to taking my hat off to a lady on shore.

The principal object of our cruising or steaming around in those days was to watch the yacht races. This was because my father had designed many of the yachts that were racing and therefore took an unusual interest in their performance. In fact, he was usually so absorbed in watching and timing the yachts at the various mark buoys that it was not safe to approach him closely—particularly if his yachts were not in the van. So we youngsters spent most of our time towing models over the stern of the yacht, often two or three out at a time, but as the scale speed of these models was some hundred miles an hour, they performed amusing antics in the boiling wake of the yacht. Some of the models had been whittled out with great care, and if they performed well, they were as fondly cherished by their owners as any of their possessions, but sooner or later the best of them took a dive and, after zigzagging around under water a few moments, parted the towropes and was last seen far astern, while the owner, half in tears, wound in a loose towline.

At such embarrassing moments, or if it became cold on deck, a favorite resort was the engine room, where a kindly engineer would set a lad down in a safe, out-of-the-way place, where he was fascinated watching the moving parts of the engine as the pant of the air pump kept time with each stroke. After the bracing air on deck, it was difficult to keep awake in the warm air of the engine room, and as the yacht rolled back and forth, the lad's head would begin to nod until the engineer thought it was time to go on deck again. But even after all these years, I can remember the pleasant smell of the engine room, with its scent of hot oil and steam, which is an entirely different odor from that of the modern engine room with either a gasoline or heavy oil engine, both of which to me are nauseating. We also cruised quite a little, and it might be safe to say that we visited nearly every navigable harbor from Bar Harbor to Sandy Hook, and now sometimes, as I study charts, I am surprised that my father ventured into some of them, on account of their shallowness.

While these trips on the water were good fun, I was generally much pleased if left at home, for then, with some boys of my own age, I would retire to a certain small pond in cow pastures back of the town. Here we held yacht races of our own. At that time it seemed stupid to me to watch an Astor Cup Race all day, and at the end of the long-drawn-out affair not always know who was the winner until the next day, on account of corrected time, etc. But in our miniature races, the first yacht that crossed the pond was at once hailed as the winner, and if things went well, we would have completed half a dozen regattas before the big yachts would have gotten well under way. The best thing about the miniature regattas was that they were so full of life, and the hopes and despairs of the various owners fluctuated back and forth every few seconds, for, although one of the yachts might have a commanding lead, when halfway across the pond, she might suddenly come about and go back to the starting line. Many of the races were between a sloop and a schooner, closely matched as to speed, so that quite a little rivalry was the result. To make the races seem more realistic, each of the yachts usually carried a miniature skipper in the form of a potato bug or a snail placed near the helm, and while we had each promised not to push our yacht at the start, each owner was so intent on watching the others' hands instead of his own that the yachts usually started off with quite a bone in their mouths, and this headway often carried them parallel a quarter way across the pond, when Captain Potato Bug on the sloop (being the leeward yacht and partly blanketed) might decide to luff, but Captain Snail, being a rather deliberate sort of individual, might be slow in meeting the luff so that a foul was the result. Both yachts would then swing around in a circle, with the gaff of the sloop between the mastheads of the schooner, and the mainsail of the schooner goose-wing over the head of Captain Potato Bug, while the yacht owners at the head of the pond, not knowing which way to run, either came to blows or were pelting each other with dry cow dung, which was always plentiful around the race course.

After making a few circles locked together, the yachts usually parted, one going toward the finish line and the other toward the starting point, and I remember one time when my sloop was nearing the finish line and I was all flushed with victory, all of a sudden Captain Potato Bug, seeing a flaw of wind come down the pond, decided to gybe over and started off on a broad reach toward the north end of the pond, where he fetched up all standing on a rock about twenty feet from shore, while the schooner, which had gone back to the starting line and put about, recrossed the pond and finally won the race, under the cautious management of Captain Snail.

These pond races so fascinated me that I often returned to them even after having a boat of my own large enough to sail in, for we boys thought it was pretty pleasant around that pond, and if the wind was too light for racing, we could sit under the shade of the willow tree at the north end with our bare feet in the cool mud, while the barnswallows skimmed over the pond, and now and then a kingfisher flitted by, and the song of the meadowlark could be heard from the nearby hayfield. Our tranquility was sometimes suddenly interrupted, for occasionally a mud wasp would sting one of the boys and he would start off running with a cry that made the mud turtles draw their heads below the surface, and might even disturb the cows that were browsing around us. In spite of such annoyances, the pond seemed to me a much pleasanter place than the deck of a yacht, where one had to sit in white duck pants and be careful not to soil the spotless pine deck.

My first command was a nine-foot sailing skiff, which, like most of my clothes, had been handed down to me from an older brother who had outgrown her, but she was a dear little ship and had been designed by the same man who designed the Cup defender *Columbia*. And if J. P. Morgan was proud to be part owner of the *Columbia*, I am sure I was as proud to be the full owner of that skiff. I remember very well the first day I sailed in her alone. It was under the lee of a very small island where the water was shallow, and as I sailed back and forth over the eel grass, her speed seemed to me to be terrific, and I have never had such a thrill since. She was a wet little boat, though, and the harbor where we lived was generally choppy, so that we usually had to sit in the water she had shipped and came home as wet as if we had been in swimming.

When about sixteen, I was put in charge of a knockabout of eighteen-foot waterline, twenty-four feet overall. She had a good little cabin and altogether was nearly as nice a boat of her size as I have ever seen. While most all of my sails in this boat were between meals, we did occasionally sail to Newport, a distance of ten miles, and on a few occasions got permission to spend the

Newport Harbor, about 1908-09. (Newport Historical Society)

night in Newport Harbor. One of these times I was accompanied by a friend who had been a competitor of mine in the cow pastures, and if possible was more of a rustic than I. The outfitting for these cruises was a simple matter and consisted of filling the water jug and refilling the riding light. Then we took on board a wicker basket of food that the cook had packed up for us, and we were ready to start. I don't remember about the sail down the bay, but we were probably so busy anticipating the sights of Newport Harbor that the sail down was but a means to an end, for we knew the New York Yacht Club fleet was in and thought there might be an illumination, as there had been some years in the past.

We anchored way up in the south end of the inner harbor (which used to be quite shallow), for this insured our not being bothered in the night by larger yachts. Until sunset we feasted our eyes on the yachts of all sizes, very many of which we knew by name or had seen pictures of. Then, as darkness came on, we lit a small cabin light and tried to stay awake until the New York-Fall River liner had gone through the harbor, for the passage of this large steamer, all lit up, was quite a sight for country boys. However, one of those damp Newport fogs was settling down with the evening, so we were glad to go in the cabin out of the drip from the rigging.

In those days I seldom wore shoes and stockings and, as we turned in all standing on these cruises, about all I had to do was to take off my cap, blow out the light, and roll up in a blanket. The cushions we slept on were only about two inches thick and were on flat board transoms, but the damp ocean air soon put

us to sleep, and it seemed no time at all until the sunlight was coming in through the cabin door. While not an early riser on shore, even in those days sleeping on a sailboat seemed to so revive me that it was pleasant to get up soon after sunrise. So, putting on my cap, I stepped out in the cockpit, unhung the riding light, and mopped the deck and cockpit seats in the morning dew, not forgetting to empty the cedar bucket that had stood in the cockpit ready for use in the night. (And I might mention that this was the first cedar bucket I was shipmate with.) It seemed a long time before there was much life on the larger yachts, but soon the crews began scrubbing down decks and chamoising the brightwork, and by seven or so, some of the afterguard of the racing yachts appeared on deck in their pajamas and soon plunged overboard nude for their morning baths. I might mention that it was an unwritten rule in those days that ladies should not appear on deck before colors, or eight o'clock, and in my opinion this, like all the olden customs of yachting, was a great improvement over present-day practice. The reason for this rule, of course, was so the yachtsman could take his morning plunge, wipe himself dry with a towel, and go below without a dripping bathing suit and its salt.

So we boys had our plunge, and I should add that the water of Newport Harbor in those days was clear and transparent. It was just the right temperature, not too cold nor too warm, and guaranteed to produce a good appetite for breakfast. In those days we boys did not drink tea or coffee, so after a good glass of water, some hardboiled eggs, and bread, we were ready for the day's fun. It was getting on toward eight o'clock, and the crews of the yachts were standing by to make colors, when we remembered we had on board one of my father's old private signals, so in great haste we bent its small staff to the flag halliards, and when the gun from the flagship echoed across the harbor, we had our flag mastheaded before most of her taller sisters, and probably even beat the flagship, which, if I remember right, was the handsome steam yacht *Delaware*. Then we settled down in the cockpit to watch the larger yachts in the outer harbor hoist their mainsails and send up their club topsails in stops, while the mastheadsmen lashed the heels of their yards to their topmasts. In those days, some of the larger yachts went out quite early, for if it was calm it took some time to get out to the lightship, a distance of perhaps five miles.

By the middle of the morning, after the steam yachts had gone out, the harbor seemed quite deserted, and we boys were trying to think what to do until the yachts came in again, when my friend suggested that we might take a walk to while away the time. Said he, "We might walk over to part of that much-talked-about Ten Mile Ocean Drive, and don't forget we've each got a nickel to get some of them Newport choc'lat sodies."

"Yes," I said, "but them sodies ain't so good as they used to be. I remember the first one I had about two years ago. Gee, but it was good. But the next one was only fair, and the last one I had was nothing much more than some water with some sweetening in it."

So we dressed up to see Newport, which operation consisted of putting on shoes and stockings, but I might say that a boy's clothes in those days were a queer ensemble. We had linen caps called bicycle caps, white shirts with stripes or dots on them or both, butterfly neckties, and linen trousers called bicycle trousers, which had a buckle just above the knee (that never stayed buckled), and that invention of the devil, long black stockings that were nearly impossible to haul on over wet feet. Well, after putting some lunch in a lard can, we went ashore near the head of the harbor and tied the skiff in a safe place. There used to be a winding road bearing southwest from the head of the harbor that went at first under shady trees and then wound its way by several ponds and well-kept country estates (called cottages in Newport, though I never knew why), until this road came out at the ocean on part of what is called the Ten Mile Drive. We boys were used to walking long distances in those days, but it was a hot summer day and the road was dusty, so when we sat down on the rocks for lunch, we were thirsty and tired. This part of the shoreline, on what is called The Neck at Newport, we found very interesting. It consisted mostly of small, rocky points on which the surf broke continually, while way out to sea the waves were combing over the outlying rocks with the racing yachts more than hull down in the distance.

This was a stylish part of the Ten Mile Drive, so what seemed like an endless procession of carriages passed us, each rolling up its cloud of dust. In those days, it was a custom among the dowagers of Newport to take in at least part of this drive every day, so as the phaetons and victorias passed us, we looked with awe at coachmen and footmen in livery, not to mention the much-belaced ladies under their parasols. We hadn't gone far along the ocean drive when my friend said, "Gee, but I'm thirsty. What do you say if we start back and git them choc'lat sodies we've been talking about, even if they ain't as good as they used to be?" About that time I was sitting on the grass taking off my shoes and stockings, for to tell the truth, in those days it was easier for me to walk barefooted than with shoes on, even if it was rough going, and here there was a smooth footpath and grass. So we both took off our shoes, tied the laces together, and threw them over our shoulders. Then with stockings stuffed in our side pockets, we proceeded to take in the sights of Newport.

We hadn't gone far when we came to quite a wide street leading back toward the town. On the signboard it said Belleview Avenue, and as we thought that a queer name, we decided to see where it led to. It turned out to be a nice wide street with shady trees, and we were making good progress, both thinking about the chocolate sodas we were soon to have, when my friend said, "Oh, look. Look at the funny lady in the carriage with a pair of glasses on a stick."

"Don't point," I said, "for maybe you look as funny to her as she does to you. Maybe she has never seen anyone walk up Belleview Avenue barefooted before."

"Well," said my friend, "I don't see nothing in that excepting the sidewalk is hard and hot and I wish there were a few nice cool cow flops to walk in along here, like the ones over around the pond at home." But as we walked along, we were so taken up with the sights that we forgot about ourselves and our appearance, although we must have caused some astonishment.

The principal things we had our eyes on were the early automobiles, and we met two or three of them along that street, and when one of them stopped, so did we, and probably walked around it to see what it looked like on both sides. Finally we came to the house with the owls in front of it, where James Gordon Bennett had lived, and then the Casino across the street, with its stylish store windows and many people promenading up and down.

This street so fascinated us that we walked on it farther north than we needed to to be opposite the head of the harbor, and came finally to a corner in front of a respectable wooden house that I was to know later in life as the Newport Reading Room. There we stopped near the stepping stone at the curb, undecided which way to go next, when a fine-looking carriage with a coachman and footman on the box drew up to the curb just where we were standing. While we looked on with astonishment, the footman alighted and helped a nicely dressed old gentleman out almost between us. He was probably one of the southern aristocracy, some of whom for generations had visited Newport in the summer. At any rate he was a tall, thin man in a broad-brimmed panama and light-colored striped trousers, and no doubt as surprised to see two sixteen-year-old barefoot boys as we were to see him. But he stopped and said kindly, "Well, what are you boys doing here?"

And my friend spoke up and said, "We've each got a nickel and we're going to get some choc'lat sodies, but they ain't so good as they used to be."

This must have struck a favorite chord in the old gentleman, for he turned round and spoke to us very slowly and distinctly, keeping time with his cane. He said, "Young men, I have been around this blasted town quite a lot in the last seventy years and I can tell you as a certainty that there's not a blooming thing in the blazing place that is as good as it used to be." Then the doorman came out of the house and, with the footman on the other side, they took the old gentleman indoors.

The old gentleman had spoken with such strong feeling that it most scared us boys to death, so we struck out for the water-front almost in a run and didn't stop until we were safe aboard. When my friend said, "By gee, we forgot all about them sodies," we had had such a very long walk and were so tired out that we decided to have a good drink out of the water jug instead. To make it a sort of state occasion, we got out an old tin cup that had hung in the cabin two or three years, and probably had been used to dip out chowder a couple of times, and maybe used for varnish, since it had been washed, for it had a very peculiar odor and usually made the water take on rainbow tints near its sides. But we each watched the other with envy while he had his turn at the cup.

By this time the yachts were coming into harbor again, so we were occupied with this spectacle until suppertime, when we had sardines and much hardtack. That evening, as I sat on the after deck jigging my toes in the water, I thought to myself, gee, this must have been quite a town once, if not a blasted thing here is as good as it used to be.

And now, some forty years later, I understand much better what the old gentleman meant, and I think, as far as yachting is concerned, there is not a blasted thing about the whole blooming game that is as good as it used to be.

The Names of Some of the Yacht Sails

Apparently some of the younger generation are beginning to collect photographs and prints of the larger yachts that were in use near the turn of the last century. I suppose the pictures of the large yachts are already becoming rare, and will be as much sought after in the future as other antiques whose scarcity has increased their value. While the large yacht was in common use or was a common sight, it was no more thought of than the square rigger was when it was a common sight, but now that the large yacht has gone, it is beginning to have a romance connected with it only second to the square rigger, and in my opinion, the yacht was far the most graceful and artistic of the two. The first might be classed as utilitarian, while the latter is purely sporting. However, now that yacht pictures are being collected, some of the younger sailors would like to have a clearer idea of the names of their sails.

While it is true that yacht sails in most cases have similar names to the corresponding sails on commercial craft, it might be stated that in both cases the proper names of the various sails are derived from the spar or stay they are set on. For instance, the fore staysail is set on the forestay; the mainsail on the mainmast, etc. But it may be well to first trace the development of yacht rigs to help the reader to remember the evolution of the various common sails.

Yachting, as a recognized sport, started in Holland just before 1600. It would be quite difficult to give the exact date, but by

1620 or so there apparently were many sailboats in Holland used for pleasure purposes, and early prints suggest that they used the spritsail and the regular fore-and-aft gaff sail. At first, apparently with their gaff sails, they used a two-masted rig somewhat like Figure 1, the type our Block Island boats are descended from. But as time went on, most of the yachts became sloops with a high narrow mainsail and a sizable jib. Figure 2 shows several such yachts, but the larger yachts, say, those of over fifty or so feet long, often had two headsails and crossed a yard. These yachts, like Figure 3, were the type of sloop with which England started yachting, for when Charles II became king of England in 1660 (after his retreat in Holland), he imported a Dutch yacht of this type, which served as the model for the first English yachts. While these yachts were pure sloops, still they had the jib set flying to clear the squaresail when that was set for running off the wind.

The next development of the single-master was made in France, where the sloop was refined for use as a fast revenue

Figure 1. Early Dutch yacht. (The Rudder)

Figure 2. Water festival in honor of Czar Peter the Great. (The Rudder)

Figure 3. Type of Dutch yacht copied by the British. (The Rudder)

cutter until a type similar to Figure 4 was developed about 1800. Here we see everything in the way of rig that the cutter used for the next hundred years, but in France, until at least after 1860, it was still called the sloop rig.

The early English yachts, say, before about 1725, were pure sloops of the Dutch style, but during the next seventy-five years England was generally at war with some nation or other, so yachting was almost entirely stopped, with the exception of some activity of the Cork Water fleet in Ireland. During this time the revenue cutters of both France and England were highly developed, and their peculiarities of rig were mostly to allow large sail area for light weather and still be able to shorten down to storm canvas when on station in the English Channel or North Sea, so these revenue cutters eventually became single-masted vessels with a housing topmast and reefing bowsprit, although several other rigs of more than one mast, particularly the lug rig, were tried in the cutter service. A single-masted cutter under full sail and shortened sail looked somewhat like Figure 4. After 1800, when yachting again became popular in England, their racing yachts adopted these peculiarities of the single-masted cutters principally because this rig allowed an enormous sail spread under the measurement rules then in use, which measured tonnage only and did not measure sail area.

In the meantime, we in this country were developing the purely Dutch sloop for commercial purposes principally on the Hudson, and this American development of the sloop looked

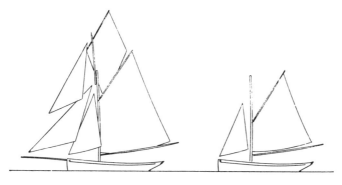

*Figure 4. Cutter under full sail and storm sail. (*The Rudder*)*

somewhat like Figure 5, with fixed bowsprit and only one or two headsails. (Folkard in his book *The Sailing Boat* says the word "sloop" is derived from the ancient word "shaloop.") It might be safe to say the word "sloop" is the proper designation of all single-masted vessels that set headsails, and that the cutter, knockabout, single-masted lug, spritsail, and leg-o'-mutton sailboats are special types of sloops and have many names in different countries that would be quite tedious to list now. However, what we generally call the knockabout rig today was formerly called a jib-and-mainsail sailboat, and the word "knockabout" only came into use about 1890 or later. Figures 6, 7, 8, and 9 are diagrammatical drawings of a jib-and-mainsail boat, an American sloop, a cutter, and a schooner, together with the numbers that refer to the names of their sails:

1. Fore staysail
2. Jib
3. Jib topsail
4. Mainsail
5. Foresail
6. Topsail
7. Main topsail
8. Fore topsail
9. Main topmast staysail

And I give you a few notes about each of these sails.

1. *Fore Staysail.* As said before, this sail sets on the forestay and thus is the sail directly before the mast. It is likely the fore staysail is the most ancient of headsails and undoubtedly was the first fore-and-aft sail used, as it was the first logical addition to the earlier squaresail. I must note that all headsails are loosely called jibs by the tyro, so that today when there is only one headsail (as on a knockabout), it is usually called a jib. At Gloucester and through Massachusetts Bay of late years, the fore staysail has been nicknamed "the jumbo," and possibly this term came from the fact that this sail on the fishing schooner is made of the heaviest canvas, the same weight as the foresail, for these two sails are usually carried in the heaviest weather. Jumbo seems a confusing name for the smallest sail on a vessel, and as it is incorrect and only a local pet name, it should be discontinued. In America in the past we have usually set the fore staysail on a boom and had its sheet self-tending, but in England the fore staysail has usually been loose-footed, principally because in that country it has been the custom to replace the heavy fore staysail by a light balloon fore staysail in moderate and light weather. For some reason or other, this light, overlapping sail adds materially to the speed of the vessel.

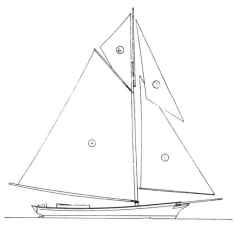

Figure 5. American sloop. (The Rudder)

Figure 6. Jib and mainsail boat. (The Rudder)

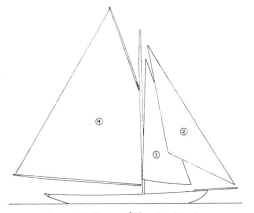

Figure 7. Sloop. (The Rudder)

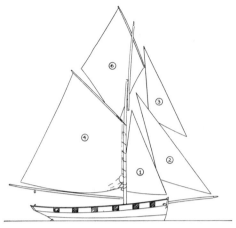

Figure 8. Cutter. (The Rudder)

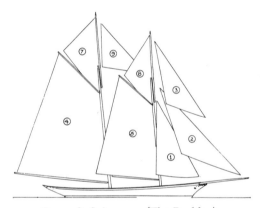

Figure 9. Schooner. (The Rudder)

2. *Jibs.* The word "jib," which I suspect is of Anglo-Saxon derivation and not often used in continental Europe, is the sail set next ahead of the fore staysail. Originally it was set flying on the early sloops and topsail schooners to give room for the squaresails they used in running. After the cutter rig came into vogue, the jib also had to be set flying because of the difficulty of rigging a jibstay on a reefing bowsprit. Also, the cutter had a so-called traveler, or ring around the bowsprit, on which the tack of the jib was set, and this traveler was hauled in and out to adjust the balance (correct the helm) with various sail combinations. The early cutters also had several sizes of jibs, the smallest of which was sometimes called a spitfire jib, and in

heavy weather set not far ahead of the stem head. On fishing and commercial vessels in America, the jib has invariably been set on a stay, but with the yacht it is usual to set the jib flying, simply because then there is no jibstay to interfere with tacking ship with a balloon jib set. After the technique of handling this sort of jib is learned, it is the handiest in light and moderate weather. In short, this jib is set in stops and taken in under the lee of the fore staysail; it can be muzzled before anyone need go out on the bowsprit to unfasten the tack. A jib set flying, however, has to have very stout halliards and generally a jig to obtain the required tautness of the luff. Of the yachts with three headsails that I have designed or sailed on, about as many set the jib flying as on a stay.

Jibs, so far as I know, have always been miter cut. (See Figure 10.) A great deal of the art of cutting a good jib depends on the curvature of the seam at the miter. Jibs were the first sails made crosscut (or with the cloth at right angles to the leech), and antedated my father's invention of the crosscut mainsail by a few years.

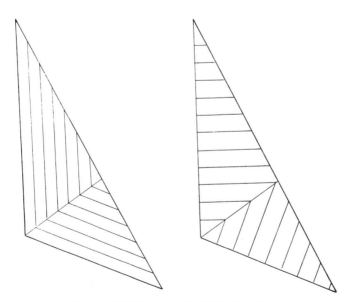

Figure 10. Miter-cut jibs. (The Rudder)

3. *Jib Topsails.* These sails are set on the headstay (some-times called topmast stay) and usually come in three or more sizes, some of which are of quite light sailcloth and all of which are intended for light to moderate weather. The smallest of these sails is called the baby jib topsail, and is the only jib topsail most yachts could carry when close-hauled in a breeze, but the next two sizes, No. 1 and No. 2 jib topsails, could usually be carried on a reach or in light weather close-hauled. The balloon jib, which also was set on the headstay and more than filled the whole fore triangle, was usually only set on a broad reach or a run. While the balloon jib and the spinnaker are rather recent inventions, coming into popular use only after about 1870, a balloon jib either on a racer or a cruiser is a valu-able sail, as in light weather on a reach it will often pull more than the other sails put together. On a cruiser a balloon jib can at times be carried all day long, and at times will keep a large yacht traveling two or three miles an hour, when under her heavier sails alone she would have been becalmed. This is particularly so if there is a ground swell running.

However, in former times topmasts were not made strong enough to carry a balloon jib in a breeze, excepting when running quite free, so that it was most important to take the ballooner in at once when hauling on the wind or with an increase of wind. For this reason, a yacht with a balloon jib set almost invariably also carried her jib set in stops ready to break out if the balloon jib was hurriedly taken in. More topmasts were carried away by hanging onto a balloon jib too long than from all other reasons put together, and many a good sailorman was lost off the bowsprit on the larger yachts when muzzling these large sails, for at times they were nearly as dangerous as the present lapping jibs, which in fact are really heavy flat-cut balloon jibs set on spars and gear strong enough to carry them close-hauled. Nevertheless, an old-fashioned balloon jib need not be dangerous if taken in in time.

4. *The Mainsail.* Originally when the mainsail was set without a topsail over it (as on the early Dutch yachts), it was a high, narrow sail with a very short gaff, and even up until about the time of the Civil War, our smaller sailboats used high, narrow mainsails. In England the use of large topsails on the cutters from 1800 on had made the long gaff stylish, so that for many years the length of the head of the sail was the same as length

of hoist. The early English cutters, large and small, carried topsails together with a multiplicity of running rigging that would astound the modern yachtsman, for their mainsails could be clewed up and brailed in, as is practiced even today on the Thames barges. This, of course, is only possible on a loose-footed sail, but the sailorman of those days could use all that gear and not only shorten a cutter down to meet any weather but steer her with her sails in making maneuvers now thought impossible.

Our American sloops had much smaller topsails that ran up and down the topmast on hoops, thus had to be stowed or furled aloft, while the English cutters' topsails were set flying from the deck. So, with a small topsail, the mainsail of our sloops was higher and narrower. Just how our large early sloops were handled in the thundersqualls of the Hudson I do not know, but both the main boom and fore staysail boom were well supplied with lazyjacks, and I imagine they let everything go on the run when caught in a squall, for the fore staysail always and the mainsail sometimes were rigged with a downhaul. While it is admitted we do not have the changes in weather that are met in the English Channel, still it is generally conceded that our thundersqualls are more severe. Our early sloops on Long Island Sound and the Hudson, in spite of their simpler gear, were adapted to our climate, a statement substantiated by the fact that our present yachts are rigged more like them than the cutters.

However, it may be that our wide centerboarders with a simple rig were well adapted to our shallow, comparatively smooth waters, while the complications of the cutter rig were best in the varying weather around England with its tide rips and steep seas. It is interesting that our early yachts used much flatter mainsails than English ones, and after 1850, when the sandbagger came into use, we tried to make our mainsails as flat as could be, and invariably had the foot of the mainsail laced to the boom. This practice may have come from the fact that a flat sail has less tendency to make a boat heel than a baggy one, and stability was a vital point with our sandbaggers, while the heavily ballasted cutter could lug a drafty sail in a knockdown and still have the virtues of a drafty sail in light weather.

While it is comparatively easy to cut or make a flat gaff sail, it was during the sandbag era that really nicely made sails were first cut, and at that time most every waterfront town had its sailmaker and blockmaker, so it was not hard or expensive to fit out a small sailboat with good gear. However, it was not until the time of the fin-keelers in the eighteen-nineties that my father invented the crosscut mainsail, and as the fin-keeler could carry her sail as well as any of our later deep yachts, sails of about the same draft as our modern yachts were used, and these early crosscut sails won so many races both abroad and here that they are now quite universal on racing yachts, but the up-and-down cut sail is still much the best for deep sea cruising, fishing boats, and even for trysails.

5. *Foresails.* On a schooner the foresail is the sail set on the foremast, and on our original schooners this was a nicely proportioned sail of perhaps three-quarters the area of the mainsail. These early schooners, both here and abroad, often used the foresail loose-footed and trimmed it as one would a jib with two sheets from its clew. This allowed the foresail to lap by the mainmast enough so that the gaff or head of the sail did not swing off unduly.

As time went on, the mainmast crept slowly forward until the schooner's mainsail became almost as large as a sloop's, and the foresail was a miserable narrow thing. By about 1890 the larger schooner yachts had three sheets on their foresails, for the foot of the foresail set on a boom that extended aft as far as the mainmast, while the sail itself extended aft some eight or ten feet more and was controlled by a pair of sheets, as the loose-footed foresails had been. The foresheet to the boom ran on a traveler and so was self-tending in coming about, but the two after sheets (which were called lugsheets and trimmed the part of the foresail that overlapped the mainsail) had to be tended. Consequently the New York Yacht Club in about 1910 barred lug or overlapping foresails. In photographs of schooner yachts before that date, you will generally see overlapping foresails. It seems strange today that overlapping foresails are barred, while headsails with an enormous overlap are allowed. Barring lugsheets or overlapping foresails made the foresail so high and narrow that it was a foolish sail, for the gaff often swung to leeward thirty degrees more than the boom, so from 1910 to 1925 the usual schooner was a poor performer when close-hauled.

In 1925 Starling Burgess designed the staysail-rigged schooner *Advance* to secure better-setting sails between the masts. At the time I was a draftsman working for Starling and drew up this sail plan under his direction. The next year I designed a staysail schooner rig for the fifty-footer *Pleione,* and with that rig she has won the Astor Cup several times and the King's Cup in 1947. So the foresail, you might say, of late years has gone out of style and been replaced by the main staysail.

6. *Topsails.* Of course a topsail is the sail set on the topmast, and the original Dutch sloops, as well as our later American sloops, only used what is known as a working topsail—that is, a topsail hooped or laced to the topmast and stowed aft. (See Figure 11A.) This is the best sort of topsail for the larger cruising yacht or fishing schooner, where the sail may be set or taken in several times a day, because it can all be done from on deck when properly rigged. In England this sort of topsail is called a "jib headed topsail" and it was often set on a wire or jackstay running from the deck to the topmast head, and then the topsail can be set or taken in from on deck. When the jackstay is rove through a certain-shaped frog at the foot of the topmast, this makes a fine rig, for the frog or switch keeps the jackstay from sagging off to leeward. However, with this rig the topsail must be set on especially shaped hanks to work well, but it is a great advantage to be able to set or take it right down on deck in any sort of weather. Those original French cutters used a topsail like Figure 11B, which was shaped exactly like the topsails of a lugger—that is, the yard crossed or extended forward of the topmast. This sort of topsail has the advantage that it can be set from on deck by stopping the topsail up on the yard, hoisting in place, and then breaking out, but it is said they sometimes were difficult to take in. However, they were used for well over a hundred years on countless French and English cutters, schooners, and ketches. I can remember when one could occasionally see one in this country. Over here we called them English topsails, for the cutters that came here were invariably rigged with them, although in England they were called jackyard topsails. When we began using a topsail on a yard so that it extended above the topmast head, we used the yard so snugly attached to the after side of the mast that it went straight up and down, parallel with the topmast, and this used to be called an American topsail. It seems to have been the fastest rig, although a man had to go aloft to lash the heel of the yard to the topmast.

As topsails for many years were not measured, very large ones called club topsails were developed. (Figure 11C.) These sails, besides having a yard on their forward side, had another spar called a club on their lower after side that carried the topsail far beyond the peak of the mainsail, and it took real sailormen to handle them. They were generally set while the yacht was at anchor, head to the wind, and taken in on the leeward side of the mainsail, even if the yacht had to come about to bring the topsail tack to leeward of the gaff. The larger yacht sometimes had two or three sizes of club topsails, and some eventually became so large that the New York Yacht Club had to pass the rule that a yacht's club topsail should not be larger than 150 percent of her working topsail. So as a general rule, photographs showing very large club topsails were taken before 1900.

The latest type of topsail used on racing yachts did not use a club but were like Figure 11D. The topsail and mainsail together, you might say, became a high leg-o'-mutton sail. On large racers in England, the mainmast, the topmast, and what had been the yard were made into one long pole mast, which required quite complicated staying, and these long masts with their particular type of staying were called the marconi rig, as they resembled some of the early radio spars. But these early marconi rigs used a gaff and topsail.

Before closing the subject of topsails I would like to say that the old sloops with sizable topsails and jib topsails were pleasant to cruise in, for when the topsails were taken in and she was

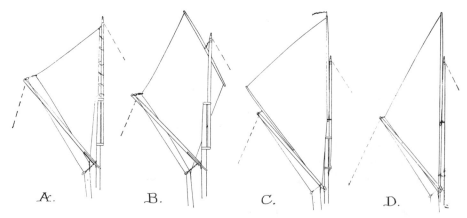

A.   B.   C.   D.

*Figure 11. Topsails. (*The Rudder*)*

under her lower heavy canvas, she could take almost any ordinary summer weather in comfort. In fact I do not remember sailing on one of the larger yachts with a reef in. However, I have sailed quite a little on them with a trysail set and the racing mainsail safely under a sail cover out of the rain.

7. *Main Topsail.* All that has been said about a topsail applies to a main topsail, the latter name only indicating that it is the aftermost topsail of a schooner and is set on the main topmast.

8. *Fore Topsail.* This is the sail set on the fore topmast of a schooner and is a miserable sail, as it has to have double sheets and double tacks to allow it to swing over the springstay and main topmast forestays in coming about. In case of being taken aback or accidentally gibing, they are a mess. We in this country, so far as I know, have never set anything but a working topsail over a foresail, but in England between 1870 and 1890 fore topsails set on a yard were occasionally used on the larger schooners, and they must have required large crews to handle them. Possibly they were never set unless they intended to stay on one tack for some time. However, you may occasionally see this sort of topsail in photographs of English schooners.

9. *Main Topmast Staysails.* This sail sets on the main topmast forestay (the wire running between the head of the foremast and the head of the main topmast) and is a sail used in several sizes. I have said "the main topmast staysail set on the main topmast forestay," and so it was on the square riggers and our large commercial schooners, but on most yachts it was set flying from the deck so that its luff was parallel with the main topmast forestay. In coming about, most main topmast staysails had to be lowered away to clear the fore topmast backstay (sometimes called the triatic stay), and all of these staysails that were quadrilateral, or hung down below the springstay, had to be lowered way down to the deck and taken to leeward of everything before resetting. These latter staysails are sometimes called "fisherman staysails," and, while often quite large wind bags, they make a vessel heel over more than shoot ahead. Because previous staysails had to be lowered away in tacking, when my father designed the schooner *Queen* in about 1908 he did away with the triatic stay and in its place ran a stay called a "freshwater stay" between the topmast heads. This staysail with which a schooner can tack is called a "Queen staysail," as it was first used on the schooner *Queen,* and then was used on most later larger schooners.

The largest main topmast staysail was called a balloon main topmast staysail and was only to be used on a broad reach or a run. This sail came down nearly to the deck and had to be set to weather of the foresail and really did little more than blanket the foresail, so it was only a nuisance and an extravagance. But in those days there were men who would go to most any expense to best someone who had almost as much money as they themselves had.

In the town where I spent my youth, there was an old drunk who could name off all of the running rigging of a square-rigged ship, and when he had a few drinks in, some of us boys used to start him off. Before he was done with the foremast, we were tired of listening and would say "to hell with it." I imagine some of my readers have said that some time ago in reading about all these stays and staysails, but if I have inspired them to a greater appreciation of our older yachts, this article may not be all wasted.

The Names of Some of the Rigging

Since the parts in a whole gang of rigging for a sizable yacht are so numerous, I will confine this discussion to the principal and most interesting parts. I suppose rigging could be classified as follows:

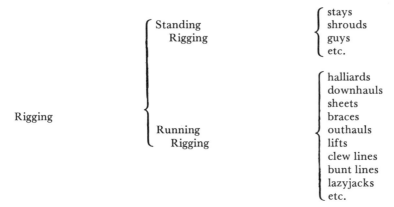

Though the names in the last column (stays, halliards, etc.) are highly generic in order to make them applicable to various rigs, on vessels of like size and sail plan they may be quite specific, particularly after the name is given in full, when it becomes nearly as descriptive as some of the Latin botanical names. For instance, a main topmast backstay is the rope or wire that holds the topmast of a schooner backward, while a topmast backstay would be a stay performing the same function on a sloop. Very fortunately, the descriptive nature of most rigging names makes them easy to learn and easy to remember. While some of the names, like mainstay, are short and sweet, still others on square riggers of olden times could be long and complicated. One like starboard topgallant studding sail boom tricing line would be quite a mouthful, but it is believed the gentle reader will not be called on to use this name unless he is a model maker who goes in for intricate detail, or one like myself who does most of his sailing in the sphere of imagination. We will now speak of some of the different classes of rigging.

Stays. The stays are the ropes that support the mast or masts in a fore-and-aft direction only, and one of the commonest mistakes you are apt to hear the tyro make is calling the shrouds, "stays." You often hear them say such things as, "The spinnaker pole is up against the stay." But this is wholly confusing, for a sailorman of course would think that under this condition the pole would be tending right fore and aft, while as a matter of fact the tyro was trying to say, "The pole was broad on the beam." Hence, using the proper names of things can save much disorder, embarrassment, and jumble, and this is very important on shipboard, particularly in a race, where time is often paramount.

There are no such things as side stays, any more than there are fore shrouds.

Forestays and backstays are among the most ancient and rudimental of all standing rigging, and several centuries before Christ the Egyptians used quite complicated fore-and-aft staying to masts. Even as late as the year 1000, some of the Viking ships only had a forestay to support the mast, and it is believed that the first shrouds were simply the halliards taken to the rails, as is still done in small luggers. However, the forestay is still the stoutest piece of rigging on most yachts, and this is so not only because of its seniority and venerable usefulness, but principally because if the forestay parts, the mast or rig will swing directly aft (held by the shrouds) and kill or crush the crew, whereas with most other dismastings, the whole rig goes to leeward. The forestay is also subjected to some wear from the fore staysail hanks, for this sail is hoisted and lowered more than any other, and is carried in the heaviest weather, although square-rigged vessels usually never set a fore staysail, for their square foresail would interfere and blanket such a sail.

On a square rigger or a staysail-rigged schooner, the stay that supports the mainmast on its forward side is the mainstay, and on the square rigger both the forestay and mainstay had to be very strong, for if the vessel were taken aback (got the wind on the fore side of her sails), there was a terrific strain on these forward-tending stays, as in the square rigger the shrouds have to lead well aft to clear the yards when close-hauled. So when a square rigger is taken aback, the shrouds and the whole sail plan are forcing the masts aft.

The next higher stay before the mast or masts on most American sailing vessels is the jibstay, though cutters and other vessels that set the jib flying use no jibstay. The jibstay is often of about half the strength of the forestay, as they are both attached to the mast at about the same point, while the lower end of the jibstay is attached to a bowsprit (which may be carried away in a collision), while the forestay can be very securely anchored to the stem head.

The uppermost of the forward-tending stays is the headstay, I suppose so called because it supports the topmast head, although it is also sometimes quite correctly called the topmast forestay. Of course the large square rigger had several other forward-tending stays, usually named for the sails set on them, but perhaps they need no particular comment except to say they usually were attached to the spars just above the yards in groups of two or three to give room in between for the squaresails. However, before closing about the stays forward of the mast, I must mention that they are often spoken of collectively as head-stays, which is quite proper.

Stays Between the Masts. The stays between the masts on a schooner have different names in different localities, but the lowermost one is generally called the springstay and runs between the mastheads. The next upper one is called the triatic stay and runs between the mainmast head and the fore topmast head, making a triangle with the springstay. This stay is also quite properly called, "fore topmast backstay." The stay between the main topmast head and the foremast head is simply called the main topmast stay. The stay between the topmast heads is called by some the freshwater stay and by others the cold-water stay, and it is a stay very rarely used before the stay-

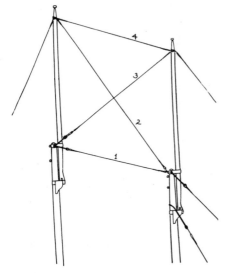

*Figure 1. Stays between the masts of a schooner. 1. Spring-stay. 2. Main topmast stay. 3. Triatic stay. 4. Freshwater stay. (*The Rudder*)*

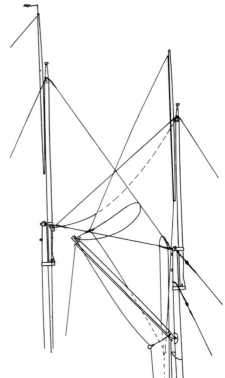

*Figure 2. The rigging of a fore jackyard topsail with double triatic stays and double sheets and tacks. (*The Rudder*)*

sail schooner came into use. Figure 1 shows these stays. Figure 2 shows an arrangement used on English schooners, which set a jackyard topsail on the fore topmast. In coming about, there were six ropes to tend in connection with this sail, for there were double topsail tacks, double topsail sheets, and two fore topmast backstays running to the deck. It must have taken three or four men to do it smartly. Figure 3 shows a schooner sailing that is rigged this way.

Backstays. The older American schooners and the Gloucester fishermen, even of late years, did not use backstays, but they did call the after shroud a backstay. Their masts were stepped with some rake at the deck but sprung forward aloft by tension

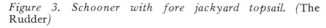

*Figure 3. Schooner with fore jackyard topsail. (*The Rudder*)*

on the forestay and springstay. This had a tendency to hold the mastheads steady, but the shrouds had to lead well aft. Figure 4 shows an early American sloop without backstays. In Holland, however, regular backstays had been in use since at least 1700 and were used on many different rigs. When the French began to develop the cutter, they used backstays at least on the lower mast, and Figure 5 shows a French revenue cutter probably built around 1775 that has everything rigged as the cutters did for the next 150 years. The inexperienced sailor has always disliked backstays, for in the case of a sudden or accidental gibe, the boom is apt to be broken. But backstays are quite necessary if one is to carry large headsails in a breeze. They also seem to increase the speed of the vessel quite a little, for when the luff of the jib stands well (does not breathe), it seems to be a more efficient airfoil, and it is rather amusing that some racers who have found that out carry their backstays unnecessarily tight in all weather.

The danger of having the boom come over accidentally can be obviated by using a forward guy on the boom, and in my youth most of the larger yachts had this forward guy permanently rigged. It was made of wire and attached to the boom nearly as far aft as the mainsheet, while the forward end, which terminated in an eye splice over an open thimble, came far enough forward so that it could be reached easily when the boom was broad off. This guy was ordinarily held in place with a few stops

*Figure 4. Early American sloop. (*The Rudder*)*

of thread and caused no trouble when not in use. When in use, the forward end was either tailed out with a piece of manila taken to the capstan or hooked to a watch tackle secured to some deck fitting suitably located for whatever angle the boom was out. W. A. Robinson, in his cruise around the world in the *Svaap,* learned to use a forward guy on his boom so successfully that it is his opinion that this piece of rigging makes the small yacht with fore-and-aft sail nearly as good for running in a sea as a small square rigger would be.

The lower backstay on the larger vessels has usually been composed of three parts. The upper leg or pendant is called the lower backstay, while the next part is called the backstay runner, and the last part the backstay runner tackle. This arrangement is used because the tackle need only be slacked off enough to unhook the hook at the other end of the runner to allow the boom to go way forward, but the backstay runner tackle blocks always get more or less tangled up and sometimes get over the side, so I got up the arrangement where the blocks slide on deck, as shown in Figure 6.

Topmast backstays have usually been rigged of only two parts, with the wire pendant coming right down to the hook in the tackle called the topmast backstay tackle. Of late years, on pole-masted vessels, this is often called the upper backstay, and since

*Figure 5. French revenue cutter. (*The Rudder*)*

large overlapping headsails and flat-cut balloon jibs have come into vogue, this upper backstay is as stout or stouter than the lower backstay and, like the latter, is generally rigged with a runner.

Shrouds. Just when shrouds began to be used on the larger vessels I do not know, but it is only since about 1700 that shrouds have been common on the smaller craft. Before that the mast was supported sideways by taking the halliard to the rails. Shrouds were also a difficult proposition on the lateen-rigged boats and the luggers, for on most (if not all) fore-and-aft-rigged boats that used a yard instead of a gaff, the leeward shroud had to be slacked off after coming about, and when running free had to be slacked up considerably. So you will find that all feluccas, pinks, tartanas, chasse marées, and other vessels rigged with lateen or lug sails had shrouds arranged to slack up readily in tacking. These shrouds were usually arranged much as lower backstays, with a pendant, a runner, and a runner tackle, the latter usually rigged with large fiddle blocks with four or five parts, of course depending on the size of the craft. And it is my opinion that some of these Mediterranean boats could not tack ship readily without a large crew.

Figure 6. Backstay runner tackle on deck. (The Rudder)

With the squaresail, which has its yard and sail ahead of the mast and shrouds, of course the shrouds became real standing rigging, with their lower ends secured with deadeyes and lanyards, and after the Dutch invented the gaff and spritsail fore-and-aft sails, which were all aft of the mast and shrouds, then the shrouds on the smaller craft were also standing. Today shrouds and turnbuckles have been so perfected that they will often go through a season's sailing without adjustment, particularly if the upper end of the shroud is so attached to the mast that there is no give, or spring.

I hardly need to mention that the lower shrouds are called lower shrouds; the intermediate shrouds, intermediate shrouds; the upper shrouds, upper shrouds, although the latter used to be called the topmast shrouds.

Running Rigging. Most of the running rigging is named after the sail it attends or is attached to, so if you can tell a sheet from a halliard, or a downhaul from a tack strap, you can nearly always name the running rigging correctly. It is said that some of the larger frigates and ships of the line between 1800 and 1850 had as many as eighty running ropes on their foremasts alone, and a great many of them ran down to the fife rail, around the mast or the pin rails under the shrouds. It is also said that some of the largest square riggers between 1850 and 1900 had more than twenty miles of running rigging, and to give the reader an idea of its complication and to amuse some old timers, I will give a partial list of the running rigging on a full-rigged ship.

Fore royal brace	2	Royal lift	2
Main royal brace	2	Topgallant lift	2
Mizzen royal brace	2	Topsail lift	2
Fore topgallant brace	2	Lower lift	2
Main topgallant brace	2	Royal sheet	2
Mizzen topgallant brace	2	Topgallant sheet	2
Fore topsail brace	2	Topsail sheet	2
Main topsail brace	2	Foresheet	2
Mizzen topsail brace	2	Mainsheet	2
Fore brace	2	Royal clew line	2
Main brace	2	Topgallant clew line	2
Preventer main brace	1	Topsail clew line	2
Crossjack brace	2	Fore or main clew garnet	2

Fore tack	2
Main tack	2
Royal yard rope	1
Royal halliard	1
Topgallant yard rope	1
Topgallant halliard	1
Fore or main topsail tye	2
Fore or main topsail halliard	2
Mizzen topsail tye	2
Mizzen topsail halliard	1
Fore topgallant bowline	2
Fore top bowline	2
Fore bowline	2
Main topgallant bowline	2
Main top bowline	2
Main bowline	2
Mizzen topgallant bowline	2
Mizzen top bowline	2
Lower leech line	6
Lower slab line	12
Topsail reef tackle	2
Lower reef tackle	2
Topgallant bunt line	2
Topsail bunt line	2
Lower bunt line	6
Peak halliard	1
Throat halliard	1
Spanker outhaul	1
Peak brail	1
Throat brail	1
Foot brail	1
Tack tackle	1
Tack tricing line	1
Vang	2
Spanker boom topping lift	1
Spanker boom sheet	2
Fore or main trysail gaff chain	2
Main trysail sheet	2
Trysail brail and vang . (each)	2
Trysail outhaul	1
Trysail inhaul	1
Flying jib halliard	1

Jib halliard	1
Fore topmast staysail halliard	1
Flying jibsheet	2
Jibsheet	2
Fore topmast staysail sheet	2
Flying jib downhaul	1
Jib downhaul	1
Fore topmast staysail downhaul	1
Jib and flying jib lacing	1
Jib heel rope	1
Flying jib heel rope	1
Top tackle pendant	5
Top tackle fall	3
Topgallant mast rope	1
Lizard pendant for topgallant mast rope	1
Jeers	3
Short jeers	3
Bill tricing line	1
Quarter tricing line	1
Topgallant studding sail halliard	2
Topmast studding sail halliard	2
Lower studding sail halliard	2
Inner halliard	2
Topgallant studding sail tack	2
Main topmast studding sail tack	2
Fore topmast studding sail tack	2
Boom brace	12
Lower studding sail tack	6
Topgallant studding sail sheet	2
Topmast studding sail sheet	2
Lower studding sail sheet	2
Topgallant studding sail downhaul	2
Topmast studding sail downhaul	2

Lower studding sail tripping line 2

Lower boom topping lift . . 1

Long lizard 1

Fore guy 8

After guy 12

Topmast studding sail boom jigger 6

Topgallant studding sail boom tricing line 6

Topgallant studding sail boom back 4

There are many other parts of running rigging on a ship not mentioned in this list, particularly if she carries several staysails, each with its halliard sheets, downhauls, and tacks. You can see from this list how futile and tiring it would be to describe many of the kinds of running rigging on the many types of sailing vessels each country has used, for no one can begin to know about them all or know their proper names in the sailor's language.

It is also strange how many people think there is only one way to rig the various sail plans, but each country, every port, and sometimes individual captains had distinct ways of arranging their rigging. Often you hear people with some nautical knowledge say, in looking at an old model, "She was never rigged that way," but if it is a logical or workable arrangement, then it is possible that that rig was used somewhere, sometime. Figure 7 shows an unusual sail plan. When I was a boy and knew men who had sailed on square riggers, there were two catch questions they used to ask, and while they are quite foolish, they might amuse you.

1. How many ropes does a full-rigged ship need? Answer: She doesn't need any if she is full-rigged.

2. How many ropes are there on a full-rigged ship? Answer: Twelve (I think), and they are the foot rope, leech rope, luff rope, head rope, bell rope, bucket ropes, limber rope, drag ropes, man rope, royal yard rope, topgallant yard rope, and the head ropes. All other pieces of running rigging are sheets, halliards, braces, lines, lifts, vangs, strops, pendants, brails, or guys, purchases, tackles, warps, cables, and hawsers.

Some of the old riggers I have known were interesting characters and took more pride in their work than perhaps any of the other mechanics in a shipyard. One of these shellbacks was Old Nick, who was a rigger at the George Lawley yachtyard for some fifty years. It is said he was an old man when he came there, thus the name. When Old Nick was about eighty-five, one day he was up aloft putting a throat serving on a throat halliard pendant of a fair-size schooner yacht. When he was lowered on deck, the superintendent of the yard came up to him and said, "Nick, I don't want you to go aloft any more."

Whereupon Old Nick took off his rigger's belt, grease horn, sheath knife, spike, and nippers and replied, "I'm through if you don't think I am a good man up aloft."

So the superintendent said, "We know you are a good man, Nick, but why don't you let one of your helpers go up?"

Old Nick walked to the rail, spat out his quid, came back and said, "Them young fellers hain't had experience enough to do a good job." At this they all started to chuckle, for one of Nick's helpers was seventy and the other seventy-five.

Old Nick is still alive and 104 years old now, and so far as I know, his only complaint is that no one seems to want to hire him, which he can't understand, for he says he is a good man with years of experience. Some of my readers may think this quite a yarn, but it is nothing to the yarns some of the old riggers can spin, and the strange part about it is that it may be true.

Figure 7. Strange sail plan. (The Rudder)

Ropes

"How many ropes are there on a ship?"

This old catch question is usually answered by saying, "Six or nine—as all the rest of the cordage has proper names that can be classed in the categories of halyards, sheets, braces, buntlines, clewlines, shrouds, stays, downhauls, cables, warps, lines, pennants, and pendants." But a closer look at the matter reveals there were about forty properly named ropes on some good-sized sailing vessels of the past.

It must be remembered that the cordage used in most tackles was called rope—for instance, gun training tackle rope—and even today we use the name backstay runner tackle rope.

The list of ropes is as follows:

AWNING-ROPE   A rope around an area to which an awning is laced.

BACK-ROPE   The rope pendant or small chain for staying the dolphin striker.

BELL-ROPE   A short rope attached to the tongue of a ship's bell.

BOAT-ROPE   A separate rope veered to the boat to be towed at the ship's stern.

BOLT-ROPE   A hard-laid rope used in several places where it is not required to flex, such as the head rope, foot rope, leech rope, and luff rope of a sail.

BREAST-ROPE   A rope fastened along the lanyards of the shrouds to secure the leadsman when in the chains, heaving the lead.

BREECH-ROPE   A rope to restrain the recoil of a gun when discharged.

BUCKET-ROPE   A rope attached to the handle of a bucket for drawing water to scrub the deck, put out fire, etc.

BULL-ROPE   A hawser rove through a block on the bowsprit and attached to a buoy to keep it clear of the ship.

BUOY-ROPE   A rope that fastens the buoy to the anchor.

CAT-ROPE   A line for hauling the cat-hook about.

CHECK-ROPE   A rope made fast to anything stationary for the purpose of bringing a moving vessel to a stand.

CLEW-ROPE   In large sails the eye or loop at the clew is made of a rope larger than the bolt rope into which it is spliced.

DAVIT-ROPE   Lashing that secures the davit to the shrouds when not in use.

DRAG-ROPES   Two ropes that trailed from the after quarters of a sailing vessel so that if a man fell overboard he could grab one of these ropes as the vessel passed him. They generally had Turk's-head knots on them, spaced about 2½ feet apart, to assist one in climbing aboard.

ENTERING-ROPES   Ropes that hung from the upper part of the stanchions alongside the ladder at the gangways.

FOOT-ROPE   A rope suspended under a yard or boom for men to stand on. Also, that part of a bolt rope to which the bottom of a sail is attached.

GRAB-ROPE   A line secured above a boat boom or gangplank for steadying oneself.

GUEST-ROPE   A rope fastened to an eye-bolt in the ship's side, and to the outer end of a boom, projecting from the ship's side, by guys, to keep the boats clear off the sides.

HAWSE-ROPE   A rope used to take the strain off the anchor warp when clearing hawse.

HEAD-ROPE   A rope to haul out jib-booms, and the bowsprits of cutters, etc. Also, that part of a bolt rope at the top of a sail.

HEEL-ROPE   A rope for securing the inner end of a studding-sail boom to a yard.

JAW-ROPE   A rope over a jaw of a gaff, to keep it from leaving the mast.

LIMBER-ROPE   A rope rove fore-and-aft through the limbers, to clear them if necessary.

LUFF-ROPE   That part of a bolt rope on a fore-and-aft sail nearest the mast.

PARREL-ROPE   A rope used to confine a yard to a mast at its center.

PASSING-ROPE   A rope led round the ship, through eyes in the quarter, waist, gangway, and forecastle stanchions forward to the knight's head.

PORT-ROPES   Ropes for hauling up and suspending the gun port lids.

RIDGE-ROPES   Ropes sewed along the center of an awning to give it the pitch needed to shed rain.

RING-ROPES   Ropes made fast to ring-bolts in the deck, and by cross turns round the cable to confine it in stormy weather. Also used to reeve off the anchor cable through the hawsehole.

SLIP-ROPE   A rope whose bight is passed through the ring of a mooring buoy with both ends on shipboard. By letting go one end and hauling on the other, the ship is freed.

SPAN-ROPE   A rope made fast at both ends for hooking a block to the bight.

SPRING-ROPE   A rope led from a ship's quarter to her anchor cable, to bring her broadside guns to bear upon a given object.

SWAB-ROPE   A rope tied to the handle of a swab for dipping it overboard.

TAIL-ROPE   A rope, attached to the clew cringle, that is made taut when the sheets are transferred.

TILLER-ROPES   Ropes leading from the tiller-head round the barrel of the wheel. Also used to secure and control the tiller of small craft.

TOP-ROPE   A rope rove through the heel of a topmast to hoist it by its tackle to the masthead.

TRIP-ROPE   Rope fastened to the tripping hook of the anchor tackle to release the anchor when the order, "Let fall!" is given.

YARD-ROPE   A temporary rope used for hoisting a yard for crossing or sending down.

Marine Pictures

Ever since man first made pictures on the walls of caves, or decorated his weapons, he has tried to make portraits of the things he loved, or the things that thrilled him most. From these early efforts, Art, as we know it today, has sprung. Pictures in general can be classed in three groups—the portrait, the story-telling pictures, and the conventional. In a portrait, a true representation of the object is essential, and it may be pretty or artistic if the subject is beautiful. The story-telling picture, or illustration, is seldom artistic, even if the technique is perfectly done. The conventional picture, design, or scroll must be entirely artistic or it is of no value.

Ship pictures, in general, come in the class of portraits; in some cases, if they represent some particular incident in the career of the vessel, they are also story-telling. Thus they are seldom, if ever, artistic and are more of a combination of a document (telling how things actually were) and a portrait (giving the true proportions and shape). But like a fashion plate, which shows a woman some nine or ten heads high, and with feet smaller than her lilylike hands, so, too, the marine artist has conventionalized his work so that a vessel is often shown in the teeth of a booming gale with all sail set and standing up straight. And some ships—like the ladies on the fashion plate—are shown more dashing and rakish than they ever were. All this is correct and desirable in a ship or yacht picture.

It is also desirable from the sailor's or yachtsman's point of view to go into rather more detail in the picture than the naked eye can usually see, and this brings up a very interesting point, for there is a big difference in people's vision. Some have eyes like a hawk and can see every shackle, grommet, or block on a ship more than a hundred yards off, while to others it all seems a blur or is mostly represented by mass or color. But no doubt the average person sees things about as shown on the paintings of Turner, or, we will say, like picture no. 1.

Undoubtedly some people see things in sharp outline; others have eyes that are more color-conscious, and others are more impressed by tone, value, shadow, etc. These differences account for the varied tastes of individuals and help explain why there is such a great difference in pictures. Right here some of our younger friends, who have been playing around with the fascinating little black box, will say, "Yes, but isn't a photograph the exact impression of the picture as it is?" Some people seem to believe a photograph to be the truth, as so many people think a thing that is in print is a fact, but this is far from so. The photograph certainly is a clever chemical trick, but it can only register the colors from the spectrum that are active on the sensitive material used, and these are surprisingly few, so that colors and values in a photograph are hopelessly mixed. The length of exposure makes for great variation. Also, two

Figure no. 1. Print by J.M.W. Turner.

photographs taken from the same spot with lenses of different focal length will produce quite different pictures as far as perspective and the shape of curved objects, like a boat, are concerned. Picture no. 2 shows a photograph that has some of the qualities of a painting.

A good picture should be a feast to the eyes, and the artist painting it must choose the savory parts of the scene and combine them to give the most pleasing effect, leaving out whatever unpalatable matter there may be in the scene, just as a good cook, in preparing a dish, uses only the most palatable parts of the fish, fowl, or beast, put together most pleasingly. But this choice in a photograph is impossible, and you must take it all—head, feathers, and feet—as they cannot easily be separated.

To make a really good portrait, the artist must be very well acquainted with his subject, and this often takes a great deal of study in order to bring out all of its subtle character. This is particularly true of a ship and any good ship picture represents an unbelievable amount of study—and, of course, it has to be done by men who make a specialty of this branch of the art.

To a great extent the ship pictures of New England were drawn to order for the captains of the ships portrayed, and these gentlemen were the severest critics imaginable. Not only

Figure no. 2. A photograph with the qualities of a painting.

were they entirely familiar with their ship, which they often had seen built and in use under all conditions, but as a class they were the most broadly educated people we had. Few of us realize today what high-grade men the sea captains were before about 1850 or 1860. Not only were they trained in higher mathematics for the type of navigation then in practice, but they were called upon to be surgeons, diplomats, and financiers, for in the days before the telegraph a vessel often went to sea to trade, as they called it, and the captain was the agent who had the responsibility of selling his cargo and buying another; or, as often happened, selling ship, cargo and all.

These sea captains were great connoisseurs of art objects and brought back to their countries the choice objects now shown in the museums of England, France, Holland, and New England. Very often, on retirement, these captains lived in homes furnished by themselves in nearly perfect taste, so it is safe to say the ship pictures that were owned by these captains were at least as carefully chosen as their Lowestoft china, East India bronzes, and unrivaled glass.

One of the last of these sea captains of this old school was Captain Arthur Hamilton Clark, born in Boston in 1841. During a very long and active life at sea and connected with shipping, Captain Clark made a hobby of collecting ship pictures. Two thousand two hundred of these were prints, which he presented to the Pratt School of Naval Architecture at the Massachusetts Institute of Technology. This collection of prints, known as the Clark collection, is perhaps the finest thing of its kind in the world, as a collection of prints of shipping and craft, although the Macpherson collection, now owned by the British government, is by far the largest and contains 7,500 items, many of which are portraits of naval heroes, seaports, etc. So, for prints of ships alone, it is not much more complete than the Clark collection.

The third great collection is that of Commander Sir Charles Leopold Cust, Bart, K.C.V.O., C.B., C.M.G., C.I.E., R.N., and is confined exclusively to naval battles.

The pictures in this article are intended primarily to show examples of the commoner types of graphic art, as used in pictures of shipping and craft, and to show oil paintings, water colors, wood engravings, lithographs, etchings; and the many types of combination prints, such as colored lithographs both printed and hand tinted, combination engraving, etching, mezzo-tints, etc. A few words about the advantages and disadvantages of these types may be of interest, although the writer realizes he is treading on very dangerous ground.

The advantages of an oil painting in general are that, at the time of painting the artist can use a greater range of colors and values than in any other way. He can paint over, or change the work almost unceasingly, and it has been said that some of the old masters worked on, or re-worked, their canvases for over a year. The disadvantages are mostly from the collector's point of view and are that good oil paintings are expensive to produce and require a lot of space to store or hang. Picture no. 3 is an oil painting.

Water colors, on the other hand, are nearly the opposite in all these respects. The range of colors or tones is quite limited, so that it would be nearly impossible, for instance, to show a shining black hull with white rail caps, etc. Water colors cannot be easily worked over or changed, so a very finished water color, like painting no. 4, requires more skill than an oil painting; and a really good water color is a cheerful thing to look at, so that they have always been popular. Some very good water colors have been made in a few hours, so it is possible to make them much cheaper than oils. A great many of them can be kept in a portfolio unframed, which is an advantage to a collector.

Paintings are individual or unique pictures, not easily dupli-

Figure no. 3. Oil painting by W.A. Fowles.

cated or reproduced, but the various forms of prints that come next are intended to be printed in numbers from the original negative, stone, or plate; strange to say, this often adds to their value, for if you are lucky enough to have a print of some picture that has become stylish (like some of the Currier and Ives prints a few years back), they often are valued more than a very well done painting, even though the print had no artistic merit or accuracy.

But before taking up the prints, I should like to say that, although they were often printed in large numbers, the plate, stone, or negative often represented an unbelievable amount of work. For instance, many of the plates of steel engravings that were about two by three feet would cost today several thousand dollars to produce, so that each print that was pulled from such a plate had to sell for quite a good price. There is no rule to go by to tell how many prints were taken from different negatives, but, in general, only a few—say, twenty first-class prints—could be taken from a copper-etched plate that had very delicate lines, for paper is a powerful abrasive, and when it was forced into the delicate grooves of the plate under the enormous pressure of the roller in the press, the paper soon polished off or changed the character of the etched line. But, on the other hand, in a picture done all with coarse lines on a wood engraving or a steel engraving, several thousand prints could be pulled. The dollar bill is an example of a steel engraving, where many thousands of prints are taken from the plate.

Figure no. 4. Water color by Thomas G. Dutton.

Almost all of the types of prints were developed with a great deal of care, as each one of them at one time was the principal means of illustration, so that the woodcut, the etching, the steel engraving, and the lithograph all had their day of being the best money-makers or the most in vogue.

In this article there is no woodcut, but since nearly everybody is familiar with the technique of making these, we will let them pass with only a mention that they are different from other negatives, inasmuch as in charging all the other types of plates with ink, the ink is rubbed in the grooves and wiped off of the original surface before printing, so that a black impression is given only at the lines. On a woodcut, the part that is cut away is cut out so far back that it does not get charged with ink or print on the paper, and only the flat original surface registers. This, in itself, makes it necessary for the artist to stick to quite simple or quaint types of pictures. A woodcut, for this reason, is not good for the necessary fine detail required in ship portraits.

Wood engraving, which is quite different, is done on the end grain of hard, fine-grain wood, like boxwood. An example of this type of print is shown in print no. 5. Wood engraving was for many years the most popular type of cheap illustration. It was brought to a very high state of perfection some forty years

Figure no. 5. Wood engraving, Marblehead, Mass.

ago by a Frenchman named Lepére, and at times wood engravings are confused with lithographs and other engravings, although, as a general rule, they are printed on cheap grades of
paper. In all engraving the lines are mostly straight, as the artist
or draftsman has to push the graver in the direction in which it
is sharpened to cut, so he does not have a free hand to make a
very pleasing picture. This is quite different from the case of an
etching, which is described next.

From the collector's point of view, etchings today are
certainly the most desirable of all prints and by far the best
medium for drawing small-scale portraits of vessels, for if the
artist has the skill, he can go into microscopic detail. In painting
the artist is hampered by the peculiarity of his tool—the brush—
which, to give it an ungraceful description, has to be dragged
around to keep the hairs in line, and the work, to quite an
extent, is done by motion of the unsupported arm.

In pen-and-ink drawing, the artist can only make sweeps in
the few directions allowed by the nibs of the pen.

In drawing with a pencil, the pencil point constantly changes
as it is deposited on the paper, so that no constant or reliable
type of line is recorded.

In an engraving, the draftsman must resort almost entirely to
mechanical aids and compose his picture of straight lines and a
few curves made under great difficulty.

But when the artist sits down to a well-prepared plate to trace
his lines for etching, he is working in a medium that is
practically only limited by the artist's ability. He can move his
needle in any direction with the same resistance, combine free-
hand and mechanical drawing, and attack the problem of
shadow and tone so unhampered that even color can be
suggested.

Unfortunately we have never had in America an etcher who
made a specialty of accurately portraying ships or yachts that
were contemporary with his life, but Mr. Wales of Boston has
done remarkably fine work of vessels between about 1800 and
1850.

England has had, and now has, several fine marine etchers,
and the best of all was undoubtedly Edwin William Cooke, R.A.,
F.R.S., 1811-1880. His work to a great extent was done when
he was between eighteen and twenty-one years old. He knew his
subjects perfectly and could draw possibly better than anyone

who had attempted marine subjects. All of his work is most painstakingly done and every detail is drawn out, as can be seen by examining his work with a magnifying glass. His work is the most perfect, from an architectural point of view, of any artist who worked in any medium. Another contemporary etcher who was very good was Henry Moses. See picture no. 6.

Next there is an etching by W. L. Wyllie, R.A., who wrote the book *Marine Painting in Water Color* in 1901. This etching represents a period a hundred years later, and it is interesting to see the tendency toward painting and away from the pure line. Picture no. 8 is a photograph that has some of the qualities of an etching.

From the collector's point of view, etchings have many advantages. They are often quite inexpensive, and good ones invariably increase in value. They will stand a lot of handling and abuse; in fact, perhaps more than any other type of picture, so a collector can have several hundred of them in a drawer, book, or portfolio; and since they go well with any type of interior, the problem of hanging them is simple. As for disadvantages, they have practically none.

Steel engravings, which are not popular at the present time,

Figure no. 6. Etching by Henry Moses.

Figure no. 7. Etching or dry point by W.L. Wyllie, R.A.

Figure no. 8. A photograph that has the values of an etching.

were once thought to be quite grand. The great amount of time necessary to produce the plate rather prohibited able artists from working on them, for they could make more money at something else, so that to a great extent they were the work of engravers, draftsmen, etc. The large one here shown of Boston Harbor (picture no. 9) is not pure engraving but probably contains some etching, stipple, etc. In general, engraving is not adapted to ship pictures, particularly the surrounding water, which is hardly ever shown pleasingly, but there have been some very fine engravings of ship designs, plans, and details, which are rare and valuable.

Lithography is the favorite medium for marine prints because it is so adapted to depicting the sky and sea. While it is not as good as etching for fine detail on small prints, it still is possible to show fine lines in the rigging, etc., and the modeling of the hull and the curve of the sails can be shown to great advantage in delicate tones and shades, so that from the collector's point of view, lithographs are only second to etchings. They are often moderate in price and can be stored compactly, although they are more easily damaged than etchings. The fact is, there are more good lithographs of nautical subjects than any other form of print, and *that* in itself makes it desirable from the collector's point of view. Picture no. 10 is a lithograph.

The technique of making lithographs is so complicated and varied that it would take a long time to describe it, but to anyone interested in studying it, I recommend the book "How to Appreciate Prints" by Dr. Weitenkampf, which is in most libraries. Lithographs were at first done on stone (thus the name), later aluminum sheets, and various substances having a somewhat porous texture were used. It is from the texture of the negative that the lithograph gets soft lines. It, too, is spoken of as a planographic process, which might be described by saying that the surface of the plate or stone is all on one level or plane, but the ink or color to print is retained in places treated chemically to absorb it. Lithographs have been made by most of the best artists in the last hundred years, and their names would number hundreds.

Before finishing with lithographs, it should be mentioned that it was possible to print large numbers of them from the original drawing, because several stones or plates, which were nearly duplicates, were taken or transferred from the original drawing,

Figure no. 9. Engraving with other processes.

Figure no. 10. Lithograph by Morel-Fatio.

which was done on paper and placed upside down on the stones. The stones received an impression chemically for the draftsman to work from. This also made it practical to make several stones for color printing, and the Cozzens print (picture no. 11) here shown is a good example of a colored lithograph. Most of the Currier and Ives prints, and many others made to sell at a cheap price, were done in this way, but the lithographs done in England and Europe about 1850 are often very fine and nice to have. Possibly the best known of the marine lithographs of that time is the one by T. G. Dutton showing the *America* running wing-and-wing as she appeared when winning the cup that has since borne her name. Dutton seems to have been the principal marine lithographer around 1850.

There are several other types of prints, such as the aquatint, mezzotint, stipple, etc., and although some prints were made in these methods alone, as a general rule these processes were only used to fill in background or make sky, texture, etc., on etchings and engravings in a much easier way than by handmade lines, and some of these processes are often seen on prints from around 1860 and later.

I will now mention some of the marine artists in an effort to help or guide those who are interested in acquiring their pictures. While I realize that I am no authority on art in general, still my work and studies have perhaps to a certain extent qualified me as a judge of their architectural correctness, and I must say that many pictures accepted as marine art are quite architecturally impossible. You know a ship has anatomy as much as a horse, dog, or the human animal, but many of the so-called marine artists seem to have overlooked this, so if their names are not included in the list below, that is one of the reasons. Also, I have left out those whose pictures are so rare and valuable that they are hopeless to try for.

Willem van de Velde: Holland and England, 1610-1693. Van de Velde is often spoken of as the father of marine painting and the first to master aerial perspective, and it may be no exaggeration to state that his distant ships, clouds, and shadows have never been excelled. He appears to be entirely familiar with the vessels of his time. It is not likely that you can acquire one of his paintings, but there are quite a few prints by good engravers and etchers of his pictures, so anything with his name on it is apt to be good. Picture no. 12 shown here is from his painting

Figure no. 11. Colored lithograph by Fred S. Cozzens.

Figure no. 12. Painting on Delft tile after W. Van De Velde. Done in 1764.

"A Fresh Gale" and was done in about 1760 on Delft tile by Johannes van Duyn, one of the best Delft decorators.

J. M. W. Turner: England, soon after 1800. While some may not think of Turner as a marine artist, still he did very impressive paintings of large ships of the time, although his smaller craft sometimes were not as accurately drawn as could be wished. Still, he must have had quite a lot of nautical knowledge. While his paintings are not obtainable, of course, still there are quite a few engravings, etchings, and lithographs available that were done for or partly by him. Picture no. 1 is a print he is said to have done some of the work on. I think anything that has his name on it is worth picking up, and most of them you will not tire of. This, after all, is one of the best tests of a picture.

E. W. Cooke, R.A., F.R.S.: England, 1811-1880. I have written about Cooke before in this article under etchings, but for those who would like to know more about Cooke, I would recommend the chapter about him in Uffa Fox's book *Sail and Power*, page 103. The best thing about Cooke's pictures or etchings is that they are still available at a remarkably cheap price.

Henry Moses, who worked around 1830 in England, did work quite similar to Cooke's, but it varied more. Some is quite sketchy and some most minutely perfect. Anything with his name on it should be very good. See pictures 6 and 13.

Robert Salmon: both England and U.S.A., circa 1814. I believe he came from England or Scotland and painted here around Boston for several years, then went back to England. He worked in oils, and his paintings are very fine indeed; there are still some of them to be had occasionally. They are sold at a good price but certainly are worth it.

The Roux family: France, 1790-1840. There were three or four in the Roux family who specialized in ship portraits, mostly in water color. Their paintings are beautiful and decorative and generally quite accurate. There are still some available at a price.

M. Morel-Fatio: France, circa 1830. He always signed his name with an anchor lying on its side after the name or initials M.F., so if you see anything with the anchor on it you had better grab it: if you don't, I will. See picture no. 10.

L. Lebreton: France, worked around 1840. Mostly lithographs. His vessels are quite architecturally correct; his small craft would please any sailor.

Thomas G. Dutton: England, 1850. Lithographs mostly. Dutton is probably the most important of marine artists from the collector's point of view, for there are a great many of his fine lithographs available. He worked both from his own sketches and from paintings by others. I can hardly find words of praise sufficient to describe his accuracy and skill. See picture no. 4.

John E. C. Petersen: U.S.A., 1860. Oil paintings. Petersen was one of our best marine painters. Many of his paintings are in the gallery at Andover Academy.

A. W. Fowles: England, 1870. Mostly oil color. He specialized in racing yachts, which are very good. See picture no. 3.

Fred S. Cozzens: U.S.A. Cozzens was probably at his best around 1880, although he continued painting up to about 1918. He made a great many pen-and-ink drawings for illustrations in books and magazines. Many of his lithographs are available, as well as quite a lot of his water colors, but they are increasing in

Figure no. 13. Print by Henry Moses.

price rapidly. His portraits of yachts are speaking likenesses and are much sought after by the few who have a knowledge of these things. He is probably the best artist we have had who made a specialty of yachts. See picture no. 11.

W. L. Wyllie, R.A.: England, 1900. Water colors and etchings. Wyllie was a thorough artist who also had an intimate knowledge of yachts and shipping in general. He was good in both line and color. He wrote the book *Marine Painting in Water Color*. See picture no. 7.

Warren Sheppard: U.S.A., mostly after 1900. I do not think you can pick up many of Warren Sheppard's drawings or paintings, but anyone interested in marine painting should look up back numbers of *The Rudder,* particularly the years 1909-1910.

Clifford W. Ashley: U.S.A., around 1910. He painted and drew the whaling industry with a great deal of understanding and feeling.

J. Spurling: England. Spurling undoubtedly knew his ships, rigging, and sails, but most of the reproductions of his paintings are in such bright colors it is difficult to hang them. I prefer the ones in black and white, or sepia, and love to look at all of them.

There are several fine marine artists in England at the present time and for that matter there always have been since 1700, but we cannot mention them all and their pictures are not easily available.

Now a few words in defense of pictures in general. Boats, automobiles, and liquor all have their thrills, but they either do not last long or they cost a lot to keep up. Well-selected pictures, on the contrary, increase in value while constantly giving pleasure. Many of the pictures shown here are a hundred years old, and some are older. They cost practically nothing to keep up and give an amazing amount of pleasure to those who understand them. Some of them were acquired for a tenth of their present value, so that they are by far the best investment their owner has ever made, and the satisfaction of acquiring them one by one is an almost continuous joy.

Some Reasons for the
Peculiarities of Vessels of the Past

Possibly you would be amused by some discourse on some of the vessels of the past, for the development of the sailboat is spread over several thousand years and is now mostly a matter of conjecture and imagination derived from Egyptian art and other ancient pictures, stone cuttings, and coins.

Most of the civilization of ancient times that we know about was on or near rivers or seas, and it is most likely that only those localities that carried on commerce acquired wealth. The ancient cities, with their magnificent temples, therefore must have followed some maritime prosperity that we do not know about. There must have been many, many ships and large ones at the time to have acquired this prosperity. The temples, pyramids, and other ancient construction were of enduring materials and in countries without frost, so we still have them; but the wooden structures have disappeared, as have the boats and ships.

When one considers the so-called Cro-Magnon race, which lived not so far from the valley of the Mediterranean 25,000 years ago, one finds the Cro-Magnon was quite a handsome fellow, certainly more intelligent-looking than many men you might meet today on the street. I am only mentioning this because the Egyptian boats and vessels indicate to me that the art of boatbuilding was very ancient even at their time. At any rate, from the models in the pyramids, the stone cuttings, and painting on pottery, it would seem the Egyptian had many types and sizes of craft, ranging from canoes to vessels with three tiers of oars, capable of carrying a huge stone obelisk on deck. In the sketch below, I have shown an average Egyptian vessel used for trading with the land of Punt. It is as my imagination would reconstruct it, and I have discounted the high ends and other prominent parts shown on the stone cuttings, for in those days—before the art of perspective drawing was mastered—it was customary to exaggerate the important parts or people by drawing them larger. You will often see the captain, pilot, or other dignitary shown much larger than the crew or slaves. As I see it, some of these Egyptian vessels of 1000 B.C. were quite similar in shape to the Venetian gondola of today, rigged with an ingenious square sail with a yard at top and bottom, and masts well stayed. They went in for overhanging ends, and this no doubt was for landing on river banks. These long ends seemed to have given some trouble from hogging or sagging, for most pictures show a large hogging cable making a truss as it went over uprights amidships, similar in principle to the hogging girders on river steamers 2,900 years later. It would appear from paintings on vases, etc., showing boats being built, that the Egyptians used about the same methods of construction as practiced throughout the world today on heavy wooden boats, or square seamed and caulked planks over sawn frames, fastened with trunnels.

Egyptian vessel about 2000 B.C.

About the year 700 B.C. there was a type of vessel trading in the Mediterranean generally referred to as a Phoenician galley. These craft had several points of similarity to the earlier craft of the Nile. They had greater draft, beam, and freeboard, as they were seagoing vessels and no doubt carried much larger cargoes for their length. Their midship section and entire stern, including the large, curled-over and decorated stern post, was the same. Also the large steering oar or rudder. But forward they had a ram or spur, probably made of a large, sharpened rock, and to carry this in a seaway it was necessary to make a full, buoyant bow so that we see that long before Christ's time, the shape of a vessel was influenced by other things than wave action and wetted surface.

Phoenician galley.

From this time on through the next four or five hundred years, the principal craft of the Mediterranean had large rams of various materials, and they must have been hard to steer or sail, but these beaks or rams were often near the water level and may not have made the lines as impossible as is sometimes pictured.

About this time, 500 B.C., the Greeks were building quite large and powerful war vessels, which were enlarged galleys propelled by oars and two small square sails. They apparently had two or three decks and must have had considerable draft and stability to carry this top hamper, but so little actual knowledge about them exists that it is hard to speculate. It is likely, however, that there were also some long, narrow vessels built for speed, as well as the ponderous, high-sided ones for battle. Otherwise the Turkish Corsairs and other piratical craft would have had easy picking.

The Roman war ships were apparently built for coast or harbor protection and were mere floating fortresses. Probably they only made short voyages from harbor to harbor in fair weather. Speed seemed to be of no object. They were like wide canal boats with a flat bottom, square bilge, with tumblehome sides above water to make boarding difficult. They were high-sided for throwing spears and rocks, and altogether uninteresting from a sailor's point of view, though they probably were formidable engines of war.

The next type of vessel of which we have accurate knowledge is the so-called Viking ship used from about 800 to 1000 A.D. They are quite different from the earlier Mediterranean types just referred to, as they had hollow lines in both ends, considerable deadrise to the sections, and were of much lighter displacement for their length. They had some keel projecting below the hull proper, no doubt originally for a runner when hauling out or beaching. The keel and the sharp deadrise of the sections allowed these boats to sail wind abeam and probably on the wind even before they adopted the lee board. These boats were of light and scientific construction; the lapstrake planking was worked out with a cleat on the inside near each frame, and a lacing or lashing was rove through this cleat and around the frame. At the lap of the planking one plank was grooved the full length, and in this groove lay a good-size packing of loosely twisted woolen yarns. For this reason the boats could twist and work without leaking, and because the frames and planking were not pierced by fastenings, they could be made very light. The frames too could be made of natural crooks, as they were mostly quite straight. These boats could stand the strain of beaching in a seaway, or the shock of collision in battle, as they were so light in themselves and so springy that they would bend or give before rupturing. These details of construction are only mentioned because they must have had a profound influence on the type of craft finally developed.

These wonderful vessels, the fastest in the world at their time either under oars or sail, were probably kept hauled out when not in use and were thus so light and lively that they went over rather than through the water. Their graceful sheer and high ends made them splendid sea boats, so that when manned with the largest and hardiest men of their time, they could attempt real ocean voyages, and the sagas tell us that they pillaged the Mediterranean ports, levied a ransom on early London, and ransacked all the coast of Europe. They discovered Iceland and Greenland and probably visited North America. They set up colonies in France, England, and Scotland, and probably many of us who are ship-minded are partly descended from them.

At the time of the Vikings, even if some of the Nordics had not been Christianized, they did have many laws that were quite civilized, and this was particularly true in regard to slavery. Their slaves or bondsmen were comparatively few and lived in the house with the family, and there was little distinction between them and the freemen or property owners, and at sea no distinction that we can make out from the sagas. To the south the ships were propelled entirely by galley slaves chained to the rowing benches. This must have caused quite a difference in the arrangement of and management of the vessels, and made it possible for the Viking ships to be long and narrow on the water line and of light displacement, depending for stability in sailing on the weight of their living ballast sitting out to windward in their flaring sides. There is no reason to doubt that these vessels attained very high speed under favorable conditions. One sixty feet long might have easily gone fifteen knots in a strong breeze of wind on the quarter with a trained crew balancing her, and one of these craft driven hard before a gale of wind, lifting over combing seas, must have made a picture never equaled since their time.

Many of the features of design in naval architecture, as well as nautical terms, are descended from them. For instance, the names of the sides of a boat—starboard and larboard—once meant the side of the steer-board or rudder, and the side of the leeboard. According to the sagas some of the Viking ships had removable figureheads, and at one time there was a law requiring them to remove the figureheads when approaching their home ports, as it was believed they would scare the women and cattle. So we can assume some of their figureheads were quite large and grotesque. Anyone who is interested in reading parts of the sagas and descriptions of the Viking ships would do well to read the illustrated two-volume work *The Viking Age* by Dr. Chaillu.

From the time of Caesar through to King Alfred's time, southern Europe used mostly wide, bulky craft, quite often referred to as the round ships, and we have no authentic data on them. Northern Europe was using the descendants of the Viking ships, which were called "long ships" in the case of the larger ones, the smaller ones being referred to as "keels." It was the merging of these northern and southern types that evolved the galleasse, the cog, the carrack, caraval, galleon, and droman. Most of these names are confusing, for at different times in different countries, the same name was used for a quite different type. For instance, today in Germany the ketch is often called galleasse. However, in general these types were designed to be seagoing craft capable of moderately long voyages, for by this time the mariner's compass was in use in Europe. The countries that made these developments or combinations were the Genoese, Venetians, and Hanseatic League. The smaller shorter and rounder craft, more after the Mediterranean type, were often called cogs if the rudder were hung on the stern post; and nef if furnished with a side rudder. They generally had one mast placed near midships. The cog, rigged with a square sail, and the nef, with the side rudder, generally had a lug sail and sometimes a lateen set from a mast raked or pitched forward. The northern types even in large sizes were built lapstrake. Roughly speaking, the northern contributions were: (1) A model built up from a quite straight keel. (2) Concave ends below water. (3) The square sail rigged with braces, etc., for sailing on the wind. (4) The rudder hung on the stern post (afterward called the rudder post).

The southern or Mediterranean influence was: (1) More beam, draft, and displacement. (2) The forward and after castle, or raised platforms on the ends to fight from. (3) The full, round bow (a survival from the ram). (4) The lateen sail, which for many years was used for a mizzen.

About this time, 1300 A.D., many things were influencing naval architecture. The square stern was coming in in the south; long voyages were being attempted; and most important of all was the use of firearms. At first, very small pieces were used, and only for defense from boarders. These were mounted at the break of the poop and fired shot along the rail or swept the main deck. These small pieces were called serpentines, pierers, demi-culverins, and murdering pieces, and must have been very efficient at repelling boarders. Fighting tops, or great castellated baskets at the head of the mainmast and other spars, were now of great importance to shoot arrows from, throw burning brands, and no doubt some early matchlock muskets were used. Larger cannons soon came into use, too, for offense or firing at broadside, and as the gun port was not invented until 1550, the guns were carried on the upper or spar deck.

All this great weight and top hamper, far above the water line, necessitated that the ships of that time be of great displacement, and they must have been heavily ballasted to have the necessary stability. They were probably very slow and many could not beat to windward excepting in light airs. No doubt the ships or naval craft of that time were as carefully planned and designed as cathedrals or any other important contemporary structures, but no plans of them are known and no models or pictures that are not wholly conventional and picturesque and impossible. In fact, our knowledge of shipping between the years 1000 to 1500 is most meager and not authentic, although several wealthy English gentlemen have dug into the subject very carefully. The church or votive models of this period, once quite common in Europe, are entirely decorative and of little help, for any sailor-

Sail plans of around 1760.

man can see a vessel was never like them; if it had been, it would have capsized at once. They also in most cases have no identity and simply represent a vessel that has been blessed.

The Spaniards were the leaders in naval architecture in the fourteenth century and they developed the great galleons and the first large seagoing ship-rigged vessels. Spain was wealthy and religiously minded at the time, and her great galleons were built to defend themselves when carrying valuable cargoes, so they were heavily armed, which called for great displacement. Their lines under water, particularly near the keel, were very sweet, and altogether they were admirably adapted to sailing before the wind, when full lines forward and an easy run aft are desirable.

On their long voyages they probably used the trade winds and laid out their courses to keep the wind aft of the beam. All things considered, they were fine designs and it was a difficult problem to build the gorgeous accommodations thought necessary for the Spanish grandees, and carry a large battery of guns generally made of bronze and therefore much heavier than iron. These ships were by far the most gorgeously decorated the world has ever known, and with their carved and gilded poops picked out with blue and other contrasting colors, they must have made a stately sight. Or at night with their great lanterns alight, rolling down the trades, their splendor must have astounded the vessels of poorer countries.

While it is probable that these fourteenth and fifteenth century Spanish ships often made good runs with fair winds, they never could have been fast because of their large displacement, but their great size may have allowed some speed. However, they were dull to windward and this was the reason why the English outmaneuvered them when the Armada made its attack on England. However, Holland was next to rule the waves, and this was no doubt because of Spain's influence while she ruled Holland, for the Dutch ships were very similar but somewhat straighter sheered, sharper forward, and neater rigged.

It is probable that the Dutch were better sailormen and more stubborn fighters than the Spanish. At any rate, many of the words in the sailor's language and the names of the parts of ships came from Holland, and Dutch contributions to small-boat architecture are felt all over the world. They made the first good fore-and-aft-rigged boats—sloops and schooners—and started yachting or sailing for pleasure. It was while exiled in Holland that Charles II became fond of the sport and introduced it to England, as is all told in Pepys' diary of the time. Holland achieved a high state of culture around 1600 and the designs of vessels, models and particularly paintings that she made then are perhaps the oldest accurate records of shipping we have, excepting the aforementioned Egyptian and Norse craft. The Dutch marine artists of the time have never been exceeded for making oil paintings, giving accurate detail combined with artistic arrangement and coloring, and in fact the Dutch school has been imitated ever since by the world's best marine painters.

The large Dutch ships, like those used by Admirals Tromp and Ruyter between 1620 and 1670, might be said to represent the highest development of the Spanish type of great galleon, or highly decorated ship. Although England and France were building copies, or similar ships, during this time, even as far back as 1514 the English Great Harry was an attempt to copy the Spanish ships. Holland also built or developed the great East Indiaman or first large passenger ships regularly sailing around the Cape of Good Hope. These superb ships resembled the battleships of the time and were heavily armed, enough to hold off any of the pirates of the Atlantic or Indian Ocean. These

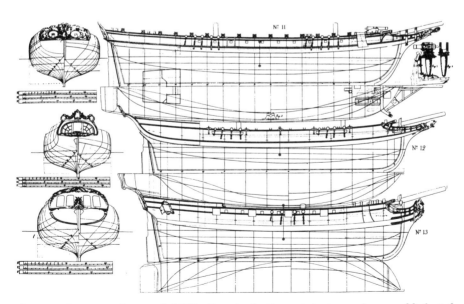

Some privateers of around 1760. Top to bottom: privateer schooner 93 feet 6 inches overall, privateer schooner 70 feet overall, privateer sloop 62 feet 3 inches overall.

great ships took several years to build and they were completely overhauled after each voyage, and some of them lasted nigh on to 100 years.

All during this time and later, England was building large, noble ships, but it is generally conceded that France led in the science of naval architecture after about 1700, and in fact up to the time of the French Revolution, when the heads of most of the people intelligent enough to master that science were cut off. But France's contribution to the science will be taken up later, and we will now consider some of the proportions of the great ships of about 1700—and there was no great difference between the ones of Spain, Holland, France, and England. Also, the large-size merchantmen were similar because it was necessary for them to be heavily armed.

At first sight these great ships would appear as great unwieldy tubs, but if you raze or remove their three or four upper decks, you will at once have as sweet a model for their length and great displacement as could well be. The great displacement is necessary to carry the battery of guns—often as many as 100—and the large amount of ballast to counterbalance this large weight so high up. In other words, these ships were designed around a large battery of guns. It was considered most important to design these vessels to roll slowly, or present a steady gun platform, as some time often elapsed after the torch was applied to the torch hole before ignition took place, so the whole mid-body of these vessels near the water line was cylindrical, and that is why they have the pronounced tumblehome and slack bilge.

These ships sometimes had a complement of 1,000 men all told, ranging from boy powder monkeys to knighted admirals, so that quartering them and feeding them must have been quite a problem in the design, and a thousand men can eat and drink quite a weight in a few months. In those days there was a vast difference in the grades of life, and the quarters for an admiral and his flag officers were thought necessary to be in keeping with their rank and to give prestige to the nation they represented when entertaining foreign potentates. As most of these capital ships were originally commissioned flagships, this accounts for the sumptuous after cabins and highly decorated poops.

The side galleries in use between 1600 and 1800 were to

allow another point of forward vision after a third gun deck was superimposed in the waist of the ship. On smaller ships the side galleries were mostly decoration. Not only were the high poops necessary for the vision of the officer conning the ship, but they made her act like a weather vane while lying at anchor. And designing a ship that would lay well at anchor was most important in those days, for unless well at sea they anchored in gales or even in head winds. The whole ground tackle was immense and designed to ride out the worst storms if caught in the open on a lee shore, and it can be rough in the Bay of Biscay and the English Channel.

The anchors, which were similar to those used today, are a monument to the smiths of the time and were much larger for the size of the vessels than is now customary. The anchor hawser was a large cable-layed rope generally of hemp, which passed through the hawser holes forward and along the manger, past several riding bitts. The hawser was never bent, but continued straight aft to the main hatch, and in securing the hawser, smaller ropes were bent to it at the various bitts, distributing the strain over some length of the ship. For this reason, it was necessary to locate the great capstan well amidships, or between the fore and main masts. The main capstan barrel was on the lower main deck, but the king pin or shaft extended up through the upper gun deck where there was another barrel. The two heads or barrels could be locked together by inserting sundry stout pins if extra power were needed to break out an anchor, at which time there would be about twenty-five capstan bars about fourteen feet long in use. Each bar would have four or five men to it so that for a short time it is possible they could develop as much as 100 horsepower. The anchor cable was not carried around the capstan barrel, for it was too large to handle. The warps are said to have been sometimes as much as eight inches in diameter. A special rope called a messenger was used. This messenger was a large loop, or endless rope. Aft it had a few turns over the capstan barrel; the forward end led over a snatch block. As part of the messenger traveled aft toward the capstan, stops were clapped around it and the cable, so that the cable was brought home in a straight line to the main hatch, where it passed below to be coiled in a gigantic coil. All told it must have employed about 150 men to up-anchor on a capital ship of this time. This description is only given to explain why the ground tackle as a whole took up so much room on these ships.

That some of these large ships of 1700 were a failure is a matter of record, and it is no wonder, for if hove down even to a slight angle, water would enter the lower gun ports, which would lessen the small amount of reserve stability. One of the tragedies was the 100-gun ship *Royal George,* built in 1756. She capsized and sank with most of her crew when careened to clean her bottom. To quote from memory part of a poem of the time—

> Toll for the brave, the brave that are no more;
> All sunk beneath the wave, fast by their native shore.
> Eight hundred of the brave, whose courage well was tried,
> Had made the vessel heel and laid her on her side.
> A land breeze shook her shrouds and as she was overset,
> Down went the Royal George with all her crew complete.

Around 1750 there was a Danish naval architect named F. H. Chapman who apparently worked in several countries. He published a large book of plates and designs covering most of the types of vessels then in use in Europe. The book or portfolio is

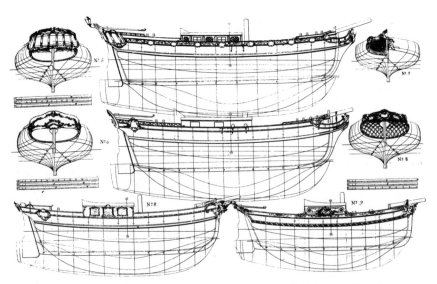

Yachts of around 1760. Top, 42 feet 3 inches overall, 14 feet 10 inches beam. Center, 35 feet overall. Lower left, 29 feet 3 inches overall. Lower right, 25 feet 4 inches overall.

named *Architectura Navalis* and is the best source of information for anyone studying the lines and proportions of vessels of that period.

The French were the great designers of ordnance in those times, and that may be why they developed faster ships than other nations, for if a ship could be equipped with a lighter battery, the displacement and ballast could be greatly reduced. So they developed the first fast frigates, which all the world copied but never equaled. A very fine rigged model of one is at the Museum of Fine Arts in Boston, where anyone can see she must have been very fast.

In as short a paper as this, it would be impossible to describe the many rigs that have been used, but anyone interested in them should get the book *Mast and Sail in Europe and Asia* by H. Warington-Smyth.

Here I will mention the lugger and cutter, which the French developed. A lug sail is the step between the square sail and a fore-and-aft sail. It is rigged like a square sail, shaped and used like a fore-and-after. The yard of the square sail is ahead of the mast and the shrouds, whereas the yard on a lugger is between the mast and one set of shrouds, so that the sail can be set right fore-and-aft, and in tacking, the wind comes on one side and then the other of the sail, but on the square sail the wind is always carried on one side, excepting while staying when the sails are said to be aback.

The French developed fine, fast, cross-Channel packets with the lug rig. They were quite long and narrow, with a sharp entrance and fine run aft. The large ones had a graceful sheer and three masts, setting a topsail on a yard above the main yard. These were the type of craft used for smuggling and harrying the coast of England during the wars, and apparently they could outsail and outmaneuver anything else. As time went on, the yard was peaked up more and the whole sail set farther aft on the mast, until eventually the yard became a gaff with jaws and the sail was entirely aft of the mast and had its luff laced to the mast.

While it is true that the Dutch had some sloops and schooners with the luff of the sail laced to the mast prior to 1600, it was the French around 1700 who developed the real cutter. It is said that its development came about in this way. Small, fast boats were needed by the customs officers to collect revenue and catch smugglers. Some of the rowing cutters from the large ships were taken to rig up for this purpose, in the belief that they would be fast under sail or oars. For a fast sailing rig they stepped one mast with a gaff mainsail and rigged a bowsprit for headsails. As these boats were successful, larger decked and ballasted ones were built, and these early French revenue cutters were rigged exactly as most all other real cutters were for the next 200 years.

In the meantime, England had started yacht racing, the first yacht race generally believed to have taken place on October 1, 1661, between the yachts owned by Charles II and his brother the Duke of York. These first yachts were sloops after the Dutch style and carried fore staysail, gaff mainsail, and a square sail. When the English took up racing in earnest, they naturally adopted the rig of the fast revenue cutters and made the rig famous in the yachting world, so that today we generally speak of the English cutter.

A true cutter is a deep, narrow vessel with a plumb stem, rigged with a single mast, and always with a gaff mainsail, a topsail, fore staysail, jib and jib topsail, and long reefing bowsprit. It is believed that there are less than half a dozen real cutters in the United States at the present time, and the young men who refer to all single-masted vessels as cutters are displaying ignorance. Almost all modern single-masted yachts, from J boats to the models racing on the ponds, are leg-o'-mutton rigged sloops.

Now that we have got to the subject of yachts, we may as well consider their history and the effect on their shape that measurement rules have had. As previously mentioned, Charles II started yachting in England, and in fact at once made it so popular that the history of yachting for the next 200 years, or up to about 1850, is entirely English. We are indebted to the diaries of Pepys and Evelyn for a record of these first yachting events. Pepys was at one time secretary of the Admiralty and was such at the time the Admiralty moved from the Tower of London to larger quarters; through his zeal and forethought, a great deal of early naval history and data of ships were saved. Pepys also owned many fine models and historical paintings, which he collected with good judgment and untiring energy. King Charles, besides being fond of dogs and ladies, loved all things pertaining to the water. He had about eight fine yachts built; he made the subject of naval architecture the court hobby;

and he would talk anywhere, anytime, with anyone on nautical subjects. This subject led him into science, and he chartered the Royal Philosophical Society, the oldest scientific society in England, many of whose early reports were of nautical matters. One of his courtiers, Sir Antony Dean, first calculated a ship's displacement in 1666. King Charles also founded the Naval Observatory at Greenwich and a home for old sailors supported by the government. On his own yachts he experimented with lead ballast and metal sheathing, and he was interested in many experiments in hull form, including some double-hulled craft, or catamarans.

Early yachting was to quite an extent for conviviality, and the food and liquor consumed would have done credit to their Viking ancestors, but eventually some means of rating had to be adopted. At first it was the tonnage rule used for the merchant service, or the product of the length of the keel times the beam, times the depth of hold, divided by the constant 94, which changed it to tons. This produced a very healthy type of vessel with lines similar to the channel luggers but with a cutter rig. However, by reducing the length of keel, the rating was reduced so that cutaway forefoots and raking stern posts were used, but the boats on the whole were very good and possibly better in proportion for cruising than any of the later types. This rule was used until 1723, when the merchant service rule for determining tonnage was changed so that, instead of using the actual depth of hold in the formula, the half beam was used instead, so the formula was approximately the length on deck, times the beam, times the half beam. This had a most important effect on model, as beam was measured twice and depth not at all. Merchant ships became narrow, deep, and slab-sided. They were cranky and slow and had to be ballasted in addition to their cargo. In fact, they developed such a poor type of vessel that the Yankees took a great deal of trade away from them between 1750 and 1850. As for the yachts, they became the typical English cutter. Why the rule was changed to measure beam twice, or take the half beam for depth, is difficult to tell, but it is likely that since most ships from Elizabethan times had averaged twice as wide as deep, the customhouse had decided that taking the half beam for depth would do away with the difficulties of measuring the depth of hold in case cargo or ballast was in the way.

In 1850 the yachtsmen used a rule that measured length in a different way from the merchant service, but in other respects was similar to the old rule. This was known as the Thames Measurement Rule and was used until about 1880, when length was measured at the water line. In the meantime a type of yacht was developed popularly called "planks on edge," or "lead mines." The most extreme probably was the five-ton *Oona*, forty-six feet overall, five feet six inches beam, eight feet draft, and a displacement of 13.25 tons, with 10 tons of lead on her keel. Her sail area was 2,000 square feet.

Yachtsmen having had enough of the "lead mines," a new departure took place, and in 1886 for the first time, sail area came into the rule. Dixon Kemp got up this rule. It was roughly the sail area multiplied by the length and divided by the constant 6,000. Many fine yachts were built under this rule, including the *Britannia,* but the Herreshoff fin-keeler *Wee Win* went over in 1892 and clearly showed how this rule could be beaten. So in 1896 Mr. Froud's Linear Rating Rule came in. This rule took the length, breadth, girth, and sail area of the yacht, which was divided by a constant, which brought R, or rating, down to a figure that approximately represented the length of the boat, and this, I think, was the first attempt of the English to measure a boat so that the rating could be used with the scale of allowance gotten up for the Boston Yacht Club in 1868 by Mr. Nathanael G. Herreshoff when he was a student at Technology. Previously the English sailed their boats in classes, such as 5-tonners, 5-raters, etc., and used no time allowance excepting in the larger classes, where they used an arbitrary allowance based on the previous performance of the competitors, as is done in horse racing. This rule, on account of its girth measurement taken at about the mid-waterline, developed yachts with very poor keels. They were practically a straight line from the forward waterline to the heel of the rudder. This profile of yacht is impossible to lay-to, difficult to dock, and generally damages its rudder when grounding. However, some very nice looking boats above the waterline were built to this rule, although they had excessive overhangs and too large a sail area.

In 1906-07, the first international conference on yacht measurement was held. Practically every country in Europe was represented, but America (who next to England is the greatest yachting country in the world) was not represented. Thirteen nations assembled, all full of scientific talent and each with the best possible rule. Under these circumstances it was obvious that nothing but a compromise could be accepted, with the usual unsatisfactory results. Thus was born the International Rule, or the Meter classes—6, 8, 12, etc. These boats are expensive to build, poor cruisers, and are slow for their cost or sail area. They are required to be built under a scantling rule, which makes it difficult to build them strong or long-lived. Personally I believe England was better off when she made her own rules, and other countries bought her yachts or built to her rules.

Because this International Rule produced heavy displacement, slow and expensive boats, the Swedes and Germans developed a rule for small racers and cruisers to be used in a part of the Baltic called the Scharen. These boats are called Scharenkreuzers or Scharen Cruisers. They do not have a rating that can be used with the time allowance tables but are divided into classes according to their sail area—22, 30, 45, etc., square meters of sail. At first this rule gave promise of developing a nice sailing boat of moderate cost, but many complicated and impractical hull restrictions were added to the rule so that now the rule is so complicated that it has broken itself down. In fact, it is practically impossible to measure a boat under it and say definitely whether she is in the class or not. Also, there is no limit to overall length, so that a type of boat quite unsuited to cruising has been developed. This class is also slow in light weather on account of its large amount of wetted surface for its sail area, and unless carrying a large lapping jib or parachute spinnaker, they are dull performers and of no interest to a real sailorman.

To go back to America—we had few and simple rules at first and in the smaller classes boats were simply measured on deck. This developed a very wide boat with a large sail and, as shifting ballast was allowed, the famous sandbaggers were the result. They were perhaps the fastest boats in the world for their overall length and good performers in light weather because of their small wetted surface, but there were so many accidents, capsizes, and drownings that shifting ballast was eventually barred. The larger boats were classified according to their customhouse tonnage, with no restrictions on sail area. Some very large schooners were built and they were undoubtedly fast sailers. In fact, the schooner *Columbia* in 1871 made as good time over the cup course as any later defender. Some of these early large yachts had very sweet hull form, but as most of them were centerboarders and carried their ballast high up, they had to shorten their sail in heavy weather, and it took real sailormen to handle them.

The medium-size yachts were wide, shallow sloops. In America the various tonnage rules used did not discourage beam, so up till the sloop-cutter controversy about 1880 we had been developing wide, shallow centerboarders with hard bilges and hollow ends. After some hot racing and hard feeling between the sloop and cutter men, American designers produced a compromise type. The *Shadow* and *Puritan* are examples. By this time sail area was a factor in the measurement, but it was not used in a way that counted up in the rating as much as the length measurements. Length was taken in a great many ways, but we can say for simplicity that it amounted generally to a mean or average of the W.L. and O.A.L., so the plumb-bowed yacht was much in style.

A great deal of the sloop-cutter controversy was centered around the Seawanhaka Yacht Club; its leaders became quite rule-minded and in 1882 brought out the Seawanhaka Rule, which measured S.A. and W.L.L. but did not measure overall length. About 1884 the New York and most other clubs adopted this rule. Yachts soon became long on deck, and in 1891 the *Gloriana* came out with nearly as much overhang forward as aft. She also had a fully developed bulb keel and could carry her sail better than the other yachts of comparable waterline length. Her great success and the continuance of the rule encouraged the building of yachts with longer overhangs and deeper keels, until a very unhealthy type of yacht was developed.

Eventually some of these were nearly twice as long on deck as on the waterline. Although the hull was shallow, they had great draft on account of their deep bulb keels and were altogether so unsatisfactory that about 1900 the N.Y.Y.C. decided a rule was needed that would encourage a more wholesome type of craft. They sent out invitations to various designers and measurers to submit rules and chose the one submitted by Mr. N. G. Herreshoff that was known as the Universal Rule. In this rule, the rating is in proportion to the sail area, provided the displacement is equal to a proportion of the waterline length and there are length measurements that prevent long or full ends. Draft is also limited and a great many fine yachts, including the J boats, M boats, P's, Q's, R's, and S's, are built to this rule. There have also been several one-design classes built to this rule. They are the New York Yacht Club 30's, 40's, and 50's, and nearly all of the larger sailboats for the last thirty years are built to it. *Queen, Westward*, and *Elena* are good examples of what was produced in schooners of that size.

So we see what a powerful effect measurement rules have when we find one country developing deep, narrow cutters while the other country is using sandbaggers. The writer has a theory that little advance has been made in hull form for speed in the last seventy-five years, although great advance in speed under certain rules of measurement has been made with one rule after the other. He believes that a model similar to some of our old yachts, like *America, Sappho, Gracie*, etc., can be made to go quite well if given outside ballast, light hollow spars, leg-o'-mutton cross-cut sails, and a smooth bottom, and this theory was pretty well substantiated in 1938 when *Tioga* sailed from New London to Marblehead, a distance of 180 miles, in eighteen hours. That is good sailing for a boat of any size or rating, but unfortunately these older models do not rate well under any of the modern racing rules.

As for our commercial craft—of course the early ones were made full-ended for carrying lumber on deck and stowing it below and, being slab-sided, it made them measure less under some of the tonnage rules. Why our whaling ships were so box-shaped I cannot say, but some oldtimers have said they were built by the mile and cut off as wanted. Why Donald McKay built his clippers with such a parallel mid-body only God and he know, but he was a Down Easter and may have been brought up on that model. At any rate, it didn't make much difference, for his ships were so large that their speed-length ratio was low. The speed record of *Lightning* was no doubt due mostly to her great size and to the fact that she was driven night and day before a westerly gale by two able captains. *Lightning*'s tonnage was 2,804, while *Taeping,* which tied with *Ariel* in the Tea Race of 1866, was only 767 tons. The small Scotch tea clippers were superb little craft and perhaps the handsomest sailing vessels ever built. They were perfect aloft and "alowe," and before closing I should like to state that I take my hat off to the Scotch for designing and building a large percentage of the world's best ships and yachts in the last hundred years.

Captain Charley Barr

It so happened that about the year 1909 there was a slight financial panic or temporary depression in the stock market, and so several of our racing yachts did not go into commission that spring. One of these was the crack sloop *Avenger* of fifty-two feet waterline, a yacht on which I had raced the two previous seasons. Very suddenly, however, the owner of the *Avenger* decided to put her in commission just before the New York Yacht Club cruise, and if he could not sell her on the cruise, he would lay her up directly afterward.

That summer, strange to say, Capt. Charley Barr was unemployed, so the *Avenger*'s owner made a contract with him to put her in commission, hire a crew, and sail her on the cruise as well as in the Astor and King's Cup races. I lived quite near where the *Avenger* was fitted out and, as I showed a familiarity with her parts when she was being rigged, plus an unbounded enthusiasm for the *Avenger* as a whole, Capt. Barr invited me to accompany him in the few days before the cruise. So we went to Newport. No doubt Capt. Barr had invited me along principally because he wanted someone to talk to in the evenings, and thought I would be an appreciative listener, in which assumption he was quite right. The next several evenings were spent by Capt. Barr in relating in great detail some of the famous races he had participated in. He had a most remarkable memory. He could tell just what sails his competitors had carried in the races, who was on board each yacht, just what tactical mistakes he or they made in each leg of the race, although the race being described may have been ten or fifteen years before.

Those evenings on board the *Avenger* with Capt. Barr were about the pleasantest of my whole life. If it were a pleasant warm evening, we sat in the cockpit and had the whole fleet of yachts at Newport as our subject of conversation. Each yacht of any consequence (either steam or sail) was described one after another in the most interesting way that could be imagined. The abilities of her designer and builder were reviewed, the peculiarities of her original owner related, and then a general review of her life was narrated, including her outstanding cruises and races, for Capt. Barr seemed to have the whole history of each yacht stored away in the archives of his memory.

Brenton Cove (a part of Newport Harbor), where we were anchored some of these evenings, was in those days a most romantic place. The few yachts that were anchored there were large fine ones, such as the steam yacht *Tuscarora, Erlking,* and *Narada*, and some of the large schooner yachts. At the head of the cove, surmounting a large gray rock or crag, stood the fine residence of E. D. Morgan, which had been designed by Stanford White with a great deal of care and was intended to be a copy of one of the strongholds of the Knights of Malta. On our southeast side we occasionally got a glimpse of the feudal walls of Commodore James' large residence, or at least we could see the weathervane on its watchtower through the trees back of Beacon Hill. Off to the westward lay Fort Adams, which in those days seemed full of life from the sunrise gun 'til the poor soldiers' work ceased with the sunset gun, for all the morning was spent in exercises and all the afternoon in reviewing the troops as each company passed in review, and the cavalry maneuvered to the sound of bugles while the parade grounds were surrounded by the bright-colored parasols of the Newport belles.

The evenings were the pleasantest times of all in Brenton Cove, for as the wind went down at sunset, the whole expanse of Narragansett Bay seemed spread out to the northward, and its many islands gave distance to the scene. The lights of the many lighthouses and of the larger naval craft in the outer harbor came into being one after another, and the quiet scene was only interrupted by the occasional passing of a ferry boat or the shrill

Avenger, *four times a winner of the Astor Cup.* (The Rudder)

whistle of a distant steam launch at the government landing. This was the setting in which many of Capt. Barr's stories were started, and as darkness came on and the dew began to form on the deck, we went below and sat in the main saloon under the subdued light of a bulkhead lamp, while above the main skylight one could occasionally see the sail cover over the mainsail as the flicker of the riding light lit up one side, then the other, as the lantern swung back and forth.

These talks of Capt. Barr were monologues, sometimes of three or four hours' duration, told in a pleasant and quiet way, and I was as much held spellbound as the Wedding Guest was under the eye of the Ancient Mariner. Not only were these talks monologues because I was spellbound, but as the story went along, each question was automatically answered and the whole description was so clear that the scene seemed distinctly before me, with each yacht in her place working up to the final climax at the finishing mark.

Capt. Barr was in some ways unique among yacht captains. He seemed perfectly content to stay aboard ship all the time ex-

cepting for the morning marketing and getting the latest newspaper. He was always neatly dressed and seemed to get up that
way very early in the morning. He planned a complete day's
work for each of the crew, and although all hands were busy all
of the time, the yacht at all times was ready to receive the
owner or guests, and could have been gotten under way at a
moment's notice. All this is in great contrast to most yacht
captains of that time, who only dressed up to go ashore to
spend the evening in some gin mill, or to boast on some pier-
head till the small hours of the morning. Capt. Barr's crews
seemed quick, willing, and contented. Their principal ambition
seemed to be to please their captain, so that everything went off
like clockwork and the meals were good and on time. Yes, Capt.
Barr loved to be aboard ship, but best of all he liked being
under way and sailing, and when everything was straightened out
and he sat at the helm with his eye on the luff of the topsail, he
was the picture of contentment. I must say I never saw an
owner who began to get the pleasure out of sailing or racing
that Capt. Barr did. He seemed never to be under tension in a
race, and could steer the yacht by instinct while carrying on a
conversation or perhaps telling some funny incident of past
yachting.

When so inclined, he could be most entertaining and agreeable
to the owner and guest, which certainly is not so of most
skippers, particularly the amateurs who seem to take racing so
seriously that they cannot bear to have anyone speak when they
are steering. However, Capt. Barr did not speak to any of the
crew when under way except in giving an order. When he was
on one of the larger yachts with first and second mates, quartermasters, etc., he was a strict disciplinarian, and after his crew
had been trained, the procedure of carrying out an order was
about as follows. He had trained his first mate (who for several
years was Chris Christiansen) to keep one eye on him, and when
Capt. Barr wished to give an order he simply crooked his forefinger slightly, whereupon the mate came close to him. Then
Capt. Barr would say very quietly but distinctly something
about as follows: "Mr. Christiansen, after rounding the next
mark I would like the spinnaker set to starboard. I would like
the jib topsail replaced with the ballooner."

The mate would then pace slowly up and down the deck,
watching the marker they were approaching until he estimated

the time and distance right to commence action, when he would roar out, "Take in the yib topsail. Raus mit the spinnaker pole to starboard. Stand by for a yibe." Before this moment everything was quiet, the crew of some twenty men all lying prone in a neat row with their heads near the weather waterways. The second mate crouched in the leeward fore rigging watching the headsails, and the only sound to be heard was the swish and hiss of the waves under the leeward bow, and a low moan of the wind in the rigging. But now the yacht's deck suddenly changed to a scene of intense activity as each man scrambled to his station and stood crouched, ready for action, some at the sheets, others at the upper and lower backstays, while the spinnaker pole was being run out and the men on the bowsprit had muzzled the jib topsail.

Now the mate nods his head at the mastheadsman, and this agile fellow runs up the mast hoops like a monkey climbing a ladder and stands on the fore spreaders in anticipation of changing the main topmast staysail. Now the mark buoy is almost abeam, and the yacht swings like a gigantic turntable as Capt. Barr crouches to leeward of the wheel and pulls the spokes toward him hand over hand. The yacht now rights herself, and the wind, which had seemed quite strong, suddenly becomes very light as the yacht, which before was heading into it at some seven or eight miles an hour, now goes with it, making the difference of some fourteen miles an hour to the wind's apparent velocity. But in the meantime there is the clicking of many winches and the chorus of many orders as the second mate and the two quartermasters call out in broken English strange words that are instantly understood and obeyed. Some of the orders are, "Stand by the after spinnaker guy," "Overhaul the leeward backstays," and the whole yacht seems to quiver from the stumping forward and aft of several 200-pound Swedes, when crisp and clear the first mate calls out, "Yesus, don't younce de yacht."

The spinnaker and balloon jib are now broken out almost simultaneously and the balloon main topmast staysail is going aloft. Soon everything quiets down again and the only movement is a few hands coiling down sheets and halliards. Capt. Barr has now moved back of the wheel and stands with his eye on the telltale pennant at the peak of the club topsail. He seems perfectly cool and quiet, and no one would have guessed his eye had seen anything but the mark buoy, the compass, and the luff of the topsail. And furthermore, anyone would have thought the maneuver had been perfectly performed, would have thought the crew had performed miracles of sail changing in almost seconds. But now Capt. Barr crooks his forefinger again and the mate approaches him, saying, "Yes, sir," and Capt. Barr says, "Mr. Christiansen, that was done very well, but the next time I would like to see the club sheet slacked simultaneously with the fore-sheet." "Aye, aye, sir," says the mate as he moves to the weather main rigging with one eye on the luff of the spinnaker.

Now the men are all sitting up on deck, ranging aft from the forecastle hatch to the weather backstays, when silently the jib topsail is handed up, stretched aft, and the men kneel in a straight row, each bending over and pulling a piece of stopping thread from the mop-like hank attached to his waist a little aft of starboard. Each man rolls the sail up to its luff rope, ties a few stops, and almost before you know it the jib topsail again disappears forward.

Now eight bells is struck, and there is a slight movement at the fore hatch. The second steward is passing up great thick sandwiches and a bottle of beer for each man. What a pleasant sight it is to see this row of big Swedes and Norwegians each with a sandwich in one hand and a bottle in the other! If the jib topsail had been stopped up rapidly, the sandwiches and beer were now being stowed away even more rapidly. Many of Capt. Barr's crew were large, handsome, fairhaired sailors of middle age with Viking-like moustaches, and many of them had sailed under him for several years and were perfectly trained. After being trained, these Nordic crews that Capt. Barr specialized in were very quick workers. Each man was a machine that could understand and execute orders without stopping to think what he was doing, so that the yacht had one head or brain (the captain), several mouthpieces (the mates), and twenty or so bunches of sinew, muscle, and leather, which acted instantly at each order.

The yacht is now rolling slowly back and forth as the spin-naker pole rises and settles, and the great billowing spinnaker and balloon sails pull alternately on one side and the other. The contrasts and shades of colors through the sails are always changing, so that the yacht seems a great iridescent being of opalescent color—the heavy mainsail of grayish white, the club topsail of creamy yellow, the spinnaker and balloon jib of transparent pinkish tan; and now and then a shadow from a spar or sail reflecting the blue of the sky and sea in a light violet shade. The Oregon pine spars of rich amber and gold, the teak rail cap, the snow-white decks and uniforms of the crew, the polished bronze—all seem alive and moving as they sparkle in the reflection of the sun. Beyond our triple wake of spindrift that narrows in the distance, where the sea has turned from transparent green to azure blue, there follow two other gigantic nautili decked in creamy rainbow hues.

This is but a glimpse of yachting at the turn of the century in the time of Charley Barr, when yachting was at its zenith, but alas, now all gone and only a memory like the squarerigger, for the large steel schooner is gone, the crews that manned them are gone, and the captains who could manage them are gone.

Charley Barr spent his boyhood on or near the Clyde in Scotland. His older half-brother was the famous racing skipper John Barr, who was captain of the cup challenger *Thistle*. So from his earliest youth, Charley was in a world of yacht racing, and as a very young boy went on Scottish yachts as a spare hand. He first came to this country in the little cutter *Clara* of only nine

The cutter Clara *of 9 feet beam. (*The Rudder*)*

feet beam. He was cook and cabin boy on the *Clara,* and I presume about nineteen years of age. This crossing of the *Clara* was in 1886, and they must have had some pleasant steady weather, for Capt. Barr used to say about the trip, "We were on one tack for so long that the grass grew on her topsides," which of course means that she was heeled over one way long enough for her to get foul above the waterline.

The American owner of *Clara* was Charles H. Tweed, and when he had a new yacht designed and built by William Fife, Jr., in 1888, Mr. Tweed sent Charley Barr, who in the meantime had studied navigation, to bring her across. The new yacht's name was *Minerva,* and she, with Capt. Charley Barr at her

Minerva, *a beautifully modeled yacht.* (The Rudder)

helm, won so consistently during the next two years that it might well be said Charley Barr's reputation as a racing skipper was at once made in the *Minerva,* but *Minerva* was a beautifully modeled yacht, so perhaps each helped to make the other famous.

Capt. Barr's next command was the forty-six-footer *Wasp,* a similar yacht to the *Gloriana,* which he generally succeeded in beating. His next yacht was the steel eighty-four-foot-waterline sloop *Navahoe,* which he sailed to England in 1893 and raced against the large single-stickers *Britannia, Valkyrie II, Satanita,* and *Caluna.* Although *Navahoe*'s season in England was not very successful, still she did succeed in winning back the Brenton Reef Cup, which *Genesta* had wrested from us in 1885. Capt. Barr used to say this race for the Brenton Reef Cup was the greatest of his life, and it is probable that it was one of the greatest and most exciting yacht races ever run. It was a match race with *Britannia,* the starting line off The Needles at the Isle of Wight, and the race to and around the breakwater at Cherbourg and return. On the first leg across the English Channel, there was a strong breeze and quite a sea. Both yachts housed their topmasts soon after the start, and in the first two hours they had covered twenty-five miles, which is remarkable sailing in a seaway. *Navahoe* reached the breakwater at Cherbourg slightly ahead of *Britannia,* but in this short weather leg, both yachts encountered some very hard squalls that nearly knocked them flat, and *Britannia* worked ahead, leading *Navahoe* home across the Channel but seldom getting more than a hundred yards ahead of her. At the finish of this long, hard race, after the time allowance was corrected, *Britannia* was declared the winner by two and a half seconds, but the mark boat had shifted due to stress of weather, making the finish line on an angle. The regatta committee of the Royal Yacht Squadron, taking this into consideration, finally awarded the race to *Navahoe,* so we can guess it was a remarkably close finish.

I wish the reader could have heard Capt. Barr tell the story of that race, for it certainly was something to listen to, and it would have given him a very high regard for yachting of some fifty-odd years ago.

A few days later *Navahoe* had a try for the Cape May Challenge Cup, which *Genesta* had also taken away from us in 1885. This time over the same course, *Britannia* beat *Navahoe*

The Navahoe *in England.* (The Rudder)

nearly an hour, but this was due mostly to a fluke in a three-hour calm when *Britannia* got a breeze that took her about three miles ahead of *Navahoe*. In her racing in England in 1893, *Navahoe* won six races out of eighteen starts, which was a very good record considering the three or four fine yachts generally racing against her.

Capt. Barr's next command I think was *Vigilant*; in 1895 she served as a trial horse against the new defender, *Defender*. Charley Barr made *Vigilant* perform very well, which caused some ill feeling and protests, and probably somewhat embarrassed my father, who had designed both yachts, and it seems remarkable today that anyone could have made *Vigilant* keep up with *Defender*, for the latter was not only a great improvement in model but was of very scientific construction, her topsides, deck, and even deck beams being of aluminum, a then (1895) quite new metal for yacht construction.

For the next two or three years, Capt. Barr sailed the large schooner *Colonia* with great success. The *Colonia* had been built in 1893 as a sloop to defend the cup but was beaten by *Vigilant*. After she was rerigged as a schooner, she was used many years, most of them under the name of *Corona*.

When the cup defender *Columbia* came out in 1899, Charley Barr was selected as her captain, and this time the new yacht had no trouble in beating her trial boat, the previous defender, *Defender*. One of the principal owners of *Columbia* was J. P.

Morgan, for whom Charley Barr had the greatest possible respect, so that when J. P. asked Charley to sail *Columbia* again in 1901, he was glad to do it. But in the meantime, in the year 1900 if my memory serves me correctly, he was captain of one of a one-design class of seventy-footers, perhaps the *Mineola* owned by August Belmont. This was our largest one-design class of sloops and had practically the same sail area as a modern J boat.

In 1901 J. P. Morgan asked Capt. Barr to sail *Columbia* again, which he did so successfully and skillfully that she beat the new cup boat *Constitution* quite regularly, and so *Columbia* was again chosen to defend the cup. Capt. Barr used to chuckle

The Columbia. *(*The Rudder*)*

when telling about that season's racing, and would say, "Mr. Morgan and I defended the cup that year for a few thousand dollars, while before that it had sometimes cost some two hundred thousand, and since then much more. You see I had laid *Columbia* up carefully in 1899 and when she was put in commission again she was in good shape, and as it turned out we could not buy many new sails that year, for the *Constitution* had taken all that the Herreshoff Manufacturing Company could make, so that season's racing cost very little." But to this I must add that Capt. Barr was so used to *Columbia* that he could handle her like a knockabout, and he knew just what he could do with her under all conditions. He has often been spoken of as a reckless, daring captain who took great chances, but I do not agree with this statement. I admit he was aggressive but believe he knew just what he was doing and seldom caused fouls or collisions. He could handle *Columbia* like a top and scared the after guard of *Constitution* most to death.

However, *Columbia* had a hard time beating *Shamrock II* that year, for *Shamrock II*, designed by George Watson, was one of the best-designed yachts that ever challenged for the cup. In some of the races *Columbia* only beat her a few seconds, boat for boat, although she did have some time allowance, which allowed her to win by a minute or two, but it is very likely that in the hands of anyone other than Capt. Barr, the *Columbia* would have been beaten by this *Shamrock II*.

Somewhere around the time we have been telling about, Charley Barr married the daughter of a nautical instrument maker of Southampton, England, and I believe she was a woman of good education and refinement, which no doubt had a beneficial effect on his career.

One of the next large yachts he was to command was the famous *Reliance*, the cup defender of 1903. By this time Capt. Barr was an experienced and extremely capable man, and he needed to be to handle *Reliance*, for not only was she the largest single-sticker ever built, but she probably had lighter spars and rigging per square foot of sail area than any yacht built before or since. Under Capt. Barr's superb management, she went through the season without an accident, and I (at least) thoroughly believe no one else could have accomplished that feat, for *Reliance* certainly was an extreme racing freak.

Reliance, *the greatest of them all in several respects.* (The Rudder)

Nevertheless, in spite of her size, Capt. Barr generally sailed her in and out of harbors without taking a tow, and often brought her up to her mooring buoy at Newport as one would a knockabout. And I might mention that, although *Reliance* was only approximately ninety feet on the waterline, still the length from the forward end of the bowsprit to the after end of her boom was 202 feet, length of the main boom was about 116 feet, and she drew nearly twenty feet of water.

The next few years were extremely busy ones for Capt. Barr, for in 1904 he took the steel schooner *Ingomar* to Europe and raced her in English and German waters, winning, I believe, nineteen firsts out of twenty-two starts. In 1905 he took temporary command of the three-masted schooner *Atlantic* to sail her in the ocean race called the German Emperor's Ocean Race, which started from Sandy Hook and finished at the Lizard in England. *Atlantic* made the crossing in twelve days and four hours, which I believe is still the record for sailing yachts.

There are some strange stories told about Capt. Barr on this

Atlantic, *holder of the transatlantic record.*
(The Rudder)

race, and one of them is that soon after the start he drove the owner into his stateroom and kept him there throughout the race, but Capt. Barr's version of that incident was about as follows:

"One night there came up a good beam breeze and I determined to see what the *Atlantic* could do on a reach, and when I had everything drawing well, the owner came to me and asked me to shorten sail, to which I said, 'Sir, you hired me to try and win this race and that is what I am trying to do.' And after we had won the race he was as pleased as any of us."

However, Capt. Barr said the *Atlantic* had too little freeboard amidships to drive hard and that, together with her low deck line and high bulwarks, she carried a lot of water on deck. "Yes," he said, "I had to wear hip boots most of the time at the steering wheel." Which makes me think he drove *Atlantic* pretty hard, and 'most anybody would have wanted to take in sail.

During the next few years, or between 1905 and 1908 (if I remember right), he went captain of several boats somewhat smaller than those before mentioned and, strange to say, one of these was an American schooner named *Shamrock*. I think he was also on one of the seventy-footers for at least two years, but you must remember it was nearly forty years ago now that Capt. Barr was telling me these things in the cabin of *Avenger*.

However, about that time (or possibly 1906), and I believe the last year that the 70's raced, Capt. Barr was frequently beaten by another 70 sailed by Harry Maxwell, an amateur skipper, but this should not detract from the captain's credit, for Mr. Maxwell was one of the best amateurs we ever had and was as much at home at the tiller of a twenty-one footer as at the wheel of a ninety-foot steel schooner.

Well, this brought the sketch of Capt. Barr's life up to the time he was telling me his story, or perhaps a few days before the Astor Cup Race at Newport in 1909. Then one morning a very pleasant young gentleman came alongside in a small steam yacht and requested to be shown over *Avenger.* For some reason or other, Capt. Barr thought I could do the honors, so I showed the gentleman everything aloft and alow from bowsprit cone to clew outhaul, and must have shown it with the enthusiasm that I felt for that fine vessel, for the next morning when Capt. Barr came out with the mail, he said, "I have a telegram saying *Avenger* has been sold to Alexander S. Cochran and that he will take her over with her crew immediately. Did you ever hear of Mr. Cochran?" "No," said I, but when he came aboard later, he turned out to be the gentleman I had shown the yacht to the previous day, and as we got to know him, he proved to be a very pleasant man. He invited me to stay aboard the next few days, and the day after this, *Avenger* won the Astor Cup Race.

During the next several evenings, Capt. Barr continued his stories about racing abroad in the *Navahoe* and *Ingomar,* and his crossing in the *Atlantic,* and Mr. Cochran became very interested. Although neither Capt. Barr nor I realized Mr. Cochran was a wealthy man, he soon signified that he would like to own a yacht that could race in Europe, and the outcome of these stories was that Mr. Cochran ordered a ninety-six-foot steel schooner from my father, and when she came out she was named *Westward.*

The next year, the season of 1910, *Westward* sailed for England with Mr. Cochran aboard and Charley Barr as captain. Their racing abroad, and particularly in German waters, was so satisfactory that Mr. Cochran's enthusiasm was raised to the highest pitch, and soon after he came back to this country, he ordered from Mr. William Gardner a three-masted schooner to be an improvement on *Atlantic,* with no expense spared. This yacht, *Sea Call,* was plated with Monel metal over steel frames, and although planned to last longer than the conventional steel schooner, was unfortunately condemned and broken up before she really had a chance to show what she could do. While I will not go into the details of why *Sea Call* was broken up, I will bewail the fact that she never had a real sail and will simply state that she was similar to *Atlantic* in size and shape but had higher freeboard and thus should have been perhaps the fastest schooner ever designed. Although *Sea Call* was an extremely expensive yacht, still Mr. Cochran's enthusiasm for yachting was so great that he alone, without a syndicate of owners, had the trial cup boat *Vanitie* built that same year, making unquestionably the greatest outlay any single person had ever made on sailboats in one year. The two yachts together would unquestionably cost over a million dollars today.

The winter after *Westward* raced abroad, Capt. Barr spent in England where *Westward* was laid up and, although a comparatively young man, he died of a sudden heart attack at Southampton in his forty-sixth year, having crowded a most remarkable career into a comparatively few years. If Capt. Barr had lived and sailed *Vanitie* and *Sea Call* (provided she had stood up better), the history of yachting might have been somewhat affected. However, the large sailing yacht has probably gone forever. Undoubtedly we shall never again have men like Capt. Barr, and the reason is simply because both here and in England the yachts now must have amateur helmsmen in the races. Thus our present yacht captains are little more than ship keepers.

I should mention that during Capt. Barr's era there were several other famous and capable captains, particularly in England, where they had Wringe, Sycamore, Cranfield, Bevis, Parker, and several other notable helmsmen. You see, in England they had more large yachts than we did, the season was longer, and they raced more days during the season, often every day of the week, and I believe the yacht captain was on the whole more respected, and therefore capable men were more apt to adopt that profession.

Although I may risk being accused of prolixity, I am now going to give the reader a copy of a letter written by Capt. Barr to my father, and I am not only doing this to show the type of man he was (which usually shows in a letter), but also because it contains several nautical terms properly used.

Yacht *Westward,*   Southampton,
16th July 1910

Dear Mr. Herreshoff:

Some time ago Mr. Cochran asked me to write you regarding the *Westward*, but I have not had an opportunity until now.

There is no criticism of the *Westward* to be made. She is a splendid boat, crossed over with some rather rough weather and got no water on deck, and practically on an even keel. She has not shown the least sign of strain, and made no creaking inside, which I think is a rare thing in a boat crossing the Atlantic.

In regard to her speed, she is fast enough in any kind of weather to win from the German schooners, but I have an impression that with her present load she would be rather sluggish compared with the *Queen* in light airs. This of course is only an idea. In a breeze of wind she would make an exhibition of any schooner in America. We have had some very strong winds racing, and she is always easily under control, no danger of getting in irons or even lying over far enough to make it uncomfortable.

In the race from Kiel to Travemunde, we ran with the spinnaker 34 knots in 2 hrs. 58 mins. and had a lead on the *Hamburg,* who was second, of about 3 minutes. We then reached on various courses 28 knots in 2 hrs. 14 minutes. At this stage *Germania* was second, about 2 minutes behind. From this to the finish was a close haul with a short tack at the line, distance 16 miles, time 1 hr. 17 mins. *Germania* was about 2 minutes behind, and had a list of 44 degrees just before she finished. *Meteor* broke her main gaff and did not finish. *Hamburg* was some distance behind. We carried working main topsails, as did the others, and were never in trouble. Distance 78 knots. Time hrs. 6, mins. 29. Strong wind and smooth sea.

Meteor and *Germania* on a close reach can do us from 12 to 15 seconds per mile if the wind is strong enough, but on no other point. We have outrun them in all kinds of weather and the same to windward. We have outreached them from close to wide in everything but strong hard winds.

The ballast is the same as when we left with the exception of one ton, which I took out. I took it out of the bow but later moved ½ ton from aft forward, which brought her trim the same as before. This was before we started racing. It seems to be

Westward *racing on The Solent about 1910.* (The Rudder)

impossible to get her down to 96 feet unless we take more lead out, and as she has done so well, there does not seem to be any need to do it.

In regard to the rig, we have had to make many changes. The anchor fell from the fish hook the first time we hoisted it after arriving here. It made a big dent in the rail and fell overboard, taking the chain with it. We had a way ahead at the time but dropped the sail and stopped the chain before it stopped us. The hook opened in some way, so I had a large, plain hook made and rove off a larger fall in larger blocks, and we have had no trouble since.

I had to condemn the manila part of the main halliards as they would not run through the blocks. I put in 2¾ in. hemp.

Our anchors are much larger than anything the German schooners carry and they have only four to our five. I do not understand this, as I have had our weights looked up, and am informed that we are only about 50 pounds overweight on the whole lot. The two iron blocks on the foremast for the M.T. mast staysail halliards did not have room to swing. They got aground on the collar of the forestay, so I replaced them with a single swivel block on the spring stay. We broke the head sheet tackle blocks because they did not lie clear on deck and had to put wire stops on them. The same with the fore topsail sheet blocks where we had to put in shackles. The flange eye under the main boom for the balloon M.T. staysail sheet broke the first time we used it.

The sails have had very hard usage with strong wind and rain, and although we have slacked them up on every possible occasion, they have stretched badly. The main luff got above the strut and I had it cut four inches along the foot and the corners cut off on the leech. It was out on the foot and head and very baggy, so I had about four inches more taken out in the middle. This was before we started racing. Now it is so large that it has to be cut again off the head six inches at the throat, and a foot off the peak, and the corners of the leech trimmed again. Ratsey has so much work to do that we cannot get it before Cowes and will have to use his sail.

The first cut on the mainsail was like this (sketched in body of letter by Capt. Barr). The lug foresail is out on the head and in the last race had to be lowered to clear the spring stay. In all the sails, that is, foresails and mainsail, we have had the peak cringle taken out and a hole cut in the sail instead. This appears to hold the sail just as well and saves the whole size of the thimble.

The main boom has been in two collisions and is as good as ever. A large tramp steamer struck the end of it with the luff of her bow, hard enough to grind ½ inch off one side as she scraped along. It was in the crutch and fast with the lifts and tackles, which I had no time to let go, although we were working at them. It was dark at the time and I fully expected to see it sprung in the morning, but there was not a mark anywhere except on the end.

On the other occasion the old Cary-Smith *Meteor* sailed into us on the port tack and stuck her bowsprit between the cap shrouds on the mainmast. The bowsprit went instantly and we could not see where it had been, but the stump hit the main boom abaft the wheel and put a dent in it, which does not appear to affect it in any way.

A great many remarks have been made about the lightness of our gear, but all three German schooners have broken down and we have not so far, and even after the *Meteor* (now *Nord Stern*) ran into us, we sailed right on in half a gale of wind and left her wrecked behind us. The only thing I think is doubtful now is the main lifts. We have had to renew the lift runners two or three times. The mainmast stands up fairly well with a very tight truss stay but not as well as it should. Although we have sailed in very strong winds, there has been no sea so far, and it looked rather bad sometimes.

Mr. Cochran is very much pleased, as I have no doubt he has told you, with the boat, and she is undoubtedly a fine boat—far ahead of any of our racing schooners. I am not talking about speed, but about her seaworthiness and comfort.

She has started nine times, won eight without time allowance, and one with the time allowance. She has twelve cups and the only thing she did not get was the handicap from Eckernforde to Kiel. I think she is the best boat you ever built.

I trust you are feeling better than when we left and remain with best regards,

Yours truly,
Charles Barr

P.S. We got a prize for the best corrected time over the course for all classes the day we lost the handicap cup, which was the day the *Nord Stern* collided with us.

I will now quote a few lines written in the English magazine *Field* at the time of his death, as it shows what our English cousins thought of Capt. Barr.

"We think that there can be no question that Charley Barr stood first among the racing skippers of the world. He had great skill, judgment, and nerve, he took the keenest and most intelligent interest in the accurate observance of sailing rules, and he was himself careful to be obedient to them. In person he was dark, small, and slight, with refined features, and he was of modest and unassuming demeanor. In fact, his manner, speech, and appearance were that of a townsman of that part of Scotland in which he was born, and unlike that of a seafaring man. Whilst we know of no sailing master who was a stricter disciplinarian than Barr, nor one to be more promptly obeyed, his manner with his officers and crew was quiet and dignified, and the extraordinary amount of shouting that goes on aboard many English vessels was absent in the yachts under his command."

Naphtha Launches

As we look at the naphtha launch today, it seems a most infernal machine. Strange to say, however, these launches had few explosions or fatal accidents, 'though most of them blazed up occasionally. Many were copper-sheathed in the engine compartment, so these blaze-ups were rather laughed at or thought to be part of the game. I have seen these blaze-ups at night when they certainly were alarming to the uninitiated.

The real, and possibly the only, reason for the naphtha launch was to get around the law that required a licensed engineer on a steam launch. Although the examinations for a license were not difficult, it was stipulated that the applicant for a steam license must have had two years' experience in tending a steam boiler, so very few amateurs had steam licenses, and it was the cost of hiring a licensed steam engineer that put the steam launch out of being, for otherwise they were delightful things to sail in or steam in. It seems quite strange today that the law then allowed one to operate a device that evaporated an explosive liquid in a boiler but could not do the same thing with water in a boiler without a license. If the law that required one to have a license to operate a steam launch had read "steam or any other vapor," the naphtha launch never would have come into use. Naphtha, as we used to think of it, was considered about halfway between gasoline and kerosene in flash point, price, etc., but it is seldom spoken of today. While the last common use of naphtha was in tailor shops for cleaning clothes, nonexplosive and odorless cleansers have taken its place since perhaps 1920.

The genius who worked up the naphtha power plant to evade the law was a German named F. W. Ofeldt of New York, and I class him as a genius, because he arranged or designed launches that had few serious accidents and because the power plants were novel and actually built at little expense. Mr. Ofeldt found a financial backer in Mr. Jabez A. Bostwick, the owner of the Herreshoff steam yacht *Orienta.* Mr. Bostwick was a wealthy man connected with the Standard Oil Company and I suppose trying to find or arrange uses for Standard Oil products. He had just built a factory to manufacture stationary gas engines, as that type of power plant was becoming much in demand both here and abroad for running small factories and shops. While we hear little about gas engines today, they were quite a factor in the 1880s, or before electricity took the place of gas. It is true that some of the early internal-combustion engine designers both in Europe and England got their early training in designing gas engines, so that several French and English automobiles were to bear their names.

Well, to get back to the naphtha launch. Mr. Bostwick's factory, which was named The Gas Engine and Power Company,

Etcetera, *auxiliary cruising naphtha launch.* (Traditions and Memories of American Yachting, *by W.P. Stephens.* © *Hearst Corp., 1945)*

was located at 131st Street and Brook Avenue. They quickly went into production with the naphtha power plants and later built the wooden hulls for these launches. Some of them that were used as launches with the smaller steam yachts and larger schooner yachts were of very nice workmanship. My guess would be that between 1885 and 1895 they built something like 3,000 naphtha launches, which may have averaged seventeen feet in length. The Gas Engine and Power Company also built many naphtha power plants for other boat and yacht builders, particularly for Kyle's Boat Shop, which was their next-door neighbor.

The naphtha launches were smaller, lighter, and cheaper and, of course, much quicker-starting than the steam launches, so they sold like hotcakes right up to around 1900, when the internal-combustion engine began to be reliable and lighter than the naphtha ones. After high-tension ignition was perfected so the gasoline engines could be speeded up, their weight per horse-power was enormously less than the naphtha power plant, which generally weighed 100 pounds per horsepower.

It was the general arrangement of the naphtha launch that made it comparatively safe. The fuel tank was as far forward as possible. The engine was as far aft as was convenient with a direct-drive propeller shaft, while the piping between them (condenser and fuel line) was outboard alongside the keel. To give the modern reader an idea of the potential danger of these infernal machines, the whistle was not blown by the pressurized vapor of the boiler but was blown by a hand-driven air pump, for if the heated naphtha gases were used, there was danger of an explosion in the atmosphere, as flame often came out of the stack. This was easily seen at night.

I will now try to describe the power plants as I remember them, together with the only suitable illustration I can find in my books. The engine itself was small and simple, consisting only of two single-acting cylinders that were on the same plane arranged in a V formation of about 90°. The connecting rods were directly connected to the pistons, as on the common internal-combustion engine, but the big ends of the connecting rods were swung by a common crank pin. Below these two power cylinders there were the pumps, which I think were activated by a crank pin of smaller throw. Some people have thought these engines were three-cylinder ones by not recognizing these pumps.

Just forward of the crankcase was an open spur gear that drove or meshed with the valve action gear. This latter gear in turn meshed with a gear that was connected with a smooth wooden wheel—perhaps made of wood so it would not be too hot for the hand. This wooden wheel was used both to start the engine, or to throw it off center, and to reverse the engine, for the engine would run in the opposite direction from which the hand wheel had been turned. This was arranged by having the gear on the crankshaft loose so it could be turned through a sector so the valves would be in the proper position for going ahead or astern. Also, if the engine was turning slowly, by turning the hand wheel faster than it was going, the engine would suddenly reverse. A similar arrangement, but called a loose eccentric, had been used on small steam engines, for it greatly simplified the reverse mechanism. These Ofeldt-designed naphtha engines are the only ones I remember where the hand control wheel came up to a handy position for working.

The whole engine was enclosed in a metal case of rectangular shape, and this made the base of the boiler or, we might say, the vaporizing unit, which consisted of a quite small and simple coil of tubing. The small size apparently was possible on account of the ease with which naphtha can be vaporized and expanded. It is astonishing how quickly these naphtha launches could be started.

The circulation of the naphtha in these launches was somewhat as follows, but it differs in starting. When these launches were running, or the vapor in the coils had been brought to an operating pressure, some of this naphtha vapor was bypassed to the burner by an adjustable bypass valve and its piping. This part of the naphtha, of course, was burnt and went up the stack, but the vapor that drove the engine exhausted into a tubular keel condenser, which condensed the naphtha to its natural size when it was pumped back to the tank in the bow.

Now I will try to describe the starting up or firing procedure, but it may be a little confusing unless you refer to the illustration repeatedly. First, please note that the dotted line *a* (or small *a*) represents a bulkhead just forward of the engine, and this bulkhead has a thwart at its top that supports two hand pumps and the handles of two valves. Capital *A* shows an alcohol lamp that, when lighted, is slid under the naphtha burner through an opening at the base of the boiler casing. Then if you turn the handle *B* the right

Naphtha engine. (The Rudder)

way and work the air pump *E*, this will force some of the
evaporated gas fumes in the bow fuel tank through a tube to the
burner. This pump *E* may have to be worked for two or three
minutes, depending on the temperature. This gas from the upper
part of the bow tank is what the burner uses at first. During this
time the tubes of the boiler are empty or dry, but the next move is
to open the naphtha valve *D* and give the naphtha pump *F* several
strokes. This forces naphtha into the coil boiler which quite
quickly vaporizes and causes a pressure, which is indicated on the
pressure gauge. After this the valve *C* at the front of the boiler
casing can be opened or adjusted when the pressurized vapor from
the boiler or retort will feed the burner.

After the engine is started, the pumps under the crankshaft will
both pump the condensed naphtha out of the condenser back into
the bow tank and force the proper amount of naphtha into the
coil boiler if they are adjusted properly. In practice, however, I

think the naphtha pump *F* was used occasionally. In the illustration, the pipe that comes out of the engine casing on the port side is the exhaust pipe, which conducts the used vapor to the keel condenser. The still larger pipe on the starboard side of the engine comes from the hood over the safety valve marked *H*. This hood and its pipe conduct the vapor that comes out of the safety valve when it blows to the keel condenser, but if the safety valve were allowed to blow into the atmosphere, there surely would be an explosion.

The naphtha launches were quite nice underwater, where they were really double-enders. Their sterns above water were of the so-called fantail type and were made so to protect the rudder and propeller. Several of these old naphtha launch hulls are still in use but are driven by combustion engines. They were not very good seaboats on account of the weights at both ends and because they had no flare and little flam at the bow, but their low speed of six or seven miles per hour saved them from being too bad in this respect.

After about ten years of success, the Gas Engine and Power Company was somewhat split up when Mr. Ofeldt, the genius of the concern, retired. It is said that the men who represented the capital of the company were a little hard on their genius, and capital is apt to be that way after it has got what it wants out of geniuses. However, Mr. Ofeldt designed a slightly different power plant called the Alco-Vapor engine, which burnt alcohol but in the boiler used water mixed with a small amount of alcohol—perhaps twenty percent—and as it was assumed that the engine ran on the vapor evaporated from the alcohol, the government allowed these power plants to be run by nonlicensed operators.

In this undertaking, Mr. Ofeldt was financed by Commodore E. C. Benedict, owner of the rather large steam yacht *Oneida*, who, I believe, made some of his money in the rubber industry. The Alco-Vapor power plants were more powerful than the naphtha ones and drove launches perhaps from ten to twelve miles per hour. These power plants used a boiler casing of rectangular shape made of some white or silver-color metal like German silver, and you can usually recognize these power plants by these features. I think the coil of tubing in the Alco-Vapor boilers was made up in a somewhat rectangular shape and had more than twice the heating surface of the naphtha boilers. No doubt the Alco-Vapors carried higher boiler pressure and perhaps their weight per horsepower was much less than the naphtha ones, but the Alco-Vapor launches quickly took the place of the naphtha launches on the up-to-date yachts. Certainly their smell was much pleasanter.

For some reason or other, Mr. Ofeldt left the Alco-Vapor concern and he or his son started the Kerosene Engine Company in South Brooklyn. Altogether Mr. Ofeldt must have done a lot of experimenting and some of it dangerous. A book about his life and experiments would certainly be interesting, but I suppose now it would be nearly impossible to get the data, for things that occurred at the edge of a growing city are soon stamped out and lost forever.

The Gas Engine and Power Company continued to grow, and somewhere around 1895 Mr. Charles L. Seabury, who had been a steam yacht designer and builder at Nyack on the Hudson, joined them, and the firm produced several fast and large steam yachts, including the famous *Kanawha,* which won the Lysistrata Cup twice so could be called the world's fastest large steam yacht. As a young man Mr. Seabury had worked in the boiler shop of the Herreshoff Manufacturing Company, and the first of his steam yacht engines were almost identical to those being made by that company when he was there.

The Gas Engine and Power Company and Charles L. Seabury Company became a large concern at Morris Heights. At the last of it, they built steam yachts, naphtha launches, electric launches, Alco-Vapor launches, and gasoline launches, for they built one of the best gasoline marine engines around 1905. It was called the Speedway and was noted for its long life, quietness, and reliability.

However, the steam launch outlasted, or was built later than, both the naphtha and the Alco-Vapor. I think the Lawley Company built their last one about 1910 and the Herreshoff Company about 1915. These, of course, were the best launches, or so-called "starboard launches," for sizable yachts.

Cutters, Laying-to, etc.

It was strangely quiet in the library of the yacht club one recent evening, for—thank God—the important tromp of high heels, the tense high-pitched voices of the ladies had gone for the season. You could even hear the tinkle of the bell buoys and the faint moan of the sea in the light easterly breeze outside; and as I settled down by the fireplace, the chirp of a fall cricket and the tinkle of glasses in the bar were my only distractions.

But presently I heard the voices of two well-known characters in our club. They must have been sitting quite close to the door, for I couldn't help overhearing them. One was Mr. Jovial Conversation and the other, who was a little older, was Mr. Precise Commonsense. They both belonged to good old Boston families, but I had heard they didn't always get along too well, so I was rather surprised now at their entering into conversation together. But the house committee had secured some rather good Scotch lately, and this, no doubt, had started Jovial off and Jovial, being a good conversationalist, had drawn Precise out. At any rate, I had not heard the beginning of the conversation, but my attention was suddenly taken by these words: "Cutter, be damned!" said Precise. "There hasn't been a true cutter in this harbor for years, and what's more there's not likely to be one again."

"Yes, I know," said Jovial, "but they all call 'em cutters now."

"No doubt," said Precise. "They also call a forestaysail a jumbo, a shroud a stay, etc. . . . only show their ignorance; damn confusing at times, too."

"Well," said Jovial, "what *is* your definition of a cutter?"

"A cutter, young man," said Precise, "is a single-masted vessel always rigged with three headsails, a running or reefing bowsprit, a housing topmast, and a gaff; and, of course, sets a topsail. She generally has a loose-footed mainsail and sets her jib and topsail flying, the latter generally on a yard. The cutter was first developed in France for the revenue service. Their first ones were pulling or rowing boats from large naval ships—hence their name. As time went on, and I am speaking of about the year 1700, they developed into a rather fixed type of small vessel supposed to be able to overhaul the cross-Channel luggers and other smugglers of the time.

"In order to do this, they adopted a sloop or single-masted rig so arranged with a reefing bowsprit and long topmast that an enormous sail spread could be made in light airs, and still be capable of shortening down to a very small sail area when caught in heavy weather. Thus we have the cutter, which is a specialized rig on a sloop. In other words, a cutter *is* a sloop and has always been called so in France, the country of their origin."

"Well," said Jovial, "I don't see any plain distinction or norm between the two."

"Maybe you don't," said Precise, "but in no stretch of the imagination can you call the wide, high-sided tubs of today cutters. You take the modern sloop—no bowsprit, no topmast, no gaff, forestay inboard, one or two headsails. They are plain sloops. They have none of the peculiarities of the cutter rig."

"Well I can't see any harm in calling them cutters if the youngsters get a kick out of it," said Jovial.

"Why, now, I don't know," said Precise. "Take the cutter—it has a distinct place in yachting history and the development of our modern racing yacht. How could we have had the heated cutter-sloop controversy between 1880 and 1890 if the difference were not important? How could we have developed the compromise type: first the *Shadow*, then the *Puritan*, etc., etc.? But this brings up the matter of hull proportion or model. Some time after 1800, Great Britain went in for taxing her shipping more exactly, so she evolved several tonnage rules, one after the other, and most of these rules left a distinct mark or, shall we say, influenced the model of sailing vessels. One rule, which measured the length on the keel, started the raking rudder post. Another, which measured the distance between perpendiculars, favored the plumb bow. Sometime around 1830 the so-called Thames Measurement Rule came into use. This rule was roughly the length between perpendiculars, times the beam, times (strange to say) one-half the beam. It is said that half the beam for the third factor was adopted because for many years the vessels measured averaged a depth of hold of one-half their beam, and cargo in the hold, etc., made the depth measurement often difficult. Well, as beam was measured twice and depth not at all, naturally the English ships became narrow and deep. Although many do not know it, this rule nearly drove English shipping off the seas by 1850, for her clipper ships were small, narrow, slab-sided craft that the large, liberal-beamed American clippers generally beat even with a larger cargo aboard.

"But to get back to the cutter yachts, or perhaps we had better say English cutters, they were rated for racing purposes by this same Thames Measurement Rule. This rule produced, or encouraged, a deep, narrow vessel with plumb bow and long overhanging stern, as the stern was not measured aft of the after perpendicular, which was at the rudder post. Now, as sail went free, they used the cutter rig, which allowed an enormous sail spread with its long reefing bowsprit and a topmast as long as the mainmast. They set a large English topsail, shaped like a standing lug sail, with the yard crossing the topmast. In anything but a calm they sailed heeled well over and in any breeze at all had to shorten down considerably, which they certainly could do in endless numbers of combinations, so that you will often see them in old prints with the topmast housed and small jib set halfway out on the bowsprit with the tack in the pigtail of the ring traveler, which was adjusted by an outhaul.

"Yes, the cutter was a sporting rig all right, but these young fellows who holler 'cutter, cutter, I got a cutter, he's got a cutter' might be surprised if they got aboard of a real cutter."

"Yes," said Precise, "I ought to know. I owned one once. She was too deep to cruise in and sailed laying on her ear; she was like all the rest of 'em—in a knockdown she would take the bit in her teeth and head off to leeward. Damn unpleasant feeling, too, if you are close to a lee shore."

"That is extremely interesting," said Jovial, "but won't you join me in another drink?"

"Don't mind if I do," said Precise. "That east wind seems damp and chilly."

"Here's to the cutters," said Jovial.

Leg-o'-mutton sloop designed by the author.

"Yes," said Precise, "and here's to the American sloops, which nearly always beat them."

Jovial then said, "I have often heard it said that a peculiarity of the cutter was that her mast was farther aft than a sloop."

"That is definitely not so," replied Precise, "and I have checked it on many sail plans and photos. You see, the thing that locates the center of the sail plan and the position of the mast is the underwater profile of the yacht; and the cutter, with her deep, sharp forefoot, required the sail plan unusually far forward. While it is true that some of the later cutters, like the *Minerva*, were cut away forward or had great rockers to the keel so their lateral resistance was far aft, still as a general rule the cutters' masts were no farther aft of the stem head than on the average sloop. Of course they both had various steppings of the mast, and this was partly dependent on the size of the fore triangle carried, be it either sloop or cutter."

"Well how is it then," said Jovial, "that the naval architects themselves call 'em cutters? Take the So-and-So's Seventeen Seas Flying Cutters, or the What's-Its-Name-Company's Deep Water Cutters."

"Well, sir," said Precise, "they are naval architects—you couldn't expect them to know about yachting history. Great big fellows, you know, rather out of their element working on the designs of yachts. But if you ask a real yacht designer, he will tell you soon enough the difference between a cutter and a sloop, and if he is an American he will not be ashamed of the American sloop, which has generally proved itself the fastest sailboat in the world."

"Now how about the marconi cutters, jib-headed cutters, and Bermudian cutters?" said Jovial.

"Yes," said Precise, "it was a pretty hard pill for the Britishers to swallow when the leg-o'-mutton sail came into popular use. You see, since colonial times, our common rig was the leg-o'-mutton sail for small craft—the Bugeye, the Connecticut River sharpie, the Block Island boat, the Isle of Shoals boat, to mention only a few. Some had short gaffs or large headboards and some were thimble-headed, but to all intents and purposes they were leg-o'-mutton rigged or had but one halliard.

"The popularity of this rig extended to the West Indies and

Three English sloops with marconi masts and staying.

even to Bermuda a hundred years ago, so that when the leg-o'-mutton sail came into popularity again, the Britishers called it the Bermuda rig or anything but its American name—the leg-o'-mutton sail. As far as the marconi part of it is concerned, that is most amusing. It seems that about 1912 or 1913, when the English large sloops or compromise-cutters adopted a pole mast, or one continuous spar for the mainmast topmast and topsail yard, a system of staying was adopted consisting of several diamond trusses like the early marconi radio masts on shore. Well, now, these yachts — the *Shamrock III* and the *White Heather*, etc.—of course were gaff-rigged and set topsails. After the war, when some of the smaller yachts were setting leg-o'-mutton sails, they too adopted this diamond or marconi system of staying the mast. But at the present time, this system of staying has been almost entirely discarded, so that it is both strange and ridiculous to call our modern leg-o'-mutton rigged yachts after the illustrious Italian who never had any connection with yachting."

"I call all of this confoundedly confusing," said Jovial.

"Yes," said Precise, "I call it damn confusing and it only shows the confusion that comes of using wrong names for things. And when you add cutter to these names—marconi cutter, jib-headed cutter, or Bermudian cutter—you add ridiculousness to confusion, for one of the principal peculiarities of the cutter rig is its long housing topmast. Now, how in thunder are you to hoist a leg-o'-mutton or jib-headed sail by the hounds, capiron, and yoke of the cutter's masthead?"

"Well," said Jovial, "they say a cutter will lay-to better than a sloop. Is there anything in that theory?"

"Yes, certainly," said Precise, "but first you must do plenty, as the modern saying is. But now we had better have an understanding about what laying-to is so we can talk so the other fellow knows what is meant. As I understand it, laying-to means heading about forty-five degrees away from the wind with no way on, either ahead or astern, of course making a dead set to leeward, as the sailors call it, which means slowly moving sideways. A small vessel under these conditions is remarkably steady, comfortable, and dry—in fact, much more comfortable than laying-to an anchor or sea anchor. But don't confuse this sort of laying-to with jogging or fore-reaching, the way the Gloucester fishermen shorten down for the night with the forestaysail sheeted to weather to kill their way. We will speak of schooners, if you like, after we have considered the cutter and sloop in laying-to."

"Now," said Precise, "I once owned the small cutter *Loon* (she was probably named so for her diving ability). It must have been thirty-five years ago now, and even at that time the cutter had gone by, so many people considered them quite passé; in fact, that's how I could afford to buy her. Well, late one summer we took a run over to Nova Scotia; had a pretty good time, too. There were four of us aboard, my old friend State Street Jack, myself, the captain, and a hand who acted as cook, cabin boy, and crew. Well, to make a long story short, after a pleasant cruise along the coast there, we started back one September evening, as we had thought it would take a night and a day to make the crossing from Yarmouth to Cape Ann. But it turned out quite calm, so our progress was slow for the first twenty hours or so. The next afternoon, however, we had a good easterly breeze and were making good progress, but the wind was increasing and slowly veering toward the southeast. We took in one sail after the other. By four o'clock it was blowing a strong breeze and we were maybe thirty miles from Cape Ann. The captain and I decided we didn't want to make Cape Ann at night in a southeaster, so we agreed to lay her to. Now this is the point I am getting at. It took us nearly two hours to lay her to. First, while we were still running or wind-on-the-quarter, we housed the topmast. Now housing a topmast at anchor is a simple matter, but in a breeze at sea, I'll tell you it is something. The boy went aloft and rove off the topmast halliards, then we slacked up the shrouds and hoisted her till he pulled out the topmast fid. We lowered her away. Then we had a wrestle to seize the topmast heel in place far enough ahead of the mainmast to allow the mast hoops to clear when we got ready to lower the mainsail.

"After lashing the topmast shrouds down, we tackled her long, noble bowsprit. It had started to spit some rain by that time and the barometer was falling rapidly. Well, it generally is easy enough to house a cutter's bowsprit. Hers had a latch arrangement on the bits so the heel of the bowsprit could come right aft and swing sideways till the bowsprit's cone or nose just extended beyond the gammond iron on the side of the stem head. Thank God, she had a chain bobstay so we lashed the bite of it up over the bitts. Now the time came to reef the mainsail, so we shot her up in the wind and let the whole sail down, which is about the only way you can do in a strong breeze. It was dark by now, raining and real rough. Well, if you have ever tucked a reef in a loose-footed sail in a gale of wind, you know what we were up against; every time she rolled, the whole bunt of the sail would swash down to leeward, taking the reef points out of your hands. No, sir, don't let anyone tell you a loose-footed sail is easy to reef in a breeze—might be all right in light weather. Worst of it is, the reefing tackle or clew lines on a loose-footed sail take the whole strain and have to be uncommonly carefully done or the whole thing will chafe and give out.

"You may ask, why didn't we set a trysail and be done with it. But a trysail's center of area is too far forward for a cutter to lay-to well. All this time we were scudding under bare poles (or running before it, if you like). But now we stood by to round up to hoist the main. I was at the helm, the captain and man forward, and my friend Jack at the cross tackles to cast off the boom the minute she lifted. Quite a sea had made up by this time and as we rounded up and came in the trough of the sea, she took a couple of rolls and a good-sized comber struck us beam-to and boarded us full length.

"Now the weight of water and the wind completely killed our headway so we hardly came in the wind at all, but the men forward managed to get the sail part up, then Jack and I worked our way forward and we finally managed to sway her up between the four of us. And she lay there pretty steady under the triple-reefed mainsail, considering the sea that was running, but we were pretty nearly exhausted after.all this work. We all went below and had a good drink. Now there are two points I am driving at with all this talk—the first is, yes, a cutter can be made to lay-to in a sea if you reduce her wind resistance forward by housing her topmast and taking in her bowsprit. The second is, all these boys who own sloops and call them cutters and think by their use of this name they can make their sloop lay-to in a breeze—well, it is a lot of tommyrot, and if you don't believe it, go out and try it."

"Well," said Jovial, "just what does happen on a sloop under those conditions?"

"I'll tell you," said Precise. "A sloop can't be made to lay-to properly; her sail and wind resistance are too far forward. First she will pay off to wind abeam; then, as she gathers headway, as she is bound to, she will shoot up in the wind and slat the daylights out of everything. Then, when she has lost headway, she will pay way off again, keep repeating these maneuvers all night till she has either driven you crazy or slatted her gear to pieces. The only thing you can do with a sloop is to shorten her down as much as possible, then put a good man at the helm. He has to be good, too, for he has to keep just headway enough on her so the rudder will control her. This, of course, is not laying-to, and you will have covered some ground in the night. So it is a thing you can't do unless you have plenty of sea room."

"Well, now, the schooner. I have always heard they would lay-to beautifully," said Jovial.

"I thought so too," said Precise, "till I tried it. I once owned the little schooner *Casco Belle*. She was a bald-headed schooner about fifty feet on deck."

"What do you mean 'bald-headed schooner'?" asked Jovial.

"Why, one without any topmasts or topsails, of course," said Precise. "Well, as I was saying, we tried to make her lay-to one night. Did everything according to Hoyle too. We had her foresail about close-hauled, backed the forestaysail to weather, and lashed her helm hard down, but she kept roaming around.

Bald-headed schooner Joann, *designed by the author.*

You see, when she got some way on, the rudder, being hard over, brought her up in the wind. When she lost headway she fell off, so she lay in the trough of the sea. You see, she went through about the same maneuvers as a sloop, but did it slower. After all, when you have lowered the mainsail on a schooner, you only have a sloop plus a lot of wind resistance aft.

"Of course a schooner, shortened down, with only a foresail drawing and the forestaysail aback, will ride quite easy, but you can never tell where they will be in the morning after jogging and fore-reaching all night in a series of moon-shaped courses—sort of roaming around, you might call it."

"Yes," said Precise, "that's how the Gloucester fisherman *Puritan* was lost—damn shame, too—for she was the last high-grade vessel built for Gloucester. She was on her first trip to the Banks, too. Well, it seems her captain tried to lay her to in the usual way, but she roamed or fore-reached in the night, so when one of the crew forward stuck his head out of the forecastle hatch in the morning, he hollered 'breakers.' Before they could fetch her about or find out which way the land lay, she took bottom. So about all they could do was take to the dories. When the fog lifted, there she was, right in the shoals off Cape Sable Island, which they had thought was about twenty miles away. Yes, the *Puritan* was a sailing fool all right; on her first trip out, they say she logged fourteen knots on a close reach. I suppose her captain was not used to such a lively vessel."

Now, as I was listening in the other room, the mention of the *Puritan* struck me with great interest, for it had so happened that when the *Puritan* was built, I had been a draftsman working for Starling Burgess and, in fact, was given the job of supervising the stepping of her masts and in other ways helping the hardy sons of Gloucester translate her proportions from the design, for there were no sixteenths or thirty-seconds on their rule of the thumb. So, although I had been rather surprised at some of Precise's conversation, I now realized he was a real thinker and man of common sense. He had stated the correct cause of the loss of the *Puritan* and was quite correct in saying what a great loss it was, for to the best of my knowledge she was the last straight sailing vessel built with the money of real fishermen. She was a fine design and would have perhaps been as great a credit to Starling Burgess as the sloop *Puritan* had been to his father. But, on account of her loss on her first voyage, few people know of her today.

French Mediterranean ballahou.

The voice of Jovial soon broke up my meditation. He said, "Now the schooner, don't you consider her our national rig? Invented in Gloucester, you know. There she schoons and all that."

"Well," said Precise, "the name schooner might have been invented in Gloucester well enough, but long before Gloucester was settled, two-masted fore-and-aft rigged vessels were in use and particularly in the Mediterranean. You will find a cut of one in Holmes' *Ancient Ships*. The picture, or cut, is called *Transportation of an Obelisque*, 1600 B. C. She is a good-size vessel with more than one mast. That was a long time ago, about 3,500 years, and I can't say there was not some Chinaman tacking to windward with a two-masted rig before that. At any rate, by 1600 the sloop and schooner and other fore-and-aft rigs were well developed in Holland, and before 1800 France in her Mediterranean ports had developed some fine vessels about like our modern schooners. To be sure, they called it the ballahou rig. And I have always thought that a capital name, for there has always been more ballyhoo about that rig than any other."

"Yes," said Precise, "the more I think about it the more I realize there are no national rigs or types. Take the English cutter, first developed in France. Take the Norwegian pilot boat. Why, I've known Norwegians to get all excited over them—rather phlegmatic race, too, as a general rule—but you just mention the name Norwegian pilot boat and they will start to breathe hard and their eyes will glisten. You would think someone had said the word 'ski.' To hear them talk, you would think their pilot boats combined the speed of a torpedo boat with the seaworthiness of a lightship. Well, what is the Norwegian pilot boat? The best of them, the ones that made the type famous, were designed by Mr. Colin Archer, an Englishman. Seems he had some tubercular trouble, moved to Norway for the drier air there. He was a wonderful designer, no doubt, and won fame by designing Nansen's *Fram*; and, if I remember rightly, the little *Fram* that made the Northwest Passage. Of course Archer had Nordic boats like the Bankfishfartöi to work from."

"Yes," said Precise, "it almost seems sometimes as if the young sailors and some writers love confusion or are carried away with romantic words. Take the word 'trunnel,' for instance, which of course means a through nail. You know they go clean through the planking and the frames and are wedged both ends. Well most writers, who have had no shipyard experience, call them tree nails and seem to get a great kick out of it. But you go to a shipyard and ask for tree nails. Like as not they will send you to some dressmaker, or give you some other feminine insinuation."

Nordic bank fisherman of 1850.

Leg-o'-mutton ketch designed by the author.

"Well," said Jovial, "I got a cat at home I generally let out about this time o' night to ease himself."

"Yes," said Precise, "and I got a dog named Carpenter, and if I don't get home soon, like as not he'll be doing some job or other around the house, but if you think that cat can constrain himself a few minutes, we had better have another drink and I will tell you about a ketch laying-to."

"Well," said Jovial, "it does seem a long time between drinks, and I would like to hear about a ketch."

"I once owned the little ketch *Ptarmigan*," said Precise. "Fact is, she was the last yacht I owned. She was a fine little vessel, leg-o'-mutton rigged, of course. Well, she was so easy to lay-to I often sailed off to the eastward of a summer or fall night just to lay-to in her. Often ran out at the beginning of a nor'wester when I knew it would be clear. All you had to do was lower her jib and mainsail, sheet the mizzen in about as you do for close-hauled; let her helm go as it pleased. Well, sir, there she would stay as steady as you please, with no way on at all, making a dead set toward the leeward beam. I used to lower a sounding lead over her weather quarter about abreast the cockpit. Used to pay out about ten fathoms. I could tell exactly by the lay of that line how she was drifting. She generally made a dead set sideways of one mile an hour. Yes, those were some of the happiest hours of my life; the stars overhead, and nothing in sight but the whitecaps. Once in a while one of them would roar under her stern. I'd just sit there in the companionway and drink in that sea air. She had a coal-burning stove, kept the whole cabin warm and dry. Yes, those were happy moments and sometimes I curse the young yacht broker who persuaded me to part with her. I hear he is in the service now; don't really wish him any hard luck, but I do hope he gets his hair singed a little."

"It's a strange thing," said Jovial, "that a ketch can be made to lay-to so easily."

"Well, I dunno," said Precise. "Depends on how you look at it. 'Tain't strange that a weather vane points up in the wind, is it? Well, the mizzen on a ketch is well aft of her center of lateral resistance. It is always working her up in the wind and gently pushing ahead just enough to overcome the tendency of the sea and wind that is trying to swing her bow off. No, you can't lay a boat to in a sea and wind unless the area of sail is well aft, and the area of sail set must be just sufficient to kill her sternway, and if you don't believe it, just go out there and try it.

"On a yawl, for instance, the area of the mizzen is well aft but not sufficient in size to hold her stationary, so as soon as she gathers sternway, she will swing off and lay in the trough of the sea, and any vessel is uncomfortable under those circumstances."

"I have noticed you use the word 'vessel' a good deal in your conversation," said Jovial. "Why don't you use the word 'ship'?"

"Well, to be precise," said Precise, "a ship is a three-masted vessel, square-rigged on all three masts, while vessel is a safe enough term to use for anything from the *Queen Mary* down to the well-known thunder-mug under the bed."

"I must be going home now," said Jovial, "so good-night."

"Good-night, Jovial," said Precise. But as he walked home, Jovial in his mind was quite confused: it was quite a shock to him to have so many myths destroyed at once, and in fact

> He went like one that hath been stunn'd
> And is of sense forlorn,
> A sadder and a wiser man
> He rose the morrow morn.

As for my part, sitting in the library listening, I must say I agreed with Precise, for there certainly is a lot of loose talk going around, and foolish writing. The use of wrong terms certainly makes it difficult to know what the other fellow means, particularly in relation to marine matters.

Lapping Jibs and
Double Spinnakers

It certainly seems that we of this generation should do some-thing to fill up the loopholes in the present methods of measuring sail area. The one or two generations before us gave us good measurement rules and we have had much pleasure and sport because of their work.

Now our present racing yachts, and this includes the so-called ocean racers, are a miserable failure, for they cannot sleep or accommodate the large crews required to sail them, and when sailed without their rule-cheating jibs and double spinnakers, they are decidedly slow and often unpleasant to steer. But worst of all, they are extremely expensive to operate; in fact, only the very rich have a chance of winning, for the one who can afford to buy the most new jibs and double spinnakers invariably wins, because the helmsmanship is of little consequence compared to the ability to set and change the innumerable rule-cheating sails.

It is a fact that many of the present racing yachts carry an area about double their measured sail area most of the way around the course. It has become the custom to set to leeward of the regular working sails a so-called flat-cut spinnaker whose tack is on a pole forward of the forestay and extending back to a clew aft of the main boom's after end (see Figure no. 1). In light weather these sails are carried even close-hauled and, of course, when running free, the gigantic double parachute spin-nakers are used. When you stop to think of it, this is a ridiculous and childish condition in classes mostly based on sail

Figure no. 1. Unmeasured sail set to leeward of measured sail plan.

area for rating, i.e., a thirty-square-meter boat sailing around the course with sixty square meters of canvas set.

Now let us look back at some of the hull measurement rules of the past and see that they broke down when their actual measurements just about doubled their rating measurements. Yachts at first were measured for rating, or classification, by their tonnage—from about the time of Charles II, or 1670, up to about 1880—and at first some very good and useful hull forms were developed, in fact, yachts far more comfortable in a seaway than our present ones. At first the tonnage was obtained by multiplying the length times the beam times the depth, but about 1800 some bright customs official discovered that most of the vessels measured since Queen Elizabeth's time averaged a depth equal to one-half the beam. Now as depth was often difficult to measure because of cargo in the hold, etc., the rule was changed to be length times beam times one-half the beam.

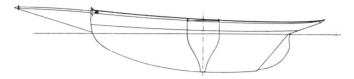

Figure no. 2. Beam measured twice, depth not at all.

(You must understand these rules were for all shipping for the purpose of taxation, etc., and used as a rating of yachts, and were changed from time to time.) Now as beam was measured twice and depth not at all, by making a narrow and deep model, the tonnage or rating was much reduced; thus the narrow English cutter was developed, and as the development went on, yachts having an actual displacement of twice their measured tonnage were finally built. These were called planks-on-edge, lead mines, and diving bells. They got to be seven times as long as they were wide, when the rule broke down and a change was made (see Figure no. 2).

We in America were playing with the sandbagger at about that time. Its only measurement was length on deck, and we finally developed craft whose length from end of bowsprit to end of boom was twice the length of hull, when that class went out of style (see Figure no. 3).

Later our principal measurements were based on waterline length, until we finally built such freaks as *Outlook*, whose length overall was twice the length on the waterline (see Figure no. 4). Then most of the yacht clubs adopted the New York Yacht Club's Universal Rule, which has quite satisfactorily controlled hull proportions.

The International Rule used in Europe and England, and a later rule, calls for the same proportion of draft and displacement for waterline length, but controls the overhang in a different way.

Well, to get back to sail area. It will be a very simple matter to bring things back to normal by simply changing the rule to measure the actual area of headsails. Certainly if the area of the fore triangle is taken at eighty-five percent of its real area, the headsails should not be allowed to lap by the mast at all. Of course the eighty-five percent was adopted as being about what

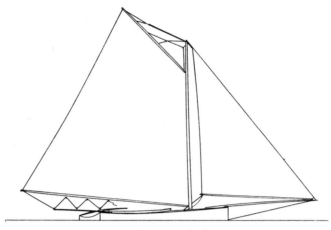

Figure no. 3. Length on deck.

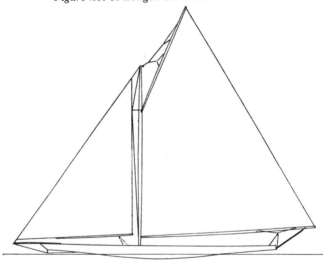

Figure no. 4. Length on waterline.

it was considered (at that time) that the jib represented of the fore triangle, and no one then thought jibs with an area of two hundred percent of the fore triangle would be common. Now the increases in area of a lapping jib naturally increased the speed of a yacht, and many who have won with these will be loath to give them up. But if one considers that the lug foresails

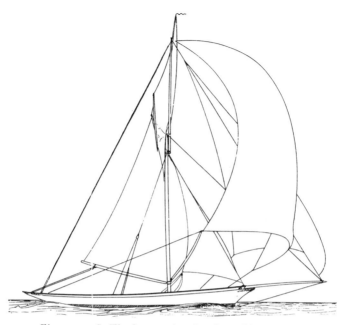

Figure no. 5. The large spinnaker is nothing new.

(that is, an overlapping foresail) on schooners have been barred since about 1912 (see Rule 16, Section 1 of N.Y.Y.C. Racing Rules), it would be hard to see how large overlapping headsails are tolerated.

Now this writer freely admits he has been one of the worst culprits in developing the lapping jib, and probably the first to design one that extended aft of the main boom, and of the American-built thirty-square-meter boats, he has designed seven out of the eight that measured into the class. (The thirty squares are mentioned because they are the worst offenders.) But, as a criminal lawyer might be sorry for some loophole in a law that allowed him to defend a client, so too a designer might be sorry there was a defect in a rule that allowed unfair practices that forced him to use them to win.

Double or parachute spinnakers. The large spinnaker is not a new thing (see Figure no. 5), but wisely our ancestors restricted the length of spinnaker booms and enforced the rule that spinnaker sheets should not be carried to leeward of the forestay.

This last-mentioned restriction is very important, but because it was so commonly taken for granted that a spinnaker would not be used to leeward of the forestay, it somehow or other was not written into the racing rules of late years. Perhaps too, it was thought that when spinnaker booms were limited to the base of the fore triangle, it would not be of any use to carry them to leeward instead of a balloon jib, but late practice has shown something different, and the double spinnaker has come into common use.

Now these sails, as set at present, are really a raffee, and under the New York Yacht Club's Rule XI—Sail Area, in the section of the rule called Total Area on Page 245 of the 1929 book, fourth paragraph down, is this wording, "In case a yacht shall carry a square sail, or square topsail, or raffee (together or separately) instead of a spinnaker, the actual area of the same shall be computed; and if such area exceeds the area of the fore triangle, the excess shall be added in computing the total area for determining the measurement." If this rule were enforced, or the rule preventing carrying the spinnaker sheet to leeward of the forestay, all the double spinnakers on large and small yachts would at once disappear.

But some will say the big spinnaker is a lot of fun and will resent giving it up just as much as did the lovers of the cutters, sandbaggers and scows in their day. Some of the freak rule-beating hulls of the past make our young sailors laugh, and it is quite likely the next generation will laugh at the sails we are carrying today, for they have not increased the speed of our boats for the actual area, but only for their measured sail area. If, with all the expense and hard work that our modern sail plans require, we did acquire a speed-length ratio equal to a sailing canoe, there would be some excuse for them.

Before the advent of the lapping jib and double spinnaker, yachting was unique among sports, inasmuch as men of seventy or even eighty could compete on even terms with men in their prime. Also, children or young ladies with a proper crew had a fair chance. Now these two things working together—the great cost and squeezing out the older men (for the older men are the only ones who have money enough to build new boats)—will either greatly reduce the size of the yachts built or much reduce the number of new yachts, or both.

Do we want to tolerate this condition—have fewer and smaller yachts—just because some exhibitionists want to show off with queer-looking sails? It will be too bad if yachts are spoiled so they are no longer good for pleasure sailing or relaxed comfort.

There is another point that I should like to mention before closing, and that is the great danger in racing yachts when the helmsman cannot see ahead. Yachting in the past has been very free of accidents when one considers the great numbers competing, but we may very well have some serious accident if we continue racing with sails that cut off the view of the helmsman, often as much as ninety degrees. Besides, the worry and anxiety of not being able to see takes most of the pleasure out of racing. Now is the time to do something before yachts and yachting are seriously harmed.

Nathanael Greene Herreshoff

Captain Nat, as Mr. Herreshoff was popularly known, was born in Bristol, Rhode Island, on March 18, 1848. He was descended from ancestors who had all been in this country since the time of the Revolution. After attending the public schools of Bristol, he went to the Massachusetts Institute of Technology and upon his graduation was employed as a draftsman in the Corliss Steam Engine Company at Providence.

While there, he worked nights and Sundays designing the boats and yachts that were built in the boatshop managed by his brother, John Brown Herreshoff, who had become blind in his youth but was an able businessman, in spite of this handicap.

The first vessel of any considerable size that he designed was the steamer *Estelle* in 1877. She was 120 feet long, with a 16-foot beam, with coil boiler and compound engine, and made 16 MPH, a high speed for the times. Captain Nat got leave from the Corliss Company, went to Bristol, and with the help of one draftsman, designed her hull, boilers, and engines. From this time on 'til 1890, most of Captain Nat's efforts were in designing steam craft and their power plants, but he designed an occasional sailing yacht, such as *Shadow* in 1871.

During the 1870s and 1880s, Captain Nat designed mostly steam craft, which included small paddle-wheel steamers, open launches, and torpedo boats, many of the latter being for foreign governments. These early steam torpedo boats, in some cases, held the speed records of the time.

Nathanael Greene Herreshoff, 1923.

Herreshoff yachts and steamers had become in such demand that Captain Nat had to resign from the Corliss Engine Company and devote all of his time to designing them for his brother, John, so that they formed a partnership and incorporated a company that was for many years known as the Herreshoff Manufacturing Company and was solely owned by them.

While the Herreshoff Manufacturing Company did not build large vessels, it did manufacture a great number of small ones, so that by 1878 the number of steamers alone was up to 49. That year the brothers, J. B. and N. G., built and took to England on the deck of an ocean liner a small torpedo boat for the British Navy. On this trip they also took over the small launch *Gymnotus*, 29 feet long; 5 foot beam; speed, 13 MPH. She was a highly developed craft for her time. In the next few years, Captain Nat designed many of the small spar torpedo boats of the time and, besides the English one mentioned, furnished them to the Russian, Chilean, and Peruvian navies. The U.S.N. torpedo boats that he designed were the *Lightning, Stiletto, Cushing, Dupont, Porter, Morris, Gwynne,* and *Talbot.*

Captain Nat is perhaps best known for the Cup defenders he designed, which defended the *America*'s Cup six times, but these craft were only possible because of the complete building plant, which was developed for building torpedo boats, their boilers and engines, and a high state of light construction, in both wood and metal, had been arrived at by 1890, so that when Captain Nat again received orders for racing sailboats, he could use new

Gloriana, *designed by Nathanael G. Herreshoff, 1891.* (Traditions and Memories of American Yachting, *by W.P. Stephens. © Hearst Corp., 1945*)

and improved methods of construction, which gave him a great advantage.

Besides the Cup defenders, some of his well-known sailing yachts were *Gloriana, Navahoe, Niagara, Ingomar, Westward, Elena,* and *Katoura,* and a great many one-design classes. In all he designed well over 2,000 craft, and if one should look over the list of yachts that have won the Astor Cup, King's Cup, and Puritan Cup, it will be found that the yachts he designed outnumber those designed by all other designers.

Captain Nat designed, or modeled, his first yacht, *Violet,* in 1864, when he was sixteen years old, and his last in 1936, making a span of seventy-two years of yacht designing. He got up the original table for giving the minutes and seconds that a larger yacht allows a smaller one, and which has been used ever since for all kinds of rating in different countries, and has made possible the racing of yachts of different size or rating. Later in life he got up the Universal Rule for the New York Yacht Club. He was made an honorary member of the Boston Yacht Club, Seawanhaka Yacht Club, and Bristol Yacht Club.

He made three visits to Europe, the first one in about 1868, when he built a small boat at Nice and crossed France by sailing up the Rhone and down the Seine. The next was in 1878, delivering a torpedo boat to the British Navy; the next in 1894, when he sailed on *Vigilant* in her first race there. In fact, he was steering *Vigilant* in the eventful moment when the *Satanita* burst out of a rain squall and sunk *Valkyrie* right ahead of *Vigilant* at the start of that first race on the Clyde.

Captain Nat had a very accurate memory of yachting history from the time of *America* on, and he had associated with many of the naval constructors, such as Admiral Isherwood, who worked on changing the Navy from sail to steam. Captain Nat invented, or brought to a high state of usefulness, the following things:

1. The light steam engine; and first fast steam torpedo boats.
2. Nearly all of the methods of constructing light wooden hulls as used today.
3. The web frame and longitudinal construction for metal hulls, afterward patented by and known as the Isherwood System.
4. The streamline-shaped bulk and fin keels.
5. The crosscut sail with the cloth running at right angles to the leech.
6. Light, hollow steel spars, combined with scientific rigging.
7. The flat stern form of steam yachts, capable of being driven at high speed/length ratios.
8. The development of overhangs on sailing yachts to allow longer lines and greater stability.
9. The sail track and slide in its present form, and a great many patterns of marine hardware in common use today.

He had been a member of S.N.A.M.E. since its organization in 1893. He died June 2, 1938, a few months over 90 years old; his life spanned most of the development of American yachting.

Tarantella (Catamaran Chronicle)

by Nathanael Greene Herreshoff
(Reprinted from *The Spirit of the Times*, November 24, 1877)
Introduction by L. Francis Herreshoff

I will make a few comments on this old article about catamarans, which was printed seventy-seven years ago, or before there were regular yachting magazines in this country (if we except *The Aquatic Monthly,* which was mostly for oarsmen).

The general interest in catamarans of that time was caused by N. G. Herreshoff's *Amaryllis,* which competed with single-hulled craft in the Centennial Regatta held on June 22, 1876, off the New York Yacht Club's Staten Island station. *Amaryllis* raced in class 3, which was open to all boats between twenty-five and forty feet in length. There were eleven starters in the race, including the best of the large-sized sandbaggers of the time. In the first part of the race, the wind was light and *Amaryllis* did rather poorly. This put her in a place where she would have to pass most of the fleet if she were to win, but when the race was about half over, a nice sailing breeze sprang up and *Amaryllis* sailed gaily through the fleet to win by twenty minutes and two seconds over the next competitor, the famous sandbagger *Pluck and Luck.* Some in the class were forty or more minutes behind.

While *Amaryllis* won easily boat to boat, she was protested by several of the competitors and subsequently ruled out, the prize being given to the *Pluck and Luck*. At that time, the papers called *Amaryllis* a life raft and several things, but created all at once an interest in catamarans, so that during the next ten years there were about twenty of them on the Hudson River and the head of Long Island Sound. However, their popularity was short lived, principally because they were barred from all the regular classes, although the Newburgh Bay Yacht Club ran special classes for catamarans for a few years. During 1876 and 1877, the papers gave catamarans much space. As I write this, I have before me a scrapbook of newspaper clippings about catamarans kept by N. G. Herreshoff in which there are sixteen articles published in 1876 and thirty-four in 1877. Some of these were quite long and illustrated, as was the one that follows.

Tarantella was Captain Nat's second catamaran, and he had worked out some of the weak points of *Amaryllis*. By the time this article was written, he had probably had several hundred hours' experience in sailing these craft, for he made long-distance cruises in them. One of the interesting things in the article is the comparison of *Tarantella*'s weight to sail area, as it seems she was lighter for her sail than most present catamarans.

The *Julia* that is spoken of in the first part of the article was my grandfather's catboat, which had a shifting ballast car on rails and so was fast to windward. The *Wm. R. Brown*, the *Wm. T. Lee*, the *Susie S*, and *Dare Devil* were crack sandbaggers of the time whose crews were fighting mad because *Amaryllis* and other catamarans had beaten them, for they thought they had the fastest sailboats of their time. The reader must remember that this was long before the automobile, or even privately owned steam launches, made much over twenty miles an hour, so the catamaran under perfect conditions could make long runs nearly as fast as any privately owned carrier. While the horse could travel fast for short distances, it could not cover 150 miles very quickly, and the speed of the catamaran was worthwhile in those days, even if it is not now.

Many of the prominent yacht designers of the past wrote a little. Dixon Kemp perhaps was more of a writer than designer. George L. Watson wrote quite a lot for the Scottish papers, mostly under a nom de plume. Colin Archer contributed copiously to the publications of the Society of Naval Architects, particularly on the wave-line theory. However, this article and one about the theoretical speed of iceboats are the only ones I know of written by Captain Nat.

L. F. H.

Bristol, R.I., Nov. 10, 1877

Dear Spirit: Starting on a cruise and the commencing of a newspaper article are tasks alike difficult. There seems to be in the mind a sort of reluctance to take the first step in an enterprise, though it may have been long contemplated. This laziness, if you would call it so, is most easily overcome by a sudden and violent effort of the will, much the same as a driver stops his horse at the foot of a hill for breathing, and then with a rush mounts it. The momentum of the will will sometimes do as much as that of the body.

In the two instances which I have cited I would, in case of cruising, rush everything aboard, hoist the sails, up with the anchor, and off. Or, in the other, fly to the desk, seize the paper, dip the pen into the pot, and fire away. Well, then, after such an effort, I and a companion found ourselves in the *Tarantella* and afloat, started on a summer cruise up the Hudson, particularly drawn thither by the great regatta at Newburgh on the 1st of August.

The day of our starting (July 26) was most pleasant and propitious. The high winds of the early summer had subsided into those pleasant breezes which the yachtsmen love best, and the fogs and rains of June were swallowed up by that invisible softness of the air, which makes a sojourn by the sea so delightful and so sought for. 'Tis our custom, when starting on a cruise, to race down the bay with the *Julia*, a cat-rigged boat whose speed is always taken as a standard, and thus we can detect any error in trim that otherwise might escape us. The one that beats the *Julia* is set down as all right.

In this case the wind was fresh from the south, and a beat dead to windward was the consequence. The four-mile point was reached by the catamaran in 43 minutes; the *Julia* was then one mile astern. She turned back disgusted and we went on contented. And now let me hasten to put right the minds of many people, and particularly the yachting reporter of *The Spirit of the Times*, on the subject of windward sailing by the catamaran.

It is true that the enormous disparity of speed between the

Cover, Spirit of the Times, *1877. (*The Rudder*)*

catamaran and an ordinarily built boat is most noticeable when sailing with the wind a little abaft of beam. Sailing to windward is a paradox at best, and a small amount thus gained is a greater triumph than much greater distances gained in the headlong, free-wind sailing. Windward sailing is not a weak point of the catamaran. I can, with a good whole sail breeze, beat to windward faster, by a mile an hour at least, than any sailing vessel afloat, or I can beat the *Wm. R. Brown*, the *Wm. T. Lee*, the *Susie S., Dare Devil,* or any other boat of that class that can be named, one-quarter, or five miles to their four, under the conditions before mentioned. I'm not making an idle, empty boast. I know well of what I am writing. I have sailed every class of vessel, from the small cat-boat up to the first-class yacht, and their performances are individually familiar to me. And further, if the owner of any yacht, or other sailing vessel, and particularly the owners of the boats whose names I have mentioned, want to be practically convinced of this, that is, of the speed of the windward sailing of the catamaran, the best way for them is to try it on. I shall be only too happy to do so anywhere and at any time.

Our first night we anchored in Newport Harbor, and, hoisting our tent, made ourselves as comfortable as could be. The tent is pitched under the boom, which is hoisted well up overhead, and the whole of the car, which is 16 feet long by 8½ feet wide, is covered by it. Under it there is plenty of room for several to sit or stand protected from wind or rain. Our preparations for sleeping were short and simple. Our beds of blankets were made, and the air cushions, on which we sat by day, we dreamed on by night.

Camping out in a catamaran is pleasanter than one would think. The tent affords such perfect shelter, and the floor of the car is so broad and flat, that it seems more like a little house on the land than a veritable flying machine. In the midst of our sleeping, a fresh northeaster came whistling in the rigging overhead. We aroused a little, only to give her more cable, which she took with great promptness. A fair wind induces an early starting, and, at six next morning, we were off, with a fresh breeze from the north and the sky slightly overcast. The run from the Torpedo Station to Fort Adams was made in true catamaran style; thought I, were there only a straight course to New York, we would get there in ten hours. But, at the Fort

Wharf, turning before the wind, everything became calm and quiet.

If, in a catamaran, you are sorely pressed by wind or wave, turn her bow to leeward. There you will find comfort and consolation, so light she is, and presents so little resistance, that the wind blows her along like a bubble floating in the air. We laid to off Point Judith, at seven, for breakfast, after which reinforcement we continued with the wind gradually dying. Off New London, at eleven, the wind shifted to ESE but still was light. When off the Connecticut River we decided to steer for the Long Island shore. We had not gone far on that course when the wind hauled back to east and commenced blowing. Now, with the wind east in Long Island Sound, and blowing a single-reef breeze, it does not take long to kick up a sea, especially with an ebb tide. At least it did not that day, and soon the *Tarantella* commenced to race, lifted, and, borne on the crest of a wave, she would shoot forward with incredible speed. We settled away on the peak halyards and made, in effect, a leg-of-mutton sail from the mainsail. This made a very easy rig, and one particularly adapted for off-wind sailing.

And now, whilst we are flying along, with the waves lifting and breaking high under the after tie-beam, let us overhaul another of the alleged failings of the catamaran, to wit: their tendency to turn over endwise or pitchpole. Now, the center of effort of the sails of the *Tarantella* is 14 feet 6 inches above the waterline. With the wind abaft of beam, the tendency to bury the bows of the hull is quite obvious. This desire to bury forward is corrected, in a measure, first by having more than an ordinarily large jib, which, on account of its inclined position, lifts strongly that part of the boat. Then the midship link, at which point is imparted most of the press of the sails upon the leeward boat, is so placed in relation to the displacement of the hulls that the downward push (to which the force of the wind on the sails is resolved) presses more toward the stern, so the leeward boat always keeps in good fore-and-aft trim. The trouble then lies only in the lifting of the stern of the windward hull. Of course, if you lift the stern of the boat, and thus make the bow bury itself, the effect is just the same, and just as unpleasant as when the bow sinks for want of buoyancy with the trim of the stern where it should be.

Building the catamaran high in the bows cannot remedy this

fault in the least degree; the only thing to be done is to take care of the stern, and the bow will take care of itself. Having stationary ballast will keep the stern down, but this is against my principles. I want to have everything about the boat as light as can possibly be; so when the stern of the *Tarantella* looks light, my companion sits on it, and says it is one of the best seats on the whole boat. It is almost always dry, and one gets there a real sense of the speed with which she tears along. It is as it would be riding on the back of the wildest horse; not nearly so wild, in fact, but a great deal steadier, having only a purely up and down motion as she flies over the waves, which is most exhilarating and exciting.

At 6 p.m., we drew near Port Jefferson, which I have always found a pleasant halfway stopping-place. The tide was nearly out, and a strong current setting in against us from the harbor. But in a catamaran nobody cares about those little places where the tide runs swiftly, and where you are mounting a little hill; the sails are so large, compared with the whole weight, that I really believe the *Tarantella* would climb the side of a mountain, if her element would only arrange itself in the position of one. The proportion of superficial area of the sails to the weight of the whole boat complete is one square foot for each 4 pounds of water displaced. In a raceboat, say, 25 feet long, with a large rig and ballast to carry it, the proportion is one foot of canvas to 8 pounds of water displaced. In a first-class yacht, such as the *Idler,* the proportion is one foot to 28 pounds of displacement. Why shouldn't the catamaran sail with such power? But what seems wonderful is that they should carry it so long and so well. The *Tarantella* will carry her sails, and carry them as well and safely as any fairly rigged yacht afloat. But their masters are apt to err in carrying sail beyond all reason. The sense of safety makes them reckless.

July 28 was one of those perfectly dead, quiet days that I have often experienced at the head of Long Island Sound. It was particularly so this day, and a decent day's work could not be made, not even in a catamaran. We anchored in Cow Bay in the early evening, pitched our tent in a sullen rain, and consoled ourselves with the idea that we were better there than in a worse place. The 29th was a little better, and we found ourselves at Hell Gate, at 10 a.m., with the lightest and most untrustworthy of breezes from SE, and the tide half flood. However, we put her to it, and by good luck, and that ability of hers to go upstairs, we got through, and finally anchored in Gowanus Basin.

On the morning of the 30th, there was a fresh breeze from the north, and we commenced the ascent of the Hudson. I kept a sharp lookout, expecting every moment to see Captain Meigs in his *Meteor*, and I thought then, as I have often since, what has become of him?

Last spring the columns of *The Spirit* were full of his effusions, everyone was in a high state of expectancy. Through him the art of catamaran building was taught to the public, and by him the whole course of pleasure-hunting on the water was turned upon and centered in the catamaran. But since the launching of his new marvel about the middle of last June, no one seems to know anything of him or his boat. I searched the columns of *The Spirit* in vain for his communications. I hope Mr. Meigs will soon reappear and give us more of his experiences, for I know he must have had some new ones since the launching of the *Meteor*.

In *The Spirit* of May 26, Mr. Meigs has much to say about the comparative merits of the flexible joint system, used in the connections of my catamaran, and the rigid or partly rigid plan that he pursues. For illustration, he makes use of a most happy simile, which, I think, serves my purpose better than it does his. 'Twas that of two drunken brothers wending their way through the streets, arm-in-arm. So long as they keep walking on a smooth, level plain, their connections are undisturbed, but if, in their erratic course, one of them would step off the curbstone into the gutter, the other one, if he undertook to keep his brother on the same plane as himself, would find it very irksome, and after several repetitions of that sort of thing, I think they would be glad to part company.

But the laws of nature, which Mr. Meigs talks about, have made most admirable provisions for this emergency. She has placed in the shoulder of each brother a perfect ball-and-socket joint, which allows one to raise himself over an obstacle, or sink into a depression, without disturbing their union, or the laying out of any strength on either side, which would tend at last to make the bond tiresome and injurious. In the afternoon, as we were near the head of Haverstraw Bay, there came a squall from the eastward, and a peeler, too. The Hudson is famous for them,

I understand, and certainly the spirit of the old navigator did his best on the afternoon of the 30th. We furled the jib, and settled away a little on the peak of the mainsail. We could not go below, so sat we grimly on the deck, protected by our rubber coats, and received meekly a perfect torrent. The catamarans seem to possess a remarkable ability to steer well under any disposition of sail. I have beat them to windward, coming about surely every time with the jib alone, or with nothing but the mainsail. With mainsail at double or three reefs, they always work well; but what seems oddest of all, I have worked the *Tarantella* under the storm-jib alone, a little sail containing only a hundred square feet. With it I could beat to windward, and come into stays every time. When the wind and rain had ceased, and the great black clouds with their thunder had rolled away to leeward, I discovered two catamarans a short distance ahead, and on coming up with them, I found my first-born, the *Amaryllis,* and the *Carrie*, a smaller one. We sailed along in company for several miles; and as we approached the old Donderberg, there came yet another squall from the same direction. There was more wind than in the first, but as for the rainfall, it defied all description. There fell nearer whole water than I've ever seen either before or since. An obstruction in the scupper of the car caused the water to collect with such rapidity that I think it must have filled it, had it not been cleared.

The *Tarantella* and *Amaryllis* stayed near Peekskill that night, and the *Carrie* elsewhere, for we saw nothing of her after the squall.

The next day commenced with a calm and an ebb tide, so the navigation of the Hudson became rather tedious. The beautiful scenery of the Highlands, however, fully compensated for the lack of wind and our consequent slow progress. Farther on, toward West Point, a fresh breeze sprung from the north, and the rest of the trip was made most pleasantly. As for the regatta next day, nothing here need be said, for it has been most fully described. I can only regret it was not a dead to windward and leeward race. In that event, the minds of many reporters would have been put to rest, in respect of the *Tarantella,* in comparison with the other racing boats.

On the morning of August 2, we started on our homeward trip and found the sailing on the Hudson just as treacherous as ever as far as the old Donderberg. A fine breeze from the eastward, and backing to the northeast, made the rest of the trip to South Brooklyn very short; for, as we neared New York, the breeze became unwarrantably fresh, and with all jib, and the mainsail partly settled away, we flew along at more than steamboat speed. Now and then a more than usually strong flaw would strike her, upon which her bows would be lifted in air, like the taking flight of a great bird who was uncertain which to make her favorite element, the sea or sky. Once comfortably at anchor at the Gowanus basin, and sitting quietly under our tent, we talked of the folly of many people who make an effort to combine the catamaran and the cabin yacht.

In my opinion, the catamaran is a perfectly distinct variety of vessel, having its own peculiarities and characteristics, and any attempt to cross it with the old form of yacht results only in a mongrel production having none of the advantages that make the catamaran so attractive, and retaining all the bad qualities of the single-hulled yacht, with unwieldiness and ugliness combined.

The catamaran should be preserved always in its pure form. 'Tis a light, airy, fantastic machine for flying and floating, and if one attempts to inflict a cabin on her, all the lightness is lost, and I feel sure that such a craft will prove in every respect unsatisfactory. At least it shall always be my aim to develop the characteristics that belong purely to the catamaran, and make the gap between it and the old craft wider and wider.

I have demonstrated, at least to my own mind, that cruising in the catamaran is both pleasant and practicable. To those who are truly in love with aquatic sports, the tent affords sufficient shelter; and if anyone wants a cabin, it is clear in my mind he doesn't want a catamaran.

The *Nereid* is an example, so far as I can learn; her performances are nothing striking—nothing that anyone would expect in a catamaran of her size.

On the morning of the third, with scarcely anything else but the tide, we started for the Sound, and, after a day of successive calms and light winds, we anchored at sunset in Lloyd's Harbor, in company with two of our Hudson River friends, the *Fidget* and the *Victoria*, both also bound to Narragansett Bay. The outlook on the next morning was most promising, and we started at six on the front of a fresh northwest breeze. Our friends fell far behind, and off Stratford Light they were dim in the distance. Then commenced a most magnificent day's sailing.

Off every point we were greeted with flaws that would send us flying at such a pace as to almost annihilate distance. Points ten or fifteen miles ahead were made and passed in an incredibly short time. But, after all, it was not a day to make continuous fast time. The wind was so unsteady, and our speed, consequently, so variable, that the fastest time made between any two points was seven miles in 28 minutes. We ran from Stratford Light to Faulkner's Island at the rate of thirteen miles an hour.

After passing the Connecticut River, the wind hauled more toward the west and became much lighter, so our hopes of reaching home that night almost failed us, but again between Watch Hill and Point Judith, fresh flaws favored us, and we turned into our home sailing ground at four in the afternoon.

The sail up Narragansett Bay was most lovely; though its banks were not as high and as boldly beautiful as those of the Hudson, the islands, now alight with the glow of the declining sun, had a peaceful beauty of their own. As is common here in summer, the northwest breeze departs with the sun, and that evening at eight o'clock it fell a perfect calm, leaving us a provoking 100 yards from our landing; however, that day's sail, though it closed in ignominy, was a great triumph. A 140-mile run in 14 hours, or in easy daylight in the summer season, was enough to suit anyone's fancy; at least I was fully contented.

I have made lately several trials of windward speed in the *Tarantella*, the best of which was a beat to Newport from Bristol, a distance of 13 miles. The wind was so nearly ahead that the sum of the length of the port tacks was 7¾ miles, whilst that of the starboard was 8¼ miles. This run was made in 1 hour 53 minutes. The tide was fair. From this and several other similar trials, I have rated the maximum speed of the *Tarantella*, dead to windward, at 6½ miles an hour. Of her speed, in free wind sailing, the fastest I have actually measured was 18 miles an hour, though on one other occasion I am positive of sailing over 22 miles an hour. It was at the first striking of a squall, and the water was nearly dead smooth. Unfortunately, I was not near any point where I could take time. These extreme speeds are by no means made every day in the week. In our average summer winds, say, about three-fourths of a whole sail breeze, the catamaran, sailing free, will go 15 or 16 miles an hour.

As the season advanced, and the winds became stronger, I had several opportunities of trying the *Tarantella* under shortened sail. With a three-reefed mainsail and storm-jib, I made as fast time in smooth water as under any condition. With a double-reefed mainsail alone, she worked admirably to windward. But what seemed to me most surprising was that, under shortened sail, she would make remarkably good time, even faster than the common style of yachts, and that in breezes when all sail might be carried.

One day, late in September, the wind in force and direction chanced right for me to race with the *Richard Borden*, our fastest bay steamer. I lay in wait for her as she was making her daily trip to Providence and pounced upon her off Papoose-squaw Point. I passed her with the greatest ease, and at Rocky Point I was a full half-mile ahead, notwithstanding the breeze, which over the last part of the course became quite moderate. The distance sailed was 4½ miles. The last act of the season was the sale and delivery of the *Tarantella* to Commodore F. Hughes, of Greenport, L. I., under whose flag she now sails. In regard to next season, and what it may bring forth in the further development of the catamaran, I do not at this moment see where I should change the construction and arrangement of the catamarans that I have built this year.

I have always in view improvement, and to that end have devised a new rig, which I shall try on my next catamaran.

Yours,

N. G. HERRESHOFF

Safety First

The person in charge of a yacht or vessel must keep constantly on the alert while on duty. Those who loll around and dream while on watch only show their ignorance of the sea.

In this locality (the North Shore of Massachusetts) you must always watch the sky to the *northwest,* for nearly all squalls come from that direction. With the exception of the white squall, which is rare in warm weather, all squalls are accompanied by clouds.

Wind, rain, and lightning are caused by sudden changes in the temperature. A thick cloud coming into a clear sky causes a shaft of shadow under it on areas where the sunlight is not heating the air. When air is cooled, it contracts, and when it is heated, it expands so that a cubic foot of cold air is considerably heavier than a cubic foot of warm air. Thus under the heavy cloud there is started a downrush of heavy, cool air, which on striking the earth rushes out to displace the warm, sunny air around it. Thus we have the wind squall, which nearly always is right below the cloud.

If you keep a sharp weather eye you can always be prepared for these squalls and can either get back to your mooring or arrange to get yourself in a good locality for anchoring and all snugged down before the squall strikes.

On a day when the wind is northwest, you can tell if it is apt to blow hard by looking at the barometer. If it is rising rapidly, it will blow hard. On northwest days there are many hard puffs;

these are miniature squalls and are caused by the separate de-tached clouds with bright sunlight between them, so do not get panicky at the puffs, for they may be of short duration.

It is not advisable to venture far away from shore when the wind is northwest. A steady dry north*east* or east wind will be the safest at Marblehead.

If it seems you are to be caught in a squall, do the following things:

1. Lower your jib first. Furl or tie it up so it will be out of the way when anchoring, and so it will not go up the stay itself when the squall strikes.

2. If you are on your own boat, take charge. If you are on someone else's boat, obey orders. At any rate, have someone in charge and do not stand for any arguing. There will be time for that after you get ashore.

3. Keep cool and do not try to do things too quickly.

4. When you anchor, try to have the land on your north side, as the squall will nearly always come from the northwest or northeast.

5. In anchoring, always remember the boat will drift to lee-ward away from the anchor about three times the depth of the water.

6. You must pay out three times the depth of water on the anchor warp in order to let the anchor lay on its side enough so that the flukes of the anchor will catch on bottom.

It is best to lower the anchor toward bottom instead of throwing it overboard with a lot of rope, for some of the turns in the rope may foul around the anchor in such a way that it may prevent it from holding. If the wind shifts or the tide makes you range up by your anchor, you may get a turn of the warp around the upper flukes, in which case the anchor will not hold. (This is the reason why Herreshoff anchors are made with a gradual taper from the crown to the flukes, and the warp seldom catches on them.)

If the anchor holds so hard on bottom that it is difficult to break out, it is best to sail the boat around some with the warp quite straight up and down. In most all cases, it can be thus broken out with a little patience.

If you are down below during a thunderstorm, do not be scared if the lightning strikes close by, for small sailboats are practically never struck. Also remember that after the rain has come, the boat is covered with a film of water, which acts as a lightning conductor and will carry the discharge off so that no harm will be done below.

You should have a sounding lead with line properly marked (not Navy markings). The lead and line have many important uses, but now we will only consider two.

1. If the lead line is marked with one granny knot at one fathom and one more knot at each successive fathom, you will have a simple, easily remembered index and one readily counted in the dark.

2. Now suppose your anchor warp is marked at every three fathoms with a whipping like that used on the end of a rope, with one additional whipping at each succeeding three fathoms. If anchored on a level bottom, you can pay out on the warp until its markings agree with the sounding lead.

Remember that in anchoring around Marblehead or any place where there is a big rise in the tides (about a fathom and a half), this must be multiplied by three or two and given out in additional warp if the tide is at the neap, so the proportion is correct at flood tide.

The lead and line also are used to warn the man on watch if the vessel starts to drag (anchor slipping on bottom). On a small boat you can lead the line below deck and watch it, or if one is taking a nap, tie it to a finger or toe. (Give slack enough for yawing.)

In hauling the anchor aboard after use, do not hook a lot of mud on deck, but drag the anchor from the bow chock a while to wash it off. Also, on a small yacht the anchor can be cleaned some with your bare feet. When convenient, tow the anchor warp after using so as to wash all mud and sand off and to make the extra turns and kinks come out. When rope swells from wetting, it tries to unlay, and if the ends cannot revolve, it will kink. By towing it, it will be wet and swelled and extended in a straight line so the extra turns will come out themselves. Thus the warp is much easier to use when required in a hurry. Because long warps twist and kink, it is sometimes customary to have them in two lengths that can be bent together when anchoring in deep water.

I believe 150 feet is about long enough for your warp and this length, if carefully towed, will give no trouble as long as it is kept stopped up in a coil not less than 2½ feet in diameter. It is well to keep the warp lashed up to the clamp so that it will be aired out. Also, on clean, bright days, get it on deck for an airing.

Small boats should carry a tow rope. On a "T" boat, it might be 1¾-inch-circumference rope about 75 feet long. The tow rope is generally the same size or larger than the anchor warp, and the two are bent together in anchoring in deep water. If you have occasion to be towed in a seaway, take one turn around your mooring cleat, then a turn around the mast, then two half hitches (never use a bowline in a rope that you might want to cast off).

You will often notice in towing that the boats will surge back and forth and at times bring a severe snap or strain on the tow rope. This can usually be greatly reduced by changing the length of the tow rope. The cause of the tow boats varying their speed is that when a boat is climbing a wave she goes a knot or two slower than when coasting down the other side. With a little care, the distance between the boats can be made to coincide with the distance between crests, so that both boats will nearly agree on their variations of speed.

Buoy or mooring ropes should be changed every month if they are so arranged that much of them is immersed. You should always have two buoy ropes so that one can be stretched out on a fence on shore while the other is in use. Rain and sunshine will kill the bacteria that weaken a rope that has been left overboard. With two good buoy ropes (preferably made of copper-treated manila—the light green rope used now for lobster pot leaders), you can be sure of going through the season in safety.

While sailing, if you should hit a rock very hard, do not become alarmed, for the vulnerable parts of your boat are about two feet above the bottom of the keel and very probably will not be touched. Also, dents in the lead keel are quite inexpensively removed by pounding the lead back into shape.

If you run aground on a level bottom, it is generally possible to get the boat off by heeling her. This can be done by holding the jib to windward and giving her a rap full, then have your crew lean out on the leeward shrouds; if you can tip the boat as much as 45 degrees, the draft will be reduced nearly a third.

With a falling tide you must work rapidly, and it is advisable to feel around with the spinnaker pole or an oar to see which side deeper water is on and try to move her in this direction. Should anyone jump overboard to push her around, it is best to do so with shoes on, for one can push much more on a rough bottom when shod.

If you should go ashore while there is a groundswell running, do not be alarmed at the boat's pounding on bottom, for a keel boat with all outside ballast will stand terrific pounding without being hurt. It is well to always keep away from the windward side of all reefs and rocks, for grounding there may lead to most serious results.

Should a fog suddenly shut in on you, always locate yourself on the chart at once, as near as possible, and take the time. If you know where you are, you can use the sounding lead to good advantage to check your progress. Every time you change your course, you must note the time.

A fog is generally accompanied by a light wind and your boat may travel two miles an hour. You can make a rough mental calculation from this as to about how many minutes to run on a course. If you should want to go dead to windward, simply run the same length of time on each tack. If you should decide to anchor in a fog, it is well to run toward shore until your lead line gives you shallow readings. Then you will know large vessels will not run into you.

Different types of vessels are required by law to make distinctive fog signals. I will note some.

A steamer will sound a whistle or siren at intervals of about a minute.

Launches, etc., a mechanical horn similar to an auto.

A sailing vessel underway on the starboard tack will sound one prolonged blast on a foghorn at intervals of about one minute. On the port tack, two blasts in succession. With the wind aft of the beam, three blasts in succession.

A vessel when at anchor will ring a bell rapidly for a few seconds at intervals of about a minute.

A steamer when towing will sound one long and two short blasts.

It is well to have on board a copy of the pilot rules and study the rules for the prevention of collision at sea. There is one very good rule not printed in the book; it is "Might is Right." By this I mean it is best to give way to a larger vessel although you might have the right of way. While sailing vessels always have right of way over power-driven vessels, a small sailboat can always turn easily and quickly, but if a large vessel is compelled to change her course, it may cause her to make a serious maneuver and she may become involved with other vessels that also have right of way over her.

Keep away from the weather bow of larger racing craft. A sudden puff may make them luff in spite of the helmsman's wishes.

In shooting for the mooring, have in mind that the boat will shoot much farther in a light wind than in heavy weather. The reasons for this are that a sailboat goes much faster in comparison to the wind's velocity in light weather. Your boat may go 2 M.P.H. in a 3-mile breeze; 4 M.P.H. in a 6-mile breeze; 6 M.P.H. in a 15-mile breeze, and after that she will not increase in speed much, no matter what the wind is.

However, her wind resistance, while shooting for the mooring, will increase tremendously with an increase in wind velocity. With a 3-mile breeze her wind resistance may be 2 pounds; with a 10-mile breeze it may be 15 pounds; in a 20-mile breeze it may be 60 pounds; at 30 miles, possibly 100 pounds, so in coming about in strong breezes or shooting for the mooring, you must remember she will not go far to windward.

It is well to have a leader between your buoy rope and your tender so that there is ample room for shooting the mooring without banging the tender. If a few corks like those used on a fish net are lashed to the leader, it will be easy to gaff the leader at any point with a short-handled boat hook.

You should have a well-thought-out place for everything on the boat and keep it there, so if necessary you can put your hand on it at once in the dark. You can tie many things up to the clamp close under the deck so they will keep dry and ready for use.

Keep out of trouble. It is a disgrace to call for help when you have gotten yourself into trouble through ignorance and carelessness. Father Neptune has no patience with those who do not respect him. If you keep on the alert, and always know what you are doing and what you will do next, you may have a long, happy career of yachting and avoid all serious accidents.

Try to be patient and speak pleasantly but distinctly to your crew, and remember that too much must not be expected from the dumb ones. Some of the bold, bad sailors who boast a lot on shore are not much help when you get in a jam, so do not depend on anyone until you have seen him perform.

With a very few exceptions, do not lend your boat to anyone—it never pays.

List of Things to Keep on Board

1. Good anchor
2. Anchor warp
3. Tow rope
4. Water bottle
5. Lantern
6. Compass (keep the lubber line parallel with keel when in use)
7. Modern chart
8. Lead line
9. Bucket (preferably wooden)
10. Lace lines, etc., for reefing
11. Well-found ditty bag
12. Foghorn
13. Oilskins or an old heavy coat
14. Ten-foot oar
15. Knife, preferably of rustless steel
16. Four life preservers
17. Parceling for anchor warp
18. Paraffin
19. Watertight jar with matches
20. Pencil and small log book for noting time and positions

H 28 or
The Building of the *Snarke*

The Editor of *The Rudder* came up to call on me about a week ago and we fell to discoursing on the H 28 and devious things— to wit: some of our early American fishing craft, and of the time when he owned the Block Island boat, *Roaring Bessie*. We talked of the progress of *The Rudder*, etc., and he asked if I would write something about building H 28, as he said during these trying times [1943] people seem to like a change—something to take their minds off the war work for the evening so that they might come up during the construction; give them something to laugh at—a conversation piece—or even one of those stories you love to tell so much.

"But," I said, "I don't think the ladies would like that very well."

"Well," he said, "the ladies, if any, who read *The Rudder* are broad-minded. Make it sort of a 'Just So' story, telling of the benefits or joys one might experience during building."

"That," I said, "is a big order for one who made a complete failure of English at school."

But now, this evening, after fortifying myself with one or two fingers of New England rum, I start:

Once upon a time, and to be more exact, it was two hundred and one thousand years ago of a Sunday afternoon, God didn't have much to do, so He thought He would amuse Himself by designing a new sort of creature for that planet of His, which lay somewhere between the sun and the moon, and as He walked over to the drawing board, He thought of the horseshoe crab He had designed several thousand years before. To be sure, that was an amusing creature that had withstood all the earth's changes. Still, it had very little nerve and brain structure. Then He thought of the little seahorses and how they jigged back and forth in the shafts of sunlight between the seaweeds, and these had given Him much pleasure to design. But of late He had developed some land creatures that had amused Him mightily. These were the monkeys and apes, and as He thought of them running through the woods, raving and throwing coconuts at each other, it occurred to Him that by leaving off the tail and lengthening the hind legs, a very droll creature might be made. So He set to work.

Now it so happened that the last creature He had designed was the pig, and to save Himself the trouble of several new detail drawings, He took the liver, the lungs, and the heart just as they were. Then He changed the scale of the other principal glands slightly and said to Himself, "These will do quite well enough." The skin also He took, but instead of having the hair evenly distributed, He arranged it in a few amusing bunches, so that on the head and face it grew quite long. Now, as this beast was to stand on its hind feet and had no tail to balance with, it seemed quite necessary to greatly increase the number of nerve cells in its feet—otherwise it would be unable to walk in the dark; and while at this work, it occurred to Him how amusing it would be if the beast had as many nerves and some long digits on its front feet.

In due course all these things were worked out, but so many nerve connections had called for a large cranium, and as He looked over the lines He thought, "Well, with this multiplicity of nerves and these digits, it would be well to greatly increase the brain, and particularly that part that had to do with the imagination, for, peradventure, if he should use those hands to their utmost, he would accomplish devious things, and if by chance he should work diligently with both the hands and the brain, he might even achieve a certain state of happiness. But I fear Me that will not often come to be. And what with the loins of a pig and the frame of an ape, his lot will not be an enviable one."

And, as He prophesied, so it turned out to be. And of all the

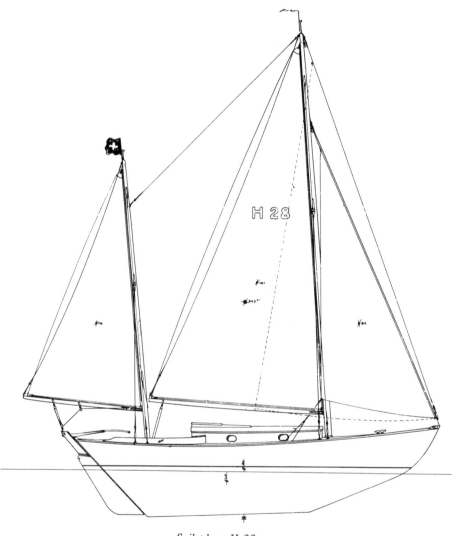

Sail plan, H 28.

beasts of the field and fowl of the air he was the most unhappy, as not one in ten thousand worked with both his hands and his head. And those who worked with their hands alone lost the use of the brain, so that some walked among them saying, "Look ye at the man who worketh with his brain, how he has a factory and a yacht and waxeth rich, while ye laboreth all to no avail."

And they talked of strikes and violence and were verily an unhappy lot. And those who worked with the brain alone were no happier, for it was their lot to have neuritis, headaches, and devious ills, both imaginary and real, and their digits hung at their sides and were only used for eating and drinking. But worst of all, before them at all times appeared the twin spectres of death and taxes; and think as they could, their brains never could quite adjust these things to their liking.

But there were among men a few, a very few, who used both their hands and their heads, and they achieved a happiness that nigh unto passeth the understanding. Such a one was Praxiteles, as he stopped to sharpen his chisel, looking out over the blue waters of the Aegean. Such another one was Grinling Gibbons, as they hoisted him in a basket to carve on the inner dome of St. Paul's (but he had the advantage of starting life as a ship's carver). So, too, were the fashioners of the rod screens, choir stalls, corbels, and hammer posts of the great cathedrals. These men felt neither cold nor hunger, pain nor weariness. To be sure, their teeth fell out and they had the other weaknesses of the flesh, but their work shows the perfect harmony that they lived in, for they worked with both their hands and their heads.

Now after many years it so came to pass that there was another whose content and happiness passeth the understanding, and we find him in a shed on the outskirts of a town and not far from the waterfront. He has before him on two sawhorses the stem of an H 28. It has been beveled from the rabbet line to the face line, and he is now cutting down to the back rabbet from the bearding line. Beside him lies the keel with its floor timbers attached, and Joe, his helper, is getting out the molds. There is quite a heap of shavings on the floor and these, together with piled lumber, give off the romantic odor of the shipyard. It is cold outside and icicles hang down from the windows, but the stove sings a merry tune as it is fed with crackling spruce and simmering yellow pine. He is beginning to feel the great content of accomplishment, for to know is all right for talkers and boasters, but to do bringeth satisfaction.

At first the work was hard for him and made him sore and stiff, but now the exercise makes him tingle with a pleasant feeling, and as he has to keep his wits about him, the time seems to fly and the days go by apace, and the H 28 takes shape.

The molds are set up and the ribbands sprung. Her shape, as it developed, fascinated him, and, so as to spend as much time as possible with her, he now brought his lunch with him. It was pleasant sitting beside the stove and the steam box to eat, for they now had a roaring good fire, and that afternoon they were going to bend frames. Joe, his helper, was a very good worker and had worked some years in the local yacht yard; he was quite an amusing conversationalist, but the only fly in the ointment was Joe's profanity—he used swear words for descriptive adjectives and punctuation, or at times for each alternate word. Joe was a French Canadian and, although he had not quite mastered the English language, he was an excellent wood worker. As they were eating their lunch, Joe said, "That frame, she is about 1⅝ square, maybe she take half-hour to steam. Every steam box, she is different, but if I work this shop long she no fool me. I think I have time to tell you wan Canuck storee while that frame she cook some more.

"I hunt muskrat, I hunt wildcat, sometime I hunt de hare. Wan time I tak' de ax an' go to hunt de skunk pole cat. My fren' Beel he say he's very good fur, sometime he's good for eat. And so I go to get fur coat, same time get some meat. I walk two-three mile, den I get de awful smell, I t'ink dat skunk has go and die and fur coat she go to hell. Den I see he is down by wan beeg tree. I sneak up close behind. I t'ink he no see me. Den I raise de ax up high, but de skunk he's t'ro somet'ing, stricket jus' in my eye. Gee-cri, I t'ink I see blind. Mon dieu, I cannot see. I go roun' and roun' till I strike de good dum tree, den I t'row way de ax and light out for de shack. I t'ink about one thousan' skunk she's climb up on my back. My wife she's meet me at the gate. She sick on me de dog. She say, 'You can't stay here tonight—go stay out with the hog.' And so I hunt de skunk no more to get its fur and meat for if he's bees he smell so strong I don't t'ink I like that meat." (With all credit to the unknown author and apologies for leaving out certain words for the benefit of the ladies.)

Well, they worked hard all the afternoon. To start with, Joe had four frames in the steam box and each time he pulled one out he replaced it with another. As he pulled the hot frame from the box, he handled it with a piece of burlap bag and handed the frame to the Man (as we will thus call him hereinafter, for there will later be one called the Woman in the case, also), who grasped it and stood it nearly upright while Joe clamped the heel against the floor timber. Then the Man bent the head of the frame toward the upper ribband and, grasping the same with one hand, he walked up the steaming frame, so that it bent perfectly on the ribbands, making the reverse curve as intended, and all this was done even more rapidly than it has been written. Joe clamped and dogged the frame in place and so as to not use too many clamps (as they didn't have many), as soon as the frame had cooled some, they put screws through the ribband into the frame after the frame had been slid and twisted into exact line, which they determined with several little measuring sticks, the exact length of the bay between each frame. Well it was fast work and hot work and almost before they knew it, the sky in the west grew pink and the east gray. Across the harbor the lights popped into view, one by one, and the icicles in front of the window stopped dripping. As Joe was putting on his coat to go home, he said, "That is some of the best damn frame I have ever bent and the reason for it is the frame is square. Each time I han' you a frame I turn it so she come slash grain (that is, so the grain of the wood is in layers parallel with the planking). Now if you try to bend him in rift grain (that is, with the grain of the wood) at right angle to planking you find plenty of him break. I think designers of that H 28 work in shop some tam' so he can know somet'ing. Lots of designers he don't know he call for frame so much molded, so much sides, that is O.K. for saw frame but no damn good for steam job."

As the Man walked home, the air was crisp and clear and the evening stars shimmered in the heavens, but he felt not the cold, for a great contentment was on him, and as is so in such cases, his perceptions were keener. How different, he thought to himself, this all is from the way I felt a month ago. Yes, the bending and stooping, sawing and drilling, were good for one after he had grown used to it, and my! how you did have to keep your wits about you. But then he thought of his wife. (Enter the Woman.)

It so happened that a young lady had lived not so far from the Man, and in fact just two streets up from the yacht club, and she, having heard devious words that some of the neighbors let fall about the time that his uncle died (to wit: that the Man was in good case, well heeled, and the like), she took it upon herself to show him good countenance and he, finding her of pleasant demeanor and comely of person, took her to wife. Now, as often happens in such cases, as the months went by she became less and less pleasant of demeanor, so at the time of which we relate, coincident with the bending of the frames, she, noting the great content which the man found himself in, took it upon herself to be gravely perplexed, and as the man rested himself before the fire in the evening, thumbing over the Merriman catalogue of yacht fittings, and Sands catalogue of marine fixtures, she said unto herself, "Woe unto me that I ever married this stick-in-the-mud who spends his evening roasting his feet while other husbands take their wives to the play and the night clubs and are merry and dance."

The Man, perceiving this disorder, put it to one side, saying, "This is naught but the ways of a woman." But one afternoon the Woman called on the wife of a man in the travel business, and seeing various and sundry pamphlets lying about, she took to looking at them, and in sooth one of them pleased her mightily and as she was departing, the lady pressed it upon her. Now this aforesaid pamphlet was intended to describe a West Indies cruise, but it gave none of the information a prudent traveler would know, such as where the ship was built, what rating she had with Lloyd's, what type of lifesaving equipment she had, or whether her paintwork and interior trim were fire resisting. In lieu of this, on the cover was depicted a great white steamer whose proportions and height would make the heart jump into the mouth of one used to nautical matters. Worst of all, hard under her starboard bow, where one of her stockless anchors would fall, was a miniature palm-clad island, and about where one would expect the steamer's port screw to be was the shelving beach of another.

But the second page was what took the Woman's eye, for there the artist had depicted a woman in a very low-necked gown, holding a fan in one hand, in the act of descending a broad flight of stairs flanked by royal palms. In the distance and hardly discernible were some pygmies dancing in a saloon about ninety feet high with a domed skylight like the apse of a cathedral. Under this artist's drawing was the simple caption, "Orchestra 4:30 and 8:30 daily."

Now the Woman took great store by this picture and many afternoons after she had finished her housework, she would take to looking at it, would mull over in her mind what kind of a hair-do she would have if she were the woman descending the stairs, and even made up imaginary conversations with the passengers. About this time the Devil, passing that way on his regular rounds and seeing the lay of things, said to himself, "This seemeth a fertile field to sow in." He got the Woman by the ear and began quoting such sooths to her as, "A woman is young but once," "Catcheth you fish while the bait has an allure," etc., which, though the Woman did not know it, were not sooths but really wiles. For, though it is true that strumpets and harlots are young but once, still those who keep themselves interesting are young always, and those who work with their hands and their heads are always interesting. Michelangelo was the life of the party at seventy, and for that matter still lives.

Well, in the meantime the H 28 prospered and grew. They lined off the planking—that is, they marked on each frame where the seams of each plank should come. The garboard, or lowest plank, was rather triangular, so that its upper edge was quite parallel with the waterline. To divide up the area above that, they took a piece of white elastic webbing such as is used to make children's garters, etc., about one inch wide. This they stretched over the longest frame amidships and divided it off with pencil lines where they wanted the seam of the plank to come, making the lower planks widest and gradually decreasing them up to the sheer strake, which again was a little wider, to be sure to take the shelf bolts. Then they restretched this elastic over each frame above the garboard and transferred the plank divisions thus. To carry the line of the plank out to the bow and stern, which were beyond the top of the garboard, they tacked a batten along each line and carried it out, and this took some care and skill, but, as Joe said, nothing was much homelier than a vessel with poorly lined-off planks.

The Man grew happier and healthier as the days went by, but the Woman was sorely perplexed and even got to the point where she considered doing the Man some grievous mischief. At one time she even considered disposing of a large pile of back numbers of *The Rudder*, which the Man kept in a cupboard beside the fireplace and solaced himself greatly therewith. At last the Woman, in despair, after many an "Ah, me" and the like, turned to cooking to quiet her nerves (and she was a good cook) and made herself a couple of mince pies. Now it so happened these pies turned out wondrous good. So, at the supper table, after first saying to herself, "I don't care about my figure any more," and such like, she did take of the pie a measure rather more than was her wont. As the evening wore on, feeling herself in slight distress, she bethought herself of some elderberry wine her aunt had given her for medicinal reasons, but not knowing the potency of that remedy, she dealt herself such portion as was more befitting of a wine than a cordial.

Soon, after feeling a certain drowsiness on her, she excused herself and said goodnight and retired, whereupon she fell into a heavy slumber and a dream came unto her wherein she heard two voices discoursing. One said to the other, "Know ye the man that buildeth himself an H 28?" The other voice answered, "Verily I do, and a happier man it would be hard to find." First voice, "Know ye his wife?" Second voice, "Aye, of a surety, I do." First voice, "What think ye of her?" Second voice, "Now so as to not mince my words, I think she is a —————— fool." First voice, "Why judge ye so harshly of her?" Second voice, "In the first place she nourisheth herself at the same loaf as the Man, and sheltereth herself under the same roof, but is too much of a fool to share his pleasure of working with the hands and the head. In the second place she is beset of a cruise on a steamer where she would only come in contact with trippers, card sharks, ham actors, and adventuresses, that human dross that frequents public places to pass away the time, for they can neither work with their hands nor their heads." First voice, "But this woman would like to go places and see things." Second voice, "Those who travel the fastest see the least, but he that would see, feel, and hear the most of life, nature, and God, let him go down to the sea in a small sailing vessel." First voice, "But the Woman would like to feel the romance of the moon rising over a tropical sea with music and dancing." Second voice, "The same moon riseth over the H 28 though it appeareth differently. Over the steamer it is cold and lifeless, as it takes its course up the heavens, while over the H 28 it is a merry thing that now peereth in through the starboard sidelight, and now through the nether end of the port hatchway, as she veers back and forth at her mooring, dancing to the tune of the incoming tide which chuckleth under the forefoot."

Well, the Woman spent the rest of the night rather restlessly, but in the morning, putting on a more pleasant demeanor than of late, made ready the breakfast things. Now the Man, as he sat down, noting the change, said to himself, "What does this forebode? I hope it is no ill omen on this the day that we were going to spring in the shelf and clamp." So he shielded himself back of the morning paper expecting momentarily the West Indies cruise to come to the fore. But as he put his coffee cup down for the second time, the Woman said in a very unconcerned voice, "Now about that curtain in front of the toilet, and the covers for the bottom of the pipe berths on the H 28." "I beg your pardon," said the Man, but to his great astonishment, they fell to discoursing most amiably on the whys and wherefores of various arrangements, and the Woman did not contradict him even once, of that which he had to say, and he marveled greatly thereat.

But Joe was waiting to bend in the shelf and clamp and this was a job for two, so he hurried down to the H 28, but often during the morning he fell to pondering about the unusual turn that the Woman had taken; and fearing lest some grievous ill was upon her, he took his lunch in his hand when the noon hour approached and went home where, much to his astonishment, he found the Woman sitting among various and sundry materials suitable for curtains, cushions, and the like, and so much did he enjoy that noon hour that he ate his lunch at home thereafter.

And the Woman, on her part, wrought wondrously well with the needle, and being one of good taste, as even some women are, began working with both hands and her head so that she, too, began to feel a measure of peace and contentment, nearly equal to that of the Man.

After the deck was laid, and the house built, the Woman helped with painting of the cabin, and she, being nearly as good a conversationalist as Joe, got to asking him where he went when he first came to the States, and how old his wife was at that time. Joe said, "Well, first we come to New Ham-sheer. That time my wife, she was dirty and I was dirty, too. We live in dat state for about two year. Then we come this place. My wife, she get job in laundry and I do somet'ing too. Was pretty hard at first but now we do pretty good. I think we clean everyt'ing up in about 'nother year."

The days now were getting longer, but the work was well advanced. The spars were glued up, the rudder and tiller finished and hung. One Saturday afternoon a rigger came up from the local yacht yard and was getting out her gang of rigging. Everything certainly was bustle and excitement, and little had they realized before how many parts there were to a small vessel, what with the shackles, the thimbles, the blocks, deck hardware, and all. Well, everything looked pretty good, and that afternoon an old uncle, a brother of the one who had died, came to look things over. Now this uncle was an eccentric old man who collected clocks; not so much for their cases did he value them, but rather for the design and excellence of their works, and like many another who has had a hobby for years, he had acquired quite a knowledge of this hobby and even could be said to be an authority on horology. In his younger days, however, he had had a yacht. Well, as he looked the H 28 over, he thought, "By golly, the planking is pretty good—nearly as good as they used to make it." When he climbed inside he was quite surprised to see the Woman painting, for he had always put her down as one who would neither fish nor cut bait.

All this pleased the old boy no small amount, and he said to himself, "My nephew is coming right along, and after this work with his hands and head, he may even have an appreciation of some of the real things of this life." So he called his nephew over to him and said, "I have at home a Chelsea clock or two, and the one that I have in mind I had on my yacht about thirty years ago. I have so regulated it from time to time that its rate is within one minute a month. It is one of their striking models. If you tell me the name the yacht will carry, I will have it engraved on the flange of the bezel."

Man speaking: "Uncle, that is the one thing I wanted most of all, but noticing the prices of them in the back numbers of *The Rudder*, I had thought them beyond my means. Now as to the name, let me call my wife down." Woman climbs down ladder and is a little cross at being summoned. Man speaking: "Uncle is going to give us a Chelsea clock for the H 28." Woman speaking: "What do you want a clock for when you have a wrist watch?" Man speaking: "Now, now, we were wondering what to name the H 28 and thought you might help us." So the Woman,

coming to her senses, said: "Uncle, what would you name her?"
Uncle speaking: "I had always thought if I had another yacht I
would name her the *Snark*, for Jack London had such an
amusing time with the one he tried to build so named, and a
few years ago, looking in Lloyd's Register, I found none of that
name." So they all did agree the *Snark* she would be, and every
one went home happily.

That night the Woman cut a stencil for the name and she was
quite deft at such work, but the next day when they went to
try it on the stern, they discovered, much to their chagrin, that
they had forgotten all about the rudder. Joe, happening around
under the stern and seeing the quandary they were in, said,
"Well, why not put another letter on him?" At first they
laughed, then the Woman said, "An old English way of spelling
it might have been *Snarke,*" so they adopted that, and the
Man said, "I bet that one isn't in Lloyd's."

Well, the days went by till it was light after supper, and one
warm spring evening they walked down to see her. It was one of
those still June evenings when all nature seemed pregnant with
life. You could almost feel the grass growing and the apple
blossoms falling. In the distance could be heard the rhythm of
the frogs as they tuned up for their evening concert, and now
and then the cadence of a robin's evening song. They opened
the big door at the end of the shed, and the evening lights and
shadows, as they played along the *Snarke*'s topsides, made her
seem almost opalescent with the reflections of the green grass
and the pinks of the sunset. My! how she stood out against the
somber background of the shed. As the Man and the Woman
stood arm in arm looking at her, they suddenly realized how
they loved her.

Nearly everything was completed now and the paint quite
hard. They had the local mover set her on the shore at low tide,
down to the water's edge. It wasn't a very thrilling launching, to
be sure, but they liked it. They expected her to float at about
seven in the evening, so the Woman (who might now even be
called the Bonnie Lassie) had put up a lunch. Uncle was there
and the three of them sat in the cabin, as the evening had
turned cool. The stove was going, so they had tea with their
sandwiches and lay back comfortably enjoying themselves, when
suddenly they heard the pleasant sound of the Chelsea clock as
it struck six bells, and they thought, she ought to float any time

now. But when the Man looked over the side, it occurred to him he had forgotten about daylight saving time, so they had an hour before them to sit and talk.

The Woman, to make conversation, said, "My husband tells me a clock like our Chelsea costs about one hundred dollars. Now, Uncle, how can that be?" Uncle speaking: "I am glad you asked me that, for I think I can tell you. Now to make a weight-driven pendulum clock that keeps fine time is a comparatively simple matter, for the driving power is constant, and the pendulum meters out the time most accurately, but when you try to equal this accuracy of timekeeping with a clock that will be subject to motion, vibration, and changes in temperature, there are some great difficulties to overcome. You will say, 'Well how about the watch?' Now, while the watch is a wonderful thing, the Chelsea clock is in reality only an enlarged fine watch with a spring large enough to drive it eight days. The escapement is full-jeweled—in fact, it has jewels in some of the important places that many watches do not. Every other gear in the Chelsea is of hardened and polished steel; the intermediate ones are of carefully cut, wide-faced bronze. Your clock here has run thirty years or more and shows absolutely no signs of wear. I do believe, with proper oiling, it may run for several centuries. The Chelsea clock is one of those unique things that is made and finished just as well all through as it is on the outside. It is manufactured with just as much care and skill today as it was fifty years ago. Now, if you take a mechanism as carefully designed and made as this and put it in a cast bronze case that is dust-, fog-, and water-tight, you have something dependable to take to sea with you."

Woman speaking: "Uncle, do you mean to say all those other clocks are good for nothing?" Uncle speaking: "Well, most of them might be used to throw at the cats on the back fence of a moonlit night, but I can't think of what use they would be at sea."

The *Snarke* began to jiggle on her cradle; then she lifted aft. Gradually she was waterborne and floated off and became that thing of life that they had so yearned for. After several trial sails, and getting well acquainted with her, they took a cruise to the eastward. They got down as far as Isle au Haut and Frenchman's Bay the first year, and cruised happily many years after, and it so happened that a son and daughter were born to them so the two pipe berths abreast the mainmast were not all in vain. They always hoped sometime to get down to the Bras d'Or Lakes, and even to visit St. Pierre and Miquelon, but I can't say whether they ever did or not. But one thing I am sure of, the Chelsea clock kept going, and so this yarn endeth more truthfully than it began.

Chelsea ship's bell clock. (Chelsea Clock Co.)

Naming the Yacht

It has been my ambition for some time to write an article that the readers of *The Rudder* would find useful enough to cut out and save. So, with this in mind, it has seemed that some discourse about the names of yachts might be as useful as any other. It is also high time that something was said on that subject, for of late years, we in America seem to have fallen down sadly in the matter of giving yachts becoming and melodious names. In using the word *melodious*, I mean names that are constructed in such a way that the succession of rhythmic tones produces a pleasant sound. I mean names that bring to mind pleasant thoughts, names that are easily remembered (and melodious ones generally are). But besides names having some romantic meaning and pleasant sounds, there are several other qualities a good name must possess.

The first of these qualities perhaps is a name that can be clearly and distinctly enunciated, for one of the important uses of a yacht's name is for the purpose of hailing. All the names that are hard to pronounce, or difficult to throw the voice into, are a continual source of annoyance to the fleet in harbor. Such names as *Jabberwock* and *Hullabaloo*, in the many ways the club squarehead may pronounce them, are wholly confusing, but a name like *North Star* will ring out across the harbor on a dark and rainy night, so that the hail soon gets an answer.

Perhaps as you sit before the fire in your city apartment, you will not think this of much consequence, but some night after you have stood on the yacht club float for an hour or two in the rain, with a suitcase in one hand and a wilting bag of groceries in the other, you will see what I mean.

Some people make the very great mistake of selecting a name that does not have a clear meaning. These are usually called "trick" names, and the owner often thinks himself very smart for selecting a name that will require much explanation; in fact, this sort of person usually gets a great kick out of making the explanation. But after six months or so, and after having recited the elaborate explanation a thousand times, and after his wife has corrected him a thousand and one times, no doubt he will wish he had named the old crate the *Mary Jane* instead of *Vivandiere.*

Unfortunately, we have named some yachts with the letters of the owner's name spelled backwards, or part of the combined names of his twin daughters, etc. Not only do these names show gross egotism but, worse still, they plainly show the owner is entirely lacking in romance, poetry, and music. Of course, if one has a wife, daughter, or mother with a nice-sounding name, then it is most appropriate to use that name, but to keep using the same with succeeding yachts is a great mistake. My grandfather named most of his catboats *Julia* (my grandmother's name), but today I can't identify one from the other. One of my acquaintances had seven or eight yachts named *Sally*, and another had perhaps even more named *Gypsy*, and several times I have been in hot arguments as to which was the *Sally IV*, or the *Gypsy VII*, for sometimes in conversation, in describing the model, etc., the identity is important.

Mr. W. P. Stephens, who for many years had charge of the listing of American yachts in Lloyd's Register, used to hate these repeat names, as they caused him endless confusion. He used to refer to them as rubber-stamp names. Charles II, the great-grandfather of yachting, named most of his many yachts after his lady friends, and in some cases he used their nicknames. At any rate, he didn't need a rubber stamp, for apparently there were more lady friends than there were yachts.

For centuries the sailor has preferred mythological names, and the sagas tell us that some of the Viking ships around the year 1000 had names from Norse mythology. Some of the Viking ships had long, compound names that, if translated, had meanings like "Deer of the Surf," "Reindeer of Breezes," "Elk of the

Fjord," "Raven of the Sea," etc. Probably the sailor and the ship owner have liked mythological names because they have come down to us from the Golden Age—the age when all things were beautiful and wonderful, for at Olympus the robes and other garments were woven by no lesser people than Minerva and the Graces, and everything of more solid nature was formed at the forge of Vulcan. He even made golden shoes for the gods so that they trod either the sea or the air and traveled from place to place with the rapidity of thought. This cunning workman could bestow on his workmanship self-motion, so that the tripods (chairs and tables) moved of themselves in and out of the celestial halls, which is quite in contrast to the clumsy products of Detroit, which must be fed fuel and have electric wires attached to them.

The Golden Age—the age of classical mythology—was one of innocence and happiness. Truth and Right prevailed, though they were not enforced by law. The actions and behavior of these gods and goddesses, as told in mythology, are so full of human nature and free of guile that the sailor, who is used to the great, free, open spaces, loves them. Artists, too, for centuries have devoted some of their best marbles and largest canvases to mythology, so that when the names from classical mythology are melodious, they are considered by the sailor the choicest of all. However, the heroes and gods of Norse mythology are quite as romantic, even if in most cases their names are less harmonious. Teutonic mythology differs but slightly from the Norse, and some of the names are very similar. Eastern and Egyptian mythology, though very ancient and abounding in names, have not as a rule been popular with the sailorman. Possibly this is because, by and large, they are collections of rather cruel stories. They never had a Homer, Vergil, or Ovid to make their myths beautiful and appealing. Druid and ancient Irish names, however, have always been popular with the English-speaking sailor, and some of these are very fine indeed.

While the names from American Indian languages are sometimes pleasant-sounding, still, as a general rule, they call for an explanation, which, as I have said before, becomes tiring. For instance, how many do you suppose know that *Istalena* is an Indian word for water lily?

The most beautiful-sounding names, as a general rule, are from the Spanish language. Italian names come next, while many

French names are both nice sounding and have very intimate, special, and pleasing meanings. I, myself, see no reason why male names should not be used more for powercraft or steamships. Certainly if naval craft and merchant ships are named after politicians, we of the smaller craft at least might use such names as *Desperado* for a high-powered motorboat; or *Ajax* for a tugboat. Many of the Spanish names end with an *o*, which gives them a nice finishing-off ring, and such names as *Stiletto, Bambino,* and *Tranquillo* seem to be good hailing names. There are also very nice-sounding botanical names, particularly those of the flowers and trees.

The reader should bear in mind that the name of a yacht often very much affects her whole prestige; at times it even affects her value, or sales price, and even a beautiful yacht can be made to seem less beautiful if one associates an unbecoming name with her. So the naming of a yacht is altogether a most important matter, but it should be a matter that gives the whole family much pleasant amusement in talking over and selecting the name, and this should be one of the greatest joys for the owner in building a new boat.

In the following list, most of the names are of yachts of the past, and I have given this list more as a guide to what has been considered suitable. A very great many of these names have been used on American yachts, but undoubtedly there are many names that would be suitable to use again, and I must note that with names that particularly suit a certain type of boat, it is excusable to use them again as long as there is not another vessel in her own home port with the same name (or if the same owner has not used the name before). I thoroughly believe that a more careful choice of names for American yachts would help the prestige of yachting in general and give the owner and his family more constant pleasure and pleasant memories.

If, in my description of the names, I have made some deviation from the accepted meaning, you must remember that even in Greek mythology there are three variations—I believe the Attic, Olympian, and Trojan; and perhaps Macedonian. And besides that, I am no scholar myself, and in most cases I have depended on my memory of conversations with a modern Greek.

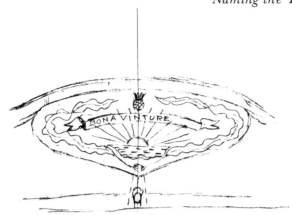

Acorn	Symbol of naval architecture.
Actaea	
Acushla	
Adela	
Adriana	
Aegir	God of the sea (Teutonic).
Aeolia	
Aeolus	God of winds (Classical).
Aglaia	One of the three Graces (Classical).
Aida	
Aileen	
Alanna	
Albatross	
Albion	A son of Neptune and founder of a kingdom in England.
Alerion	Young eagle.
Alert	
Alfreda	
Allegro	Fast, lively (in music).
Alpha	
Amaryllis	
Ambrosia	Food of the gods.
Amphitrite	Goddess of sea; wife of Neptune (Classical).
Andante	Good name for a cruiser; moving moderately slowly (music).
Anemone	Marine flower.
Angelica	
Antelope	

Aphrodite	A butterfly; another name for Venus.
Aquila	Northern constellation, the eagle.
Arcturus	
Arethusa	Wood nymph (Classical).
Ariadne	
Artemis	Goddess of Nature (Greek).
Atalanta	
Athena	Goddess of wisdom. Presided over art of navigation. (Roman name: Minerva.)
Aurora	Mother of the winds (Roman). (Greek name: Eos.)
Avaunt	
Aventurière	
Bagatelle	
Ballerina	
Bambino	
Banshee	Irish ghost.
Bee	
Bel Ami	
Bella Donna	A heart stimulant.
Belle Brise	
Bibelot	
Bona	Meaning "good."
Bonaventure	Good venture.
Bonnie Doon	
Boomerang	
Boreas	North wind.
Brunhild	
or Brynhild	A Valkyrie.
Cala Mara	Suggested for a houseboat.
Calumet	Peace pipe.
Calypso	Sea nymph (Classical).
Camargo	
Camilla	Fleet-footed maiden queen.
Caprice	
Caress	
Carina	
Cetacean	
Charmer	
Cheshire	
Chimera	Wild fancy.

Cinderella	
Circe	An enchantress (Classical).
Clytie	Water nymph.
Comet	
Connoisseur	
Constance	
Consuelo	Spanish for "comfort."
Coquette	
Cormorant	Sea bird.
Corsair	A Mediterranean pirate.
Creole	
Crystal	
Curlew	Shore bird.
Cygnet	Young swan.
Cymbelline	Daughter of river god.
Cynic	
Cynthea	Hunting goddess (Classical).
Cyrene	
Czarina	
Daphne	Daughter of river god.
Dart	
Dauntless	
Dawn	
Delight	
Desire	
Diadem	
Diana	Hunting goddess.
Dilemma	
Discus	
Dolphin	
Druid	
Dryad	
Duenna	Good name for tender of racing yacht.
Dulcia	
Dwarf	
Eagle	
Echo	Greek nymph.
Eclat	
Eider	
Electra	One of the Pleiades.
Elf	

Elfin
Elixir
Elysium   Any place of bliss.
Emblem
Enchantress
Endymion   Greek youth beloved by Selene.
Enigma
Eos   Aurora (Greek).
Epigram
Epilog
Epitome
Epode
Erlking   A malicious spirit.
Escape
Esperanza
Eureka
Express
Falcon
Fancy
Fandango
Fanfare
Fanita
Fan-tan
Fantasy
Fascine   Bundle of sticks bound together.
Faun
Fawn
Fay
Fearless
Fetish
Fidelio
Filly
Finesse
Fingerling
Flash
Fledgling
Fleetwing
Fleur de Lis
Flight
Flirt
Fortuna

Freelance	
Freya	Goddess of love and beauty (Teutonic).
Frolic	
Fulmar	Large sea bird.
Galatea	Sea nymph
Gamin	
Gar	
Gavina	
Gavotte	
Gazelle	
Gem	
Genie	Good or bad spirit.
Gew Gaw	
Gillie	Scottish word meaning "attendant to a sportsman."
Gitana	
Gleam	
Gloriana	
Gnome	
Godiva	
Gondola	
Grampus	A cetacean.
Grayling	Freshwater fish.
Gudrun	Norse mythological heroine.
Haidee	
Halcyon	
Harbinger	
Harlequin	
Harmonia	A daughter of Venus.
Hawk	
Hazard	
Hebe	Goddess of youth.
Heidi	
Hesperia	Western lands.
Hildegarde	
Hope	
Huntress	
Hygeia	Goddess of health.
Ianthe	
Ibis	
Idalia	

Incognito	
Infanta	
Ingomar	
Intrepid	
Iolanthe	
Iota	
Iris	Goddess of the rainbow.
Isis	Chief Egyptian female divinity.
Ishkoodah	Indian name for "comet."
Isolde	
Ituna	
Javelin	
Jessamine	
Joyous	
Juniata	
Karina	
Kelpie	Water sprite.
Kestrel	Small falcon.
Kingfisher	Good name for sportfisherman.
Kismet	Fate.
Kite	Bird of hawk family.
Kriemhilde	Wife of Sigurd.
Ladoga	
Lance	
Lantana	
La Paloma	The dove.
La Petite	For a small boat.
Lap-wing	Suggested for boat with lapping jib.
Lass	
Latona	Roman goddess.
Leander	
Leda	Classical goddess.
L'Esperance	
Lethe	
Leto	
Lilliput	For a small boat.
Linnet	
Lissome	Swift and light in motion.
Livonia	
Lode Star	
Lolita	

Londa	
Loon	
Lotus	Water flower.
Lure	
Macushla	
Mademoiselle	
Madge	
Madrigal	A light lyric song.
Magic	
Magnet	
Magnolia	
Maid	
Maid Marion	
Majesty	
Mañana	
Mariana	
Marionette	
Mariposa	A butterfly.
Mascot	
Mavis	A song thrush.
May Queen	
Mazurka	A lively dance.
Medea	Sorceress.
Medora	
Medusa	
Melody	
Memento	
Memory	
Mentor	
Mercury	
Merle	A blackbird.
Merlin	
Merry Maid	
Meteor	
Mignon	
Mimosa	
Minerva	Goddess of wisdom.
Minnehaha	"Laughing Water," Indian name.
Minstrel	
Minuet	
Mirage	

Mirth
Mist
Mistral
Mogli
Mona
Moonbeam
Myrtle
Mystic
Myth
Nahma
Naiad   Water nymph.
Narada
Nebula
Neptune
Nereus
Nimble
Nimbus   Halo.
Niobe
Nocturne
Norn   Any one of the three Fates.
Norna
Nymph
Onward
Owl
Pandora
Papoose
Peri   Mythological elf (Persian).
Persephone   Wife of Pluto.
Pirouette
Pixy or Pixie
Plover
Polaris   Pole star.
Portia
Primrose
Privateer
Psyche
Ptarmigan
Puck
Querida
Quickstep
Qui Vive

Ramona
Ranee
Rapier
Ray
Reaper
Regina
Reposo
Reverie
Ripple
Romance
Rowena
Sabrina
Sagittar
Samara   Winged fruit of elm, maple, etc.
Samba
Sanderling   A sandpiper.
Sans Gêne
Santiana   Sailors' chantey.
Sappho
Saraband   Slow dance.
Satanella
Satellite   Name for tender.
Sayonara
Scarab   Egyptian beetle and charm.
Scud
Scup   East coast fish.
Scylla
Seal
Sea Mew   European gull.
Selene   Goddess of moon (Greek).
Serene
Shona
Sibyl
Siesta
Signora
Siren
Sirocco
Siva
Sleipner   Odin's horse.
Snark
Solace

Sorceress
Sparrow Hawk
Spook
Sprite
Spruce
Stellar
Stiletto
Surf
Sylph
Talisman
Tamara
Tangerine
Tango
Tarantella   Spanish dance.
Tarantula   Spider.
Tatiana
Tern
Terpsichore
Thalia   One of the three Graces.
Themis   Personifies physical law, custom, and justice.
Thetis   Goddess; mother of Achilles.
Tioga   Indian name for "beautiful wife."
Titania
Tithe
Titwillow
Tranquillo
Trident
Triton
Trivia
Trixie
Troll
Turquoise
Undine   Water nymph.
Valhalla   Sailors' heaven.
Valiant
Vamoose
Vanity
Varuna
Vassal
Vedette   First fast steam launches built in France.
Vega   Star.

Ventura	
Venus	Goddess of beauty and love (Roman).
Verbena	
Verve	Energy, vigor.
Vesper	Evening star.
Vesta	Goddess of home (Roman).
Viator	
Vim	
Violet	
Viva	Long live!
Vixen	
Volant	
or Volante	Nimble, quick (name of a famous English cutter).
Wag	
Waif	
Walloon	
Wee Winn	
Whim	
Whippet	
Whisper	
Whist	
Winsome	
Wisp	
Worry	
Zephyr	

Trailboards and Figureheads

I have been asked to write something about trailboards, and as this harks back to a time when people cared something about the looks of their vessels, I am pleased to do it, but cannot help thinking it a queer request when most boats in this day are modeled after a red-painted and chromium-plated coffin. Also, there are things about heads that the ladies might not like to hear.

Trailboards are sort of an adjunct to the figurehead, and their development came about as follows. In early times, before the year 1000, many vessels had beaks, or abovewater rams, with little decoration. This was true of both the Mediterranean and Nordic craft. See Figure 1. By 1000 A.D. the Viking ships apparently had rather upright figureheads mounted over an overhanging bow. These might be called figureheads without trailboards, but as the gunwale, washboard, et cetera, were carried up in a graceful curve, perhaps the whole vessel in a way became the trailboards. In some of the sagas, mention was made of the laws requiring that the Viking ships either remove or cover up the figureheads as they approached their home ports, for it was believed they would scare the women and cattle. So we can imagine that these fierce dragon heads and grotesque sea serpents with open mouths were more fear-inspiring than beautiful. Perhaps the object of these figureheads was to intimidate the enemy in that age of fables when monsters did exist in the mind, if not on the water.

As a matter of fact, most of the Nordic craft that have been exhumed from burial mounds and bogs had either the above-water ram or very gracefully carved spiral scrolls. These latter figureheads are somewhat reminiscent of the bow and stern decorations that had been used on the Egyptian and Phoenician vessels, showing that for several thousand years the sailor was not happy without some fitting finial to the ends of his vessel. Nevertheless, there were to be three separate periods when the figurehead was conspicuous by its absence, and one of these times was when the fighting castles, forecastles, and aftercastles came into use, about the year 1200. Of course fishing vessels and boats were too small for these superstructures, but they could run into shallow water on the approach of the enemy, though apparently all seakeeping vessels of that time had to be armed like a fighting ship or they would be taken as a matter of course, war or no war.

The heavily armed or high-superstructure vessels were hard to propel by oars, so that sail was depended upon more and more as time went on. The race to crowd on more sail necessitated sticking a sprit out over the bow to support the foremast, which had been crowded well forward. However, this noble spar, the bowsprit, was unable to stand the strain without support, so that rope lashings or gammon strops were carried to the beak, which had descended from the abovewater ram, and from 1400 to perhaps 1600, these beaks became quite large and long to support the bowsprit. I might note that the beak of a vessel is or was at times also called a head, a false piece, a prow, or a cutwater. But in the times we speak of, before the bobstay, these beaks were hard-working parts of the vessel. On account of

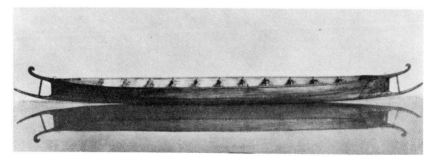

Figure 1. Early Nordic craft.

the side strain from the bowsprit, they were finally built into complicated structures in which the trailboards for the first time, and perhaps the last, were a structural part of the vessel quite necessary before bowsprit shrouds came into being.

While this complicated structure under the bowsprit is not clearly shown on many models and plans, from 1600 to 1850 it often was arranged to serve as the sailorman's latrine, and this was worked out about as follows, depending on the size of the vessel. You must bear in mind that the older vessels were very full forward, or apple-bowed. Well, on the larger ships the trail-boards swept aft from the figurehead in three or more strips separated by cross braces, as you can see in Figure 2. The upper strip was a back rest, the middle strip a seat, and the lower one a foot rest, as shown in Figure 3. This must have been an airy perch at times if beating to weather in a channel northeaster, or even a Mediterranean winter Levanter. If one looks at hundreds of plans, paintings, and models of the larger vessels between 1600 and 1850, he will almost always see these three strips sweeping aft from the figurehead.

In those days, the man in charge of the various spars aloft was called either the captain of the foretop, the captain of the maintop,

Figure 2. Group heads for larger ships.

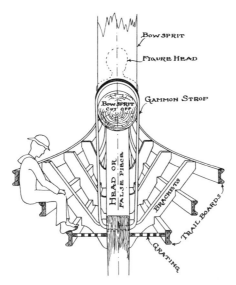

*Figure 3. An old-fashioned figurehead as
seen from astern.* (The Rudder)

or the captain of the mizzen top. The bowsprit also had its
captain, and he was designated the captain of the head. Strange to
say, that designation still persists in our navy, since the man
responsible for the sanitary conditions of the toilets is now
called the captain of the head, no matter where the toilets are
located in the vessel.

After the bobstay, martingale, and bowsprit shrouds were
developed, the bows of vessels were much simplified and the
head made very neat. At this time, perhaps 1750, the rage of
simplifying bows, particularly in Holland and Sweden, went to
such extremes that many vessels were built without any head
proper, or false piece, and these craft were called catts (generally
spelled with two t's) and spoken of as a ship-rigged catt, a snow
catt, or a sloop catt. In Falconer's marine dictionary of 1730,
the definition of catt (chatte) is "a ship employed in the coal
trade, formed from the Norwegian model. It is distinguished by
a narrow stern . . . and by having no ornamental figure or prow."
The French word for these vessels was *chatte,* which I believe is
feminine for cat, and I suppose that since a cat has a short nose
or flat face, it described these bows well. It may well be that
our name catboat also was meant to describe a boat with little
forward of the mast.

After 1800, the head was only used as a latrine on large ships,
men of war, and sometimes whaling ships, and by 1850 the

clipper ships had developed very graceful ornaments forward, which were usually a scroll of some sort on a flat board or the trailboards as we think of them today. Some of the handsomest of them were on the early steamers, which had clipper bows, and the finest of all were on the steam yachts designed by G. L. Watson in Scotland, who, it is said, developed his designs of heads from much study of the clipper ships that were still running in his time. I am sorry I do not have a suitable photograph of one of his heads large enough to use as an illustration, but after studying several of them in the past, I am under the impression that the scroll on the trailboard should be quite simple and use the reverse curve repeatedly in its composition, so that the whole theme is classic or Grecian, and this usually is the most successful on outdoor things seen from the distance. You know, Doric architecture was comparatively simple but quite striking as seen from some distance. This was accomplished to quite an extent by the use of the shadow on a white background so that the cornice, the dentil, and the fluted column were distinctly seen at a distance when the more complicated structure would have meant nothing. For this reason, I try to have the border of a trailboard raised some and the scrollwork raised from the trailboard three-quarters of an inch or more. I believe a complicated motif like the acanthus leaf is poor for the trailboard scrolls, even if Grinling Gibbons did use it in some ship garnish when he was starting his career. Certainly too much gilt spoils the whole effect.

I prefer the lanceolate leaves, like laurel, bay, and olive. Figures 4 and 5 show a pair of trailboards that did not turn out very well. The motif was the oak leaf and the acorn, the symbols of naval architecture, and while I worked some time drawing this one full size, it is not nearly as good as the one shown in Figure 6, which was done quickly. Figure 7 shows a white trailboard on a black hull, and while this works out well, it does not look well if a colored trailboard is used on a white hull, perhaps because that kills the shadow from the scroll, but it also looks more overdone than neat and classic. It is something like gilding the lily.

Many yachts, and particularly the Gloucester fishermen around 1900, tried painting and lightly carving a scroll on the bow without raised trailboards, but they were never very successful, though in some cases the rest of the vessel was handsome enough to cover this defect.

Figure 4. The trailboards
of the Ticonderoga.

Figure 5. Trailboards with an
oak leaf motif.

Figure 6. The trailboards of Mobjack.

Figure 7. White trailboards on a black hull.

Figureheads themselves are generally classed in three groups. First is the billet head, sometimes called the fiddle head, from its resemblance to the head of a violin. These are frequently carved with much detail, like the sprouting frond of a fern, but fine detail is lost in the distance and the fiddle head is usually best on small craft. The second group is composed of the figure or half-figure of a man, beast, or bird, and of course on the larger vessels, a well-shaped woman or goddess has been the most popular, and when it can have some connection with the name of the vessel, it is extremely fitting. Perhaps the young sailor likes the nude figure, but since this class of figurehead looks by far the best when white, it will be found that the drapery of the classical dress adds much charm, with the shadow giving folds of the drapery. The human form, or the mermaid, should not be used on small craft unless it is very carefully done with a rather small figurehead. Figure 8 shows such a rather messy head on a small yacht. However, the head alone of an eagle, hawk, or other bird is often very successful, even if much stylized. This has been the favorite finial on the Friendship sloops and Chesapeake bugeyes for a century or more, and some of them were very nice. The bird's head looks all right gilded, but the female figure never looks just right as a figurehead when painted in color or gilded. The male figure in armor is correct gilded, or the males and females of the red, yellow, and black

Figure 8. A rather messy figure-head on a small yacht.

races seem right when painted, but all in all the white figurehead with gilded trailboards is the most successful.

The third type is the group figurehead, which was common on large battleships and East Indiamen between 1750 and 1800. They sometimes represented a whole mythological scene with mermen, seahorses, and gods, every empty space being filled with cherubs, wreaths, and emblems, and while no doubt these group heads were very fine on the ponderous vessels they decorated, I think we need not consider them in these democratic times.

During the last two centuries and perhaps before, artists have been employed to draw figureheads and head decorations, but they have seldom been suitable or in harmony with the rest of the vessel. It seems that the general proportions and effective shapes must be worked out by the designer who made the outboard plan, or the head will look wrong. The artist is apt to go in for complication and produce something that is out of proportion. Perhaps they have been lacking in nautical tradition, and as heads change their style with the times, they cannot compete successfully in this specialty. In the past, most of the shipbuilding ports had figurehead carvers who took the designer's sketches and produced in wood figures that in some cases compared favorably with the best sculpture of the time.

Up until about 1910, there was a figurehead carver at Glasgow or Dumbarton.

As to ways of making trailboards cheaply or easily today, I would say it is best to make them in several layers glued together as follows: Take several strips of soft-bending wood like soft pine, about one-quarter-inch thick and several inches wider than the finished trailboards. Bend and fasten one of these strips on each bow, so that it will conform to the flare or flam forward and the false piece. You should use small, easily drawn copper nails for the fastenings, for the reason described later. Now coat the outer surface of this first layer with water-resisting glue and tack on the next layer. Repeat this process until all layers are in place. Wait until the glue has hardened, then remove the nails that are at the surface and mark out the borderline of the trailboards from the designer's paper pattern, when the trailboards, port and starboard, can be pried off the bow. After this, you can cut off the points of the copper nails, which are on the inner surface, and take the trailboards home or to some warm, comfortable shop.

Now, if the design of the trailboard is put in place, you can prick through with a sharp nail or scribe so that when the paper is removed, you can connect the lines and have the scroll in pencil right on the trailboard, which will much facilitate the work.

After the raised border pieces are in place, the scroll can be attempted. It will be found best to make this in short lengths, usually not much over six inches long, for the trailboards will be curved and twisted if they belong to a full-bowed vessel. It is well to make the joints of the scrolls at the intersection of branches or leaves, and the parts can easily be cut out on a jigsaw and smoothed up with knife, file, and sandpaper. As I have said before, it is best to make the scroll quite thick, from one-half to three-quarters inch, and the outer edges should be quite sharp, for only the outer surface is to be gilded. Also, when it is necessary to repaint the trailboards, this sharp outer edge makes the work much easier, while with the rounded edge, some sort of line will have to be struck with the brush, which is seldom neat-looking.

Figure 9 is the pattern of the smallest trailboards I have drawn. My larger ones are all in pencil, for they are larger than the standard sizes of drawing paper used for reproduction.

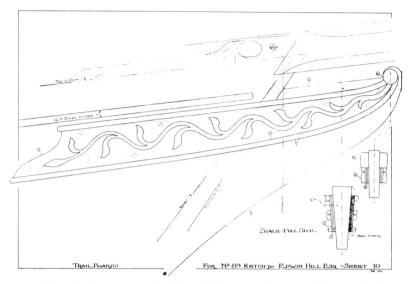

*Figure 9. A pattern of trailboards for a small yacht. (*The Rudder*)*

Before closing, I should like to say that proper trailboards and a small fiddle head can be used on very small boats or on most any craft that has a bowsprit and not too much overhang to the bow. Even a boat like *The Rudder*'s Prudence H-23 would be improved with a bow decoration that had some of the romance of the sea.

Small Coal-Burning Stoves
Aboard Ship

All good coal-burning stoves will burn wood, various briquets, and charcoal. The last, however, can give off a poisonous gas if there is a backdraft. However, to get a long-lasting fire that can be controlled—from only warm to baking hot—a good grade of stove coal is necessary.

While it is often said that the water south of Cape Cod is too warm for keeping a stove going night and day, this is a matter of opinion and it is affected by the amount of ventilation. In warm weather, the best arrangement is to use Sterno, with the can supported by a bent-up wire cradle, which fits in the hole from where the cover was removed. The wire frame should be made so the Sterno can is about 2½ inches below the top of the stove. This makes a very good and safe arrangement for boiling and frying things in hot weather—of course, light aluminum cooking vessels should be used.

Kindling a Coal Fire. First, see that the grate is clean, then crumple three or four pieces of paper (about as much as three or four pages of newspaper). Spread this over the grate with one small piece sticking down through the grate so the fire can be lighted from below the grate when the ashpit door is open. Now place small slivers of kindling diagonally across the firebox, with a second layer of kindling crossing the first layer. Now place larger pieces of wood on top 'til the firebox is ¾ full, then light the fire from the ashpit door and leave this door open, as well as the damper in the stack. If the fire does not roar within 10 seconds or so, there is something wrong with the draft that must be investigated.

The next move is to put some more chunks of wood in the firebox, and when the whole lot has become a roaring mass, then begin to add the coal—say, five pounds.

On a small yacht, the cleanest way to handle coal is to buy it in paper bags (usually twenty-five pounds) and keep it in the paper bags until it is poured into the stove from the bag. This is much the cleanest method.

After the coal has snapped and crackled perceptibly for about five minutes, you can fill the firebox up to within about two inches from the top. Now let it run this way for about ten minutes or more, or until the whole top of the coal is covered with a blue flame. Then you can close the ashpit door and adjust the slide draft adjuster in the door so it is perhaps half open. Then, after the whole mass of coal in the firebox is glowing, you can open the upper draft adjuster, which will let the draft of air in on top of the fire and take the burnt gases up the stack.

The fire should run steadily now for several hours. If heat for cooking is wanted, close the upper draft slide and open the lower one. Some stoves can be run with the damper in the stack open all the time and all adjustment in wanted heat done with the upper and lower draft adjusters. If this can be done, it has the advantage of keeping the air in the cabin fresh and clean, even if several people are smoking, for the bad air will be drawn in the upper draft, across and above the fire, and up the stack.

I must warn you that there must be a good wood fire in the firebox when the coal is introduced, otherwise the whole fire may go out before the coal starts to burn—one can tell usually if the coal is lighting, for it will make quite noticeable crackles and snaps if all is going well.

If the fire goes out on you after the coal is put in, you are in quite a mess, for you will have to wait 'til the stove cools down—then dump the grate. Always remember that coal cannot be lighted from above, no matter how hot a fire you have made over it.

The best kindling is dry, seasoned hard pine, soft pine knots, and other resinous wood. Most of the scrap of a boat shop is excellent. So, if you cannot purchase good bagged kindling, you should get someone to saw up several large paper bags of it,

Shipmate coal- or wood-burning stove. (Stamford Foundry Co.)

with some chunks nearly as large as the firebox, for sometimes in the cool of the evening, it is nice to have a wood fire to dry things out.

To bank the fire for the night, proceed as follows: first, make the fire burn up brightly by opening the lower draft and closing the upper one. When it is all aglow, rake it down with the poker running between the grate bars until most of the ashes and ash dust have gone to the ashpit (this must be done quite briskly if it is an old fire, for there is danger of its going out). Now, let it burn a while, and when it is going well again, add green coal a little at a time 'til the coal is up to about two inches from the stove top. Then let it burn ten or fifteen minutes or until you can see glowing coals nearly up to the top. Then you can let the stove run a while with both upper and lower draft slides open, but from then on to bedtime, if more heat is wanted, open the lower slide and close the upper slide a little—or vice versa if there is too much heat. At bedtime, close the lower slide and open the upper one and the fire should burn slowly and steadily 'til morning.

In getting breakfast, it is a mistake to rake the fire down first, for it will take too long to get green coal going well. Instead, it is best to close the upper draft slide and open the ashpit door.

Then, when the fire is giving off much heat, get the breakfast and rake down afterward and build up the new fire by adding a little green coal at a time. Then control the heat, as above, in relation to a newly kindled fire.

All the time you must watch carefully so that the ashes in the ashpit do not get up to the grate, for if this should happen, the grate is apt to warp and sag so it will no longer dump properly.

It used to be the custom on yachts to wet down the ashpit before shoveling out the ashes, for this prevents much dust in the cabin during the operation—perhaps two or three cups of water will do in your small ashpit. The ashes were usually kept in a galvanized pail 'til out of harbor, and anyone who dumped them over the weather rail was called a "spit to windward"—a very degrading epithet in the sailors' language.

I am afraid that after this dreary description of the management of a coal stove on shipboard, you will prefer anything else. But some cold fall evening, after the *Alaria*'s anchor has taken bottom and all hands have gone below wet, I am sure you will think the coal-burning stove is the best inorganic thing on the vessel.

Wooden Plates

Although not generally known, wooden plates were in common use in the sixteenth and early seventeenth centuries, and the few that remain are in museums. The large, fancy-grained burl bowls were highly prized and have been saved so that they are more often seen.

It is possible to make woodenware quite cheaply—that is, finished with modern lacquer or paints—but this should not for a minute be confused with the hand-turned, oil-polished ones that require a carefully prepared surface on the wood and must be made from selected pieces of interesting wood, so that each one has its individuality and charm. Unfortunately, the knotty and gnarly ones are the hardest to make, and thus are of the most value.

Nice wooden plates are useful, for they harmonize with almost any style of interior and are pleasant to handle, being light and warm to the touch. While they can be used for almost anything, they are particularly nice at teatime, or to serve crackers and cheese with the wine. They will stand hot things, and after a good oil polish is acquired, they will stand a great deal of abuse of all sorts.

A word about oil finish and its care. It is said that Chippendale and Hepplewhite would not tolerate anything but a hand-rubbed oil polish on their nice pieces, and time has shown that they were quite right. Shellacs, French polishes, and varnishes do not make a permanent finish. They scratch, chip, and crack. An

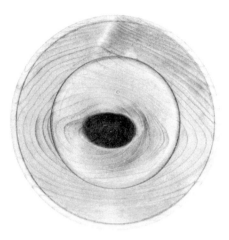

Wooden plate. (Mystic Seaport, Mary Anne Stets)

oil polish, on the other hand, penetrates the wood, making it of similar texture below the surface, so as it wears away it still retains the original look, or can always be polished by a little rubbing.

A good oil polish can only be acquired with time and many applications of oil. These plates have only had one or two rubbings with oil, and although they can be used at once, they should not be washed for six months or so, or until the oil below the surface has hardened. To clean them at first, it is best to use a paper napkin or rub them with cloth, while linseed oil—raw, not boiled—generally builds up the most pleasing and durable surface. Olive oil can be used and the original polish brought back or improved upon. In fact, after several years of rubbing with oil, a surface will be acquired that cannot be imitated by any other process.

To apply the polish, pour a few drops of oil of vegetable origin (such as raw linseed, China wood, or olive oil) near the center of the surface to be polished. Spread it over the whole piece with a small rag or your fingers, then take a dry rag and try to rub it all off, rubbing hard. The coats can be applied as often as wanted—three or four a day, or once a month—and the results will be in proportion to the rubbing.

Even after a good surface is acquired, it will not stand washing with strong washing soaps, and it will not stand continued damp, such as under a flower pot, etc., but the plates will stand almost anything else, and scratches, cuts, and mars often make them more interesting.

Some Hints on Model Making

There are a great many forms and types of model making, perhaps as many as there are different schools of painting, and that fact is a very fortunate thing, for tastes and skills vary so greatly that some can do best at one form of work while another's dexterity will allow him to enter the more artistic fields of the craft. But quite apart from the skills of craftsmanship or perfection of manual dexterity is artistic skill, which, when present, makes the model a joy forever, but when lacking (as I am sorry to say is the case with most models), then the model maker has produced only a gewgaw and a dust catcher, and his pains have all been wasted. Nevertheless, all forms of model making are so much to be recommended that I do not want to belittle any of the types. Working on a simple model that can be completed before it becomes tiring is a most exhilarating, healthful pleasure. When the model is also durable (not easily broken), interesting, or even artistic, then it is really one of the most satisfying endeavors the sailor can attempt in the winter months.

After some experience at making models of different types, I am so much impressed with the advantages of the so-called designer's half model that generally speaking, I think it is the only type worthwhile. The half model can be hung on the wall like a picture, and it can stand a certain amount of judicious handling, dusting, etc. If a half model is nicely made, that is, shaped exactly like some existing yacht, then it has a personality and is of great value as a standard of comparison in evaluating the characteristics of other models or yachts. However, if it is not accurately made, then it is of no value in these respects, and we might even say it is an evil thing, for it is nothing but a lie that deceives the eye. While models of existing yachts are quite necessary for comparison's sake, and of decorative value if the prototype is beautiful, still, making models of contemplated yachts is by far the most fun, for if the shape represents some carefully thought out combinations of curves to give stability, seaworthiness, and grace with little head-on resistance, then the model represents a solution of these scientific and complicated problems. If the model maker or designer has made a logical shape to best perform the functions of some special type of yacht, the model at once becomes a piece of sculpture of absorbing interest. Not only will it have a never-ceasing fascination to the sailorman, but if it is graceful and functional it will also be of much interest to the artist.

The reader may wonder why I have used all these words in describing the difference in half models, but as they are only to represent shape, their shape must be very exact or they are worthless. So I will tell about methods of securing correct and fair shapes, and while the description applies particularly to half models, much that is said is applicable to shaping up hulls for rigged models, or making sailing models.

The first thing to be considered is the scale of the model, and that is often affected by the size of the block of wood you have or can easily procure. Now, as this will often be a quite different size from the lines drawing you are to work from, it is helpful to have or use a proportional divider to change the scale. A proportional divider looks like Figure 1. This instrument changes the scale to any proportion within its range by shifting the center pivot along the slot in its central portion, and for model making the cheapest variety will do as well as any

Figure 1. Proportional dividers.

other. Although proportional dividers are not very common instruments, still they can usually be procured from any of the large dealers in drawing instruments, and it is not unusual to pick them up in antique stores.

The next thing to be considered is the vise to hold the work, and Figure 2 shows a carriagemaker's vise, which is the best sort for all woodwork. The jaws are smooth inside and so will not mar the work. The carriagemaker's vise also has high, narrow jaws so cut away that they will not much interfere with the drawknife and spokeshave. Generally a vise with high, narrow jaws requires a lower bench than usual, but in Figure 2 you will notice that the vise is attached to a stout piece of wood from under the bench so that the tops of the jaws are at elbow level. I might mention that a slightly lower level is even better, particularly if the work is large and extends upward much. The vise must be very strongly attached to the bench, and the bench absolutely solid and stationary, for if there is the least movement or quiver, it is very difficult to do nice work with a gouge.

The first operation on a half model is to plane up the backside for what represents the center line of the vessel, and this must be done accurately, for this center line will be the base line on which much of the later work will depend. Not only should this backside be straight fore and aft, but it must be at right angles to the top plank and the lifts or layers under it, so use a try square as you are planing, and keep the surface as straight and square as you can. This is not very easy until you have become used to rocking the blade of the plane crossways

Figure 2. A carriagemaker's vise attached at elbow level.

so it will cut most on the side that needs cutting. Now give the backside of the model a thin coat of white shellac, and after the shellac has dried several hours, either go over it with a very sharp scraper, only pressing down enough to take off what we might call a little dust, or rub it lightly with fine sandpaper.

The next operation is to lay off the station lines of frame stations, which can be done by scratching lines in the shellacked backside of the model, guiding the scratch awl with a carpenter's square, which is held at right angles by the upper edge of the top plank. After the frame stations are scratched in (and I use a scratched line instead of a pencil line because it will not rub out or so easily disappear), next, with the proportional divider set to the difference in scale between the drawing and the model, lay off the heights that the sheer line is above the waterline at each station, and then tack a batten along this line, using very small brads either through the batten or beside it. With the batten as a guide, scratch in the sheer line. After this, scratch in the profile of the bow, bottom, and stern, using the waterline as the base line, but to get the exact profile of the bow, stern, and after edge of the rudder, it is often necessary to make accurate drawings of these parts on a small piece of tracing paper, which, besides the profile, also shows at least one frame station, the sheer line, and the waterline.

Now, when the tracing is put in the exact place, take a sharp prick and prick a line of dots through the tracing onto the model to give the exact profile. Then, with various curves, battens, and straightedges, scratch in the profile to the depths marked on the stations, and to the prick marks just mentioned. These scratched lines along the sheer line and round the profile, as scratched into the shellacked backside of the model, are very convenient, and exact lines to cut down to, for the eye can see them in various lights far better than a pencil line.

The next operation is to cut the sheer line, and the model can easily be held in the vise for this operation, for both sides are straight and parallel so far. The sheer is usually cut down roughly with a drawknife, and I often cut down on an angle at first, as shown in Figure 3. Then by using a try square, drawknife, and various planes, make the sheer (or deck line) perfectly level crossways. The crown of the deck is not shown on half models. Because the sheer line is curved fore and aft, it is convenient to do the last finishing off with a sharp scraper, and then sand-

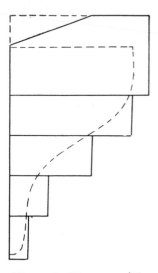

Figure 3. First cut. (The Rudder)

Figure 4. Model block with stations and profile scratched in, sheer cut, and inner surface squared.

paper used on a block. I must admit it takes considerable skill to produce a sheer line that corresponds with the scratched line on the backside and still is at exact right angles to the backside, besides being a fair sweep. Now give the deck one or two coats of thin, white shellac and, after that has dried and been lightly scraped, carry the station lines athwartships on the deck, using the square and scratch awl as was done on the backside of the model.

Next, with the proportional divider lay off the various widths at the stations, then spring a batten to these points and scratch in the deck line. In doing this, it is well to have the batten outside of the line, then the marks of the brads that held the batten will be outside the deck line in the wood that will be cut away later. Figure 4 shows a model block in this state, i.e., the inner surface squared, the stations and profile scratched in, and the sheer cut.

The next step is to secure or screw the model to a block of hardwood so shaped that the model can be held in the vise at different angles. See Figure 5. Figure 6 shows several of these blocks for holding models of various sizes. Be sure the block is well secured to the model with good-size screws, since at times with the drawknife or the gouge and mallet, the model will be severely wrenched. (This, of course, is only in the first heavy cuts.) Now put the model over the vise so that the outside or side line is uppermost, for now with the help of the block just mentioned, the model can be securely held at several angles, so

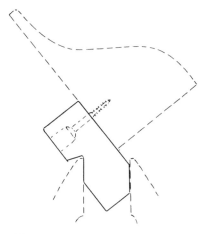

Figure 5. Hardwood block attached to model so it can be secured easily in the vise. (The Rudder)

Figure 6. Several hardwood blocks of various sizes for securing models.

that with the deck vertical and toward the workman (so he can see the scratched line that he is to cut down to), he can go to work without fear that the model will shift. The best tool for these first heavy cuts is a drawknife, and as the work is now securely held in place, you can do great execution with this tool. Not only can you rip off enormous shavings, but with a little care, you can cut down to about an eighth of an inch from the scratched deck line.

I would like now to say a few words about the drawknife, principally because it is practically useless unless kept very sharp, and because it is about the most difficult tool to sharpen. A good drawknife for model work should be fifteen or more inches between the handles. In the past, the best ones were made in England or Germany, since in this country they were manufactured to sell but not to be used, so possibly you will

Figure 7. Cross section of position for sharpening blade of drawknife. (The Rudder)

have to find yours in some secondhand shop or among the tools of a boatbuilder or cabinet maker who lived when hand tools were used, for a drawknife that is made of steel that cannot be sharpened is worthless. The section of the blade should be something like Figure 7, and the bevel of the cutting edge about 18 degrees (never less than 15 degrees or more than 20), for the blade should have a splitting as well as a cutting action. The underside of the blade of the drawknife should be on about the same angle that the handles pull. The underside should be quite broad and slightly rounded off at its after end, as the section in Figure 7 shows.

In sharpening, the drawknife is held as shown in Figure 8, and a small stone called a pocket axestone is slid up and down the blade in a slightly rotary motion. These small stones, which have a coarse and a fine side, should rest on the rib at the back of the blade and bear down or grind at the cutting edge. With a little practice, in this way the drawknife can be kept sharp and useful, but to get the best results, the cutting edge must also be stropped with a piece of leather on a stick to remove the wire

Figure 8. Position for sharpening drawknife.

edge. This can be done on a rag wheel, but it is a dangerous operation. When properly sharpened, the drawknife is a dangerous tool anyway, so the blade should either be kept in a wooden sheath or wrapped with an oiled rag. The drawknife should never be used on work that might slip, or be left where children can get at it.

I have given the drawknife these many words only because when properly sharpened and used, it is capable of such execution that it will often take the place of power tools in heavy cuts, and still, when properly controlled, it will pull off a shaving as thin as a plane can.

After the model has been cut down to nearly the deck line, the last trimming can be done with a plane, preferably a very small one that will follow the curve much better than a longer and heavier one.

The next operation is to make the templates that will guide the model maker in shaping the various sections. These templates are generally made of soft pine, about ⅛ inch thick for models about 2 feet long, and comparatively thicker for longer models. The templates are made as follows: after determining what sections will be the most useful in giving the shape (say, a midships section and two forward and aft, five in all), then draw these sections up on a piece of tracing paper brought down to the scale of the model either by using the proportional divider on the various waterlines, or, if you have the table of offsets of the yacht, use the dimensions given therein, which of course is the most accurate method. Now lay the piece of tracing paper over the strip of wood to be used for the template and prick through along the line representing the section's shape, also the center line of the vessel, the deck line, and the LWL, the last three of which will be a series of dots on straight lines. After the tracing paper is removed, fill in with pencil lines the section line, deck line, center line, etc. This should be carefully done with French curves and a straightedge so that the pencil lines run right over the pricked points. Now, with a very sharp patternmaker's paring knife, or a narrow sharp jackknife blade, cut out the part of the template that represents the body of the vessel. The last of this cutting out or shaping should be done with a small piece of medium sandpaper, rubbing down carefully so that finally you come to the marks the prick has made in the template. Some people make the template for each section on a separate piece of wood, but I prefer to cut them all out on one strip, so that it looks like Figure 9.

Mark the station number of each template and give the whole strip a light coat of white shellac. Now perhaps the model should be placed in the vise so that it lies at about 45 degrees, which our screwed-on block will allow. Then, after cutting away the superfluous wood at the ends and at the bilge, you are ready to commence working the rest down with what is called an inside sharpened paring gouge, like Figure 10. This sort of gouge with a little alteration can be the only gouge necessary in making small half models. The blade is ⅞ inch wide and very flat. I prefer the very flat ones, say, with a radius of about 8 inches, and when bought, these gouges have a section near the working end like Figure 11A, but I change the section to that shown in Figure 11B by grinding off the outside lower corners on a wet grindstone. Then by holding the gouge flat, or rocking it up on its side, curves of varying radii can be accommodated.

Another great advantage of the very flat gouge is that it can be sharpened on a regular flat oilstone, while sharpening the inside bevel of the smaller-radius paring gouges must be done with curved slipstones of more or less appropriate curve. Perhaps the difficulty of sharpening this tool is what has made it rather unpopular or uncommon, but as it is capable of such fine work, the paring gouge is indispensable to the model maker and the patternmaker.

When the model has been roughed to approximate shape (but of course oversize) with the paring gouge, we will commence to use the template to get the exact shape of each section. This is done by rubbing some blue lumberman's crayon (or dark-colored chalk) on the curved part of the template that represents the curve of sections. Now put the template in place on the model, with the upper part at the station mark on deck and its lower

Figure 9. Templates for shaping sections. (The Rudder)

*Figure 10. Paring gouge. (*The Rudder*)*

part at the station mark at the keel. If the template is moved about slightly, it will mark with transferred chalk the high spots to be chiseled away.

The work must now be slowly and carefully done so that you never cut too deeply, and as you go along, cut down the high spots between the sections. Eventually, with careful work you will have all the sections cut down so the chalk on the template registers in several spots on the section when the top of the template should be near the deck line and its center line near the profile. We can now put the template aside for a few minutes and take up a soft pine batten about 3/16 inch square and nearly as long as the model. Rub one face or side of this batten with chalk, as you did the template. Place the batten fore and aft on the model, and, after springing the ends down to bear on the bow and stern, rub or move it about until it has marked the high spots between the sections. By alternating back and forth with the section template and chalked batten, and carefully cutting down with the flat part of the paring gouge, you will have the model down to approximate shape, and then the work can best be continued with a very small plane. (The larger planes are no good on a curved surface.)

These small planes are made by Stanley and are called No. 101. When I was a boy they cost about ten cents, but after two or three Democratic administrations their cost has jumped, so

*Figure 11. (A) Section of paring gouge. (B) Section of paring gouge after outside lower corners have been ground on wet grindstone. (*The Rudder*)*

that today I understand they cost sixty-five cents or more. Nevertheless, they are the best buy of any tool, if you know how to sharpen them and set them. As for the sharpening, I generally grind a little off the heel with an emery wheel, touch up the cutting edge with a fairly fine oilstone, then strop the edge on leather until it is nearly as sharp as a razor. To set the blade, I place the plane on the bench and slide the blade down until it touches the surface of the bench, then with a light piece of brass rod, tap the blade down until it cuts as required, as shown in Figure 12. Needless to say, if the plane goes too deep, tap the back of the plane and the blade will move up slightly. If one side or the other cuts too deeply, tap the upper end with the brass rod so the blade rocks sideways until it cuts properly. With some practice, these little planes can be set very quickly and accurately in this way. Stanley also makes a similar plane called No. 100. This has a handle cast on and is better for heavier work, but not so good as No. 101 for working on half models, where the plane is held between the thumb and fingers in such a way that it can run over a curved surface more freely. If much model making is to be done, it is most desirable to have several of these small planes that have had their soles filed to be curved in different ways. Figure 13 shows several such planes.

After the model is all worked down with the gouge and the plane until it is perfectly fair fore and aft and like the sections, sandpapering can begin, but you must be sure that all traces of chalk or crayon or even pencil marks are removed (either scraped or planed off), for if not, the rolling action of the sandpaper dust will only smooch up the model and not remove the crayon as a shaving will. The sandpapering should be done

Figure 12. Tapping down blade of small plane with brass rod.

Figure 13. A selection of small planes.

with several grades of paper, first fairly coarse, then medium, then fine. At the very last, with the finest paper, you should keep away from the deck line profile and ends, and this requires some skill. I must caution that the final sandpapering must be kept up a long time, at least an hour of steady work, until all parts are smooth, even, and fair, besides being as nearly as possible the same appearance all over. If this final sandpapering is not well done, the model can never be given a fine finish later that will not show some marks.

When the bare wood is complete, the model should first be brushed off with a fine brush and then carefully wiped with a clean rag until the wood is perfectly clean and bare. Next give the model a coat of very thin white shellac so thinned down with alcohol that it is almost like water. The wood will quickly absorb the first brushfuls, so it is well to go over the model rapidly three or four times until the brush starts to drag. Then put the model aside ten or twelve hours to dry, at the end of which time you will find the surface quite rough, for the shellac has raised the grain of the wood.

Now this next sandpapering is more difficult than the previous ones, as the gums used in the modern shellac will soon ball or gum up the sandpaper so that the paper, instead of cutting evenly, will have a tendency to cut small grooves or depressions in the surface of the model. While these usually cannot be seen by the eye, they will much affect the eventual finish, so it is best to use a piece of sandpaper only a very short time and then throw it away and take a clean piece.

After this sandpapering is completed, the model will appear

almost as if it had never been shellacked, but the grain of the wood will be partly filled and hardened up. The next several coats of shellac should be of a thicker consistency and rubbed down with steel wool, excepting at the ends and edges. The model will in all probability require four or more coats, all well rubbed down, before a hard, smooth surface is acquired. Then the polishing can be continued with wax in the same way that a wax finish is put on furniture. While it is true that a so-called French finish gives the highest gloss, I do not recommend this process for the amateur, as it requires much skill and practice to polish the edges and ends the same as the central surfaces. A French polish is applied by saturating the rubbing felt or rag with both linseed oil and shellac and rubbing down with fine pumice, but only one with considerable practice can keep the proportions of oil and shellac just right so that the rag will polish and build up a surface at the same time. Also, I must note that a French polish is not as durable as wax over shellac, for the French polish will often become cloudy and turn white (to become attractive again, it will have to be taken down to the wood), while the waxed surface can be improved by later rubbings almost indefinitely.

So you see that altogether the tools required for making half models are very few and inexpensive, and the principal secrets are to have the model held firmly at the right height and in such manner that it can quickly be shifted from being on its side to a bottom-up position or to an angle of forty-five degrees. Secret number two is the use of chalk on the templates and battens to mark the high spots. And finally, the great secret: only use very sharp tools!

The making of models of new shapes, where the modeler or designer uses no plans or drawings to work from, is in some ways much simpler, for he generally only uses a midship-section template. On the other hand, he must have an extraordinary and highly developed sense of proportion, which I believe few today possess. In former days, most American vessels had their lines developed from the model, and while this is a process nearly the opposite from that described above (where the model was made from the lines drawing), still, I will say something about it. The layers or lifts of which the model was made were planed down to a thickness that represented the scale spacing of the waterlines. Either these various layers were held together with wood

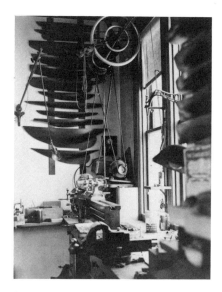

Figure 14. Corner of one of Nathanael G. Herreshoff's model rooms.

dowels running right down through the model from deck to bottom, as you will often see on old half models, or the layers were held in place by screws in the alternate layers. After the model was completed, the layers or lifts were taken apart very carefully and each was laid on a paper. A pencil was run around their borders and then, after the stations were drawn in, the offsets could be taken off. Many of these builders' models were later glued up or had their layers permanently fastened together, so that today they appear as if they had never been taken apart. My father preferred to develop the shape of his yachts from models, and had developed an instrument or measuring device that took the offsets or builder's dimensions directly from the model. This, besides being a most accurate method, also saved much eyestrain. So it is a fact that there are no lines drawings of the several hundred yachts he designed. Figure 14 shows a view of the room where N. G. Herreshoff made his models, and Figure 15 shows a larger room where he kept many models and did his drafting.

Some people, and most yacht clubs, prefer the models to be painted, but to the real connoisseur this rather takes away from

Figure 15. Three sides of Nathanael G. Herreshoff's drafting and model room.

the simple representation of shape, just as a painted piece of sculpture would seem overdone. Also, to properly paint a half model, the work must be so skillfully done that only a most expert painter can accomplish this feat. It is also interesting to note that the work of properly painting a half model will take longer or cost more than making the model itself, so that if paint only lessens the refinement of the model, it is of doubtful benefit. However, to some, a painted waterline, stripes, etc., help to establish the waterline and visualize the proportions of freeboard, etc., more clearly.

Figure 16 shows a painted model as seen from below, but quite similar effects can be achieved by putting a layer of contrasting wood at the waterline, and this saves the cost of painting. I have also made many models that were of soft pine below the LWL and mahogany above, and some vice versa, but on the whole I much prefer one of nice clear, soft pine throughout.

Even if the sole function of the half model is to give or describe shape, there is no reason why the full or two-sided model should not be nearly as carefully made. One often sees

rigged or exhibition models (which represent much painstaking work) that have wretchedly shaped hulls, and this fact has made these models nearly worthless. This misrepresentation of shape in rigged models is not at all a peculiarity of modern times, for, sad to relate, most of the models made before 1600 were quite ridiculous, and this discrepancy alone is one of the chief difficulties in unraveling the history of naval architecture. However, many of the models made in England, France, and Holland between 1600 and 1800 seem to be quite correct in their shape.

Model making is so much akin to sculpture that when well done, it is a higher means of expression than the arts that are all on one plane, like drawing or painting. There is no doubt that sculptured objects, which cast a shadow and can be seen from

Figure 16. Painted mold of 12-meter yacht Matena as seen from below. (The Rudder)

hundreds of points of view, require much more skill to make correctly. Perhaps there have always been but few with sufficient sense of shape to produce things in three dimensions, and the trend of today is almost entirely toward planographic art. Yes, today there are hundreds of millions making or taking pictures. While Mr. Eastman has made it possible for millions to take pictures who could not make pictures, still, putting the camera in the hands of millions, and millions into his hands, seems to have accomplished little toward a true appreciation of form. Now that each Boy Scout, stenographer, and what-not creeps from park to park, and slinks from bush to bush with his candid camera, the whole effort seems to be to reduce form to one plane. And if it were not that some objects of art with form have been made, there would be little of interest to photograph beyond the works of nature.

But model making can be a true manifestation of art, and one within the means of most all who have a sense of proportion, so it has always been popular as a pastime for the sailorman during the winter months. Perhaps there are few undertakings that will keep a man happily at home more than model making, and certainly there are few that will give him a better understanding of ship construction and the history of naval architecture, and none that will give him a higher appreciation of workmanship.

The reader may wonder why I have used so many words before giving some hints about model making, but the reason for it is that I would like to see amateur model making looked on as a more artistic endeavor than it is at present, and that can be done easily by being more careful with shapes.

One of the great mistakes of the amateur model maker is to attempt a more complicated model than is practicable. A model with complicated rig becomes very tiring before it is completed, and then it must be kept in a glass case or it most certainly will be damaged in dusting, moving, etc., so that it is much the best to make the hull only, as was done with many of the so-called Admiralty models. If one likes complication, he will find that by the time he has made all the deck erections, fittings, etc., properly to scale, he will have done quite enough. For instance, if one made a sloop of war of around 1800 with her complete battery of guns properly mounted, the deck fittings alone would be a winter's work, and while such a craft could be a nice thing to have, still, much more fun could be had by making several boats like our Block Island boats, or the Chesapeake log canoes,

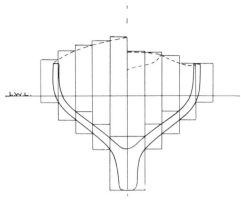

*Figure 18. Model layers made according to the "buttock system." (*The Rudder*)*

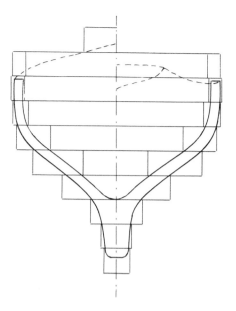

*Figure 17. Model layers made according to the "bread-and-butter system." (*The Rudder*)*

or the bugeyes, for the beauty of hull form in itself would make these types interesting.

However, almost all models of any size must be hollowed out. If it is to be a sailing model or a model to tow, it must be quite thin, but even the exhibition model must be hollowed out some, or else it will crack or warp in a few years as the wood shrinks with age. So now we will consider the easiest ways to do the hollowing out. Previously, most models were glued up of layers running horizontally, and this was generally known as the "bread and butter system." The layers represented waterlines, and thus were sawn out to the shape of the same. (See Figure 17.) This system had so many disadvantages that about 1920 I started gluing up models with the layers running vertically, or on the buttock system. (See Figure 18.) Now many others are using this method of gluing up, for it has the following six advantages:

1. The layers may be sawn out on their inside as well as their outside, which cannot be done in the bread and butter system, except with a jigsaw.

2. The layers may be clamped together much more easily while gluing up, particularly if each half of the model is done separately.

3. The central seam makes a permanent center line that cannot be lost while paring down the profile.

4. The sheer line of the model can be sawn out on the layers; the various port and starboard layers are tested by laying them on the lines drawing and trimming down with a plane until perfectly correct. But acquiring the proper sheer line on both sides of a model glued up horizontally is quite difficult.

5. It is most convenient to hollow out both sides of the model separately before gluing the two sides together, for then one can use various gouges and round-bottom planes in this work and cut down to an exact inside center line. Figure 19 shows a model hollowed out in this way as it appears after the two halves have been glued together.

6. When sawing out the layers or lifts of a model glued up on the buttock system, every other layer can usually be made from the piece sawn out of the second layer preceding. With the bread and butter system, this seldom can be done.

There are many advantages to hollowing out the inside of a model before shaping up the outside, and this may be done perfectly well where there are several layers sawn out as guides to cut down to. (See Figure 20.) During this process, the half can be held in the vise by a block of wood screwed to part of one of the layers that will be cut away later. (See Figure 20.) The first part of the hollowing-out should be done with very sharp outside-sharpened gouges of various radii, preferably with long handles, which very much help to control the cutting angle of the gouge. The gouges must be sharpened so that there is no so-called wire edge at the cutting point, for if the edge is not clean and fair, it will not be easy to control. The best way to get a clean, fair edge is to polish the cutting edge on a rag wheel, first one side then the other, until all trace of wire edge is gone and the gouge is as sharp as a razor. The last part of the hollowing-out may be done with small planes with curved soles, or a violin-maker's plane. Then the inside should be carefully sandpapered and shellacked.

Figure 19. Hollowed-out model (both halves) glued up on the buttock system.

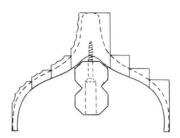

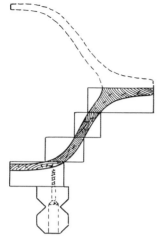

*Figure 21. Hardwood block secured to inside of hollowed-out model. (*The Rudder*)*

*Figure 20. Hardwood block attached to model block for insertion in vise. (*The Rudder*)*

After the two hollowed-out halves have been glued together, a block of wood like Figure 21 should be screwed on the inside of the model so that it can be securely held in the vise, so the shaping up of the outside may be done as was described for a half model. However, if it is a model of one of the older types of ships that had a pronounced angle at the rabbet line, then it is best to make the model only down to the rabbet line, and afterwards make up separately the stem, keel, deadwood, etc., and fasten them in place after the shaping-up of the model is completed. Sometimes in this case it is advantageous to fasten the keel on very securely by using several good-size screws, and the model can later on be held in the vise by the keel itself.

If the model is to have bulwarks, or the shape of her hull is to be carried up above the deck level, then in order to get the proper shape, it is best to make the model right up to the level of the rail cap. This will ensure the proper flare forward and tumblehome aft. With a carpenter's gauge, scratch lines along each side where the deck should come, after which, either with a very sharp knife or the blade of a hacksaw held between the fingers, you can saw or cut along the line until the bulwarks are removed. Now fair up this line with a small plane, and to get the proper bevel along the sides to fit the crown of the deck, you must make a so-called beam mold, that is, a small piece of wood curved like the deck beams. Rub this beam mold with chalk and slide it along the sheer line so it will mark the bevel to which the sides should be cut. After this is completed, you are ready to lay the main deck, and you will find in most cases that the saw cut and the fairing-up of the sides have lowered the freeboard about one-eighth inch, which is apt to be approximately the thickness of the deck.

The next job is to set in the deck beams, which is usually done by cutting notches in the inner side of the model at each side to receive the beam ends. In my younger days I used to fit the beams snugly and either glue or fasten the ends in place, but I found that later the deck either cracked in dry weather or buckled up in damp weather. You see, wood shrinks and swells *across* the grain but not *with* the grain, and the grain of the deck ran fore and aft, while the grain of the beams was athwartships. So now I set the deck beams in so they have some athwartships play; then, as the deck shrinks and swells, it will spring the side of the model without resistance from the deck beams and the deck does not crack. Figure 22 shows a model with the beams in place and the two strips that will represent the gunwales later. This construction is strong and neat and, after the rail cap has been put on top of the gunwales or bulwarks, is most realistic looking.

Another operation that bothers some model makers and often spoils the looks of the model is marking or laying off the waterline. Even if it is a glued-up model built on the bread and butter system with a seam at the actual waterline, the painted waterline should be somewhat higher.

One good way to scratch in the waterline is to place the model upside down over a smooth, flat plane, like a table top or

Figure 22. Model with deck beams in place. Strips in foreground will represent gunwales later.

drawing board (as shown in Figure 23), and scratch in the water-line with the point or scribe of a surface gauge. I find that it is well to use a chisel-shaped point on the scribe which, when properly sharpened, will cut a very neat line in the shellacked surface of the model. Of course the model must be blocked up with sundry small pieces of wood and wedges so that it is not only level athwartships but so that the gauge will mark the right height fore and aft. Other lines for curved painted stripes can at times be marked with the gauge by having the model tipped the proper amount, but if you are to scratch in lines that represent planking, copper sheathing, etc., it is best to tack a thin batten on the model for the guide of the scratch awl. The holes that the brads have made through the battens may be filled up generally by touching them with the end of a toothpick that has previously been dipped in fairly thick shellac, and of course this is sandpapered down after the shellac has dried. I myself am not very skillful at painting models, but I have found various colored shellacs (which you can mix yourself) quite satisfactory, for they dry quickly and as many coats as desired may be put on with little trouble. If the model is to go in the water, the final coat should be a transparent varnish that will keep the water from the shellac.

As for brushes, I find fairly broad ones with short hairs are satisfactory, but for painting up to or along a straight line,

Figure 23. Model positioned for scratching in waterline with surface gauge.

sometimes a very old or much-worn-down brush is the best, and if you can have quite a little of the brush lie on the wood, it will steady the hand. Of course you must have just the right amount of paint on the brush, and the paint must be thinned to run exactly right, or the job will be a mess. It is always best before putting the brush on the model to try painting up to a line on a piece of wood that has a shellacked surface just like the model. Then when the brush and the paint are just right, you can do the painting quite rapidly, and that is usually necessary with shellac, or it will show brush marks. Camel's-hair brushes seem to work well with shellac, and although they are expensive, they will last for years with care.

The brush should always be kept with its hairs in alcohol, or else cleaned at once after using. The first can be accomplished by tying a string onto the top of the brush handle that is just the right length to hang the brush in a milk bottle without touching on the bottom. At the top of the bottle there should be a cork or plug with a hook for the string. Then, if the bottle is filled with alcohol to a level that will cover half the length of the hairs, the brush will always be ready for instant use. I might mention that I have kept a brush this way for over twenty years, but the modern denatured alcohol has a tendency to eat the ferrule of the brush even if it does not damage the hairs.

To clean a shellac brush that is to be put away dry, proceed as follows: first squeeze the shellac out of the brush by holding it between the thumb and fingers inside a folded piece of paper. Wash the brush in a little alcohol and squeeze it out between paper again, repeating this process several times. Then put the brush in a mixture of Oxydol and water, about equal parts, for an hour or so, and wash it out in cold water. After it has dried, the brush should be soft and flexible. But the shellac brush that is kept hanging in alcohol is the best. It is always ready to use and can be put away instantly.

I speak at some length about the painting, for perhaps nothing will spoil a model more than poor painting, and certainly from an artistic point of view, the painting is only next to shape in importance. Few amateur model makers realize the great amount of skill that is necessary to do a good painting job, and they often ruin their models with hasty or inartistic painting. If you happen to dislike painting, then it is best to make up the model of contrasting materials, which can often be done with marked success. The older bone models are an example, and some of the finest models in existence, the so-called Admiralty models, are fine-grained wood simply finished in shellac or lacquer rubbed down.

The making of the small metal fittings for a model is a fascinating undertaking, but unfortunately it requires many tools, and some of them are quite expensive. Most of the tools have to be obtained from the firms that supply the jeweler, the watchmaker, and the dentist. The small cutters and burrs used by the dentist in his flexible shaft arrangement are wonderful tools to use in the milling attachment of a watchmaker's lathe, and they cut wood or brass very well. While a whole book could be written about making model fittings, I will now only mention a few common errors.

First, turning and drilling speeds. It is a common mistake when turning small objects in the watchmaker's lathe to have the lathe going too slowly. If, for instance, the object is one-eighth or one-sixteenth inch in diameter, then the lathe should revolve either eight or sixteen times as rapidly as a piece one inch in diameter, and the same is true of small drills. Their speed should be in proportion to their size. In turning small objects, one need only take a very light cut, really only a sort of scraping action with a very sharp graver not sharpened too obliquely, for the small object, if revolving rapidly enough, will bring its various surfaces under the cutting tool very frequently. In fact, one piece revolving sixteen times as rapidly as another need not take off a shaving more than one-sixteenth as thick in order to be cut down at the same rate. This small cutting tool or graver, and the small drill, must have their cutting surfaces sharp and correctly shaped or they will heat up the work. The small drill must be removed from the hole it is drilling very frequently, or it will clog with shavings, heat up, drill oversize, or break. The cutting tool in a small lathe should never bear on the work with a broad surface, in fact, not much more than a sixteenth of an inch of its edge should bear on the work, or it will chatter, but the art of turning in the small lathe must be almost entirely acquired by practice. When done right, the surface will be so smooth that it cannot be improved by the fine file or sandpaper.

Second, materials. Some of the small rods, steel, bronze, and Monel, become very tough when drawn to small sizes, and these should not be used for small turnings except where strength in the finished article is required. Instead, you should use a free-turning brass, which in most cases will be strong enough. However, if the object is to be bent or forged much, Everdur bronze is most excellent. The other materials that turn well are bone, boxwood, lancewood, white holly, and pearwood. The woods, of course, must be finished off with sandpaper, then shellacked, and when the shellac has dried, it can be given a French polish, which is easy to accomplish in the lathe simply by pressing against the revolving work a piece of flannel that has both raw linseed oil and shellac on it. But keep the rag moving about, for if it is left in one place long, it will heat and spoil the finish.

There are a surprising number of small files made today, and at very cheap prices, so the model builder can make many of his small fittings entirely with these various shaped files, all of which have special uses, but he should have both a pin vise and a small, high-grade jeweler's vise at table height, where he can sit comfortably in a chair during his intricate work, and it is quite worthwhile to arrange the light just right.

All files naturally get dirty soon, or have their teeth filled up, and that is particularly so if oil or grease gets on the file, so it is necessary to clean the files often. The small files can be temporarily cleaned by pushing the end of a small stick of wood along the teeth parallel to the way the teeth are cut, and this will always remove a surprising amount of dirt, but it is well once in a while to wash out all the files in hot water and fairly strong dishwashing compound, using a stiff brush parallel with the teeth. Then dry the files at once either in a stove oven or on a radiator, and sometimes they will cut almost like new again. However, it is very foolish to waste your time with a worn or dull file, since, as I have said, the small ones are very cheap today. [I highly recommend the sets made by the American Swiss File and Tool Company of Elizabethport, New Jersey. A set particularly adapted to model making is called "Sets of Knurled Handle Needle Files, 6¼ inches long, cut #2." This set consists of twelve files of very useful shapes in a wooden box that holds them from biting one another.]

I hope these few hints on model making will be helpful and make pleasanter the winter pastime of some sailorman, which they will if his work is shaped to give lasting satisfaction to the eye.

Discourse on Displacement, etc.

I have been requested to give a little discourse on such subjects as:

(1) Light and Heavy Displacement
(2) Shapes of Rudders
(3) Keels
(4) Bows, Sterns, and Overhangs
(5) The Advantages and Disadvantages of Various Sailboat Rigs
(6) The Pros and Cons of Gaff and Leg-o'-Mutton Sails, and Some Discourse about Bowsprits.

While these subjects may require quite a few words, I will try not to burden the Gentle Reader with hard-to-understand phrases, or confuse him with a lot of old-fashioned formulas; in other words, I will try to cut it as short as I can.

1. **Light and Heavy Displacement.** The terms "light," "medium," and "heavy" displacement are very confusing, for in both yacht design and in the rules of yacht measurement, displacement is compared with the yacht's length on the waterline, so that some of our older yachts of, say, before 1880—which were long on the waterline, on account of their sharp clipper bows and short overhang aft—were lighter displacement yachts for their length on waterline than our later short-waterline yachts, though they may have had the same proportion of actual sail area to the displacement.

During the last fifty years or so, most sailboat measurement rules, both here and abroad, have required a certain minimum amount of displacement for the LWL. This was originally done for two reasons:

1. To make what was called a wholesome type of yacht, or one that could be handled in strong winds under reduced sail.
2. To ensure decent cabin accommodations.

These displacement rules throughout the world are the cause of the pot-bellied tubs now used for both ocean racing and inshore racing. Two examples of light displacement boats, or, we might say, long-on-the-waterline boats, are the ketch *Araminta* and the ketch *Ticonderoga*. They are faster, cheaper, and better looking than the usual run of tubs today that have to depend on a multiplicity of light sails to get up to a good cruising speed. I am afraid we shall not have boats as good as these until the rules allow longer length on the waterline. I must mention, though, that a heavy displacement keel sailboat is often the fastest in light weather for her waterline length, for she usually has less surface and thus less surface resistance. However, as surface resistance or surface tension reduces with each following foot of length, then with two vessels of similar surface area but different lengths, the longer one will be fastest under most all conditions. If this were not so, it is doubtful if the racing rowing scull would be twenty-eight feet long, nine-inch beam, and less than three inches deep. Altogether the subject of displacement in relation to length is both interesting and confusing.

2. **Shapes of Rudders.** The shape of rudders is influenced by such things as draft and construction, but the ones way aft, like the steering oar on a surf boat, have the most power to control the craft or prevent it from broaching to. They will not, however, turn a boat as quickly as a rudder that is nearer the turning point of the boat, which, by the way, is normally quite a little ahead of the center of weight. But rudders that are down in solid water have more power or lateral thrust than those at the surface, just as the lower blades of a propeller develop more side thrust than the upper blades.

On racing sailboats, the rudder hung on the after end of the keel has proved to be the fastest arrangement and, while separate rudders have been tried in most every class of yacht

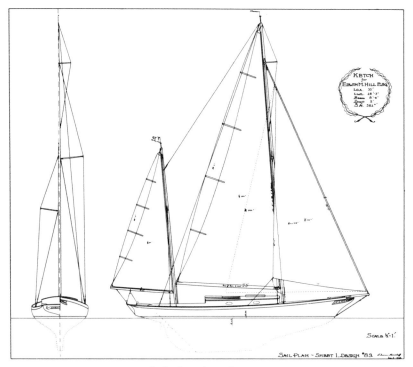

Sail plan, Araminta.

during the last seventy years, it has only been with the fin-keelers of the Gay 90s and with model yachts that the separate rudder was best. With the fin-keelers, the after end of the keel was too far forward to make a good location for a rudder, and the fin bent some, which, of course, made this location impractical. With the model yachts it has been mostly a matter of attaching the steering gear and the vertical rudder post, which is much the best for this, for it is important to have the rudder and its steering gear work very freely.

Some of the reasons why a rudder on the keel is fastest are that the rudder in this location has little resistance as it is running in the following surface eddies of the keel. Still, when the rudder is swung over, its tip at least affects solid water. The separate rudder has more surface resistance, for it is passing through water that is nearly as stationary as that entered by the forward end of the keel.

A rudder hung on the keel can often be on an angle of 45 degrees, and this materially helps the steering of a vessel that is well heeled over. When the keel and rudder are combined in one aquaplane, they make a very efficient hydrofoil to resist the side thrust of the sails, for none of the pressured leeward water can pass across forward of the rudder as it does on yachts with a separate rudder.

Rudders on racing sailboats are often farther forward than on other craft, and that is to allow the rudder to be carried on a slight angle when sailing, for in this case the combined rudder and keel have much lateral resistance. However, on cruising and seagoing craft, I prefer the rudder hung over the stern, or at least to have the rudder post above water, for such rudders are both strongest and easier to repair. This often makes the yacht too long on the keel and thus too slow in turning to be safe in crowded harbors.

On powerboats the rudder should be aft of the propeller so that it can work in the slipstream when maneuvering at slow speed.

On twin-screw craft there should be a rudder directly aft of each propeller, for this materially increases the maneuverability of the craft when in close quarters.

On most modern power craft, the rudder is too small to steer with at low speed, or with the power shut off. Apparently this is done to save cost or to allow a smaller rudder stock. It used to be the rule to have the rudder stock the same diameter and strength as the propeller shaft, but with a high-speed propeller the rudder stock should be considerably stronger than the propeller shaft on rudders without a lower support. So we see many things affect the size and shape of a rudder, and the best rule to go by is a little common sense. A few dollars saved on the size of a rudder is poor economy if it involves a collision or impairs general maneuverability.

3. **Keels.** Around the year 1000, most northern craft were built on a keel, while the Mediterranean vessels were often flat-bottomed or used a keel of little prominence. The Saxon invaders of England called the vessels they came over on *keeles,* and old British names for long vessels were Ceol and Cyulis. From that time to perhaps 1600 AD, the word was in common use to denote a vessel of several sizes. It is well known that the Viking ships had quite a pronounced outer keel to protect their lapstrake planking when taking bottom or hauling out. These keels must have had some lateral resistance, for the Scandinavians are credited with being the first people to sail to wind-

ward, but apparently these early craft, or keels, made more leeway than was desirable, for these Nordics are also credited with inventing the leeboard. Before this, they had a strange oar-shaped board hung over the after right hand side of the vessel to steer with, so naturally the newfangled leeboard was hung over the other side, and, as is quite well known, the two sides of a vessel were called starboard for steerboard and larboard for lee-board. Many years later, there were collisions and other confusion when the names *starboard* and *larboard* were misunderstood when hailing at night or in some of the fogs of the Thames, so the question came up at the Admiralty as to what to do about it. When one of the Lords, who apparently knew well the color of port wine, suggested that if a green light denoted the starboard side, why not have the name *port* denote the side with the red light.

But to get back to keels. For many years, perhaps from 1660 to 1830, English sailboats were rated for racing by the length of keel alone. This caused the forefoot to be much cut away and brought the raking rudder post into style, so that the racing yacht was perhaps two-thirds as long on the keel as on deck. This was a good thing, for too long a keel makes a vessel turn slowly and makes her try to head up in the wind as she gains headway, or carry a hard weather helm. Later, when the English racing yachts were rated by tonnage, as measured under the Thames Measurement Rule, they became very narrow and deep and began to use the plumb bow again, while the stern that was not measured was carried out in a long, graceful overhang. On account of their deep, sharp forefoot, the rig of these so-called "cutters" had to be well forward; otherwise, they would have carried a strong weather helm in light and moderate weather. But on account of their deep, narrow hulls, they would head off when heeled over much, so they were rigged with three headsails and a jib set on a pigtailed traveler, which was a ring around the bowsprit that could be let in and hauled out according to how she steered. Altogether these cutters of, say, 1860, were bad-steering craft because of their long keel and narrow beam. The later cutters were much improved in their steering qualities by having the forefoot cut away and using a keel that was much deeper aft, but they still tried to head off in a knockdown. If you don't think an English cutter is a bad-steering craft, just make a model cutter and try to sail it.

A statement that one often hears is that a long-keeled boat

holds her course well and is thus best for the singlehanded sailor, for this gives him time to go forward or below for a few minutes at a time. While it is true that a long-keeled boat swings or turns slowly, still it is extremely hard to make her self-steering, and that is what you really want, for then you can go forward or below for an hour, or several hours, at a time. On a ketch with fairly short keel, or with the forefoot well cut away, if other proportions are correct, you can make her steer herself in several directions in moderate sea and wind, and in light weather and no sea, you can even make her steer herself dead before it, while a long-keeled boat with a sharp forefoot will be difficult to make self-steering in any direction. She will be a beast to steer wind-on-the-quarter in a seaway, as she will keep trying to yaw one way or the other with such power that the sails cannot bring her back on course.

The English cutters were the first ones in general to use outside ballast, and it first was thought that this leverage would strain the hull, so quite complicated structures were used to strengthen the lower regions of these yachts. As time went on, deeper and deeper lead keels were used until the early 1890s, when the fin-keelers came out. Since then the structure of keels has caused little worry and keels became deep, narrow, and short fore and aft. Perhaps the shortest keels fore and aft were on the Sonder boats and Buzzards Bay 21-footers of about 1905, but in that year the Universal Rule came out and, as this rule required a liberal amount of displacement for the LWL, keels were again made longer and wider at the garboards to use up some of this excess displacement. Since then, the International Rule and most ocean racing rules require a liberal amount of displacement. All of these rules now have draft limits, so at present keels throughout the world are quite similar in shape and construction on racing sailboats, and, on the whole, they would steer very well if the modern yacht did not make such drastic changes in headsail area.

4. **Bows, Sterns, and Overhangs.** The styles of bows and sterns have changed back and forth many times in the last six thousand years, but apparently before the year 1000 AD, they knew more about them than now, for, from the time of early Egyptian river boats to the Viking ships, the double-ended vessel was the usual arrangement. While most every experienced person

Sonder boat. (The Common Sense of Yacht Design,
by L. Francis Herreshoff. Caravan-Maritime Books)

today admits that the double-ender is the best sea boat, few
seem to have a clear understanding of why, although it is a very
simple matter. When one end is larger than the other, then,
when the ends are each in a wave, the large end forces the small
one under, so that a large-sterned vessel will not let her bow rise
properly to meet a head sea, and in a following sea, the large-
sterned vessel will force the bow down until it has excess lateral
plane forward, so the vessel is bound to yaw one way or the
other. When the rudder is used to correct the yaw, then the
rudder and the forefoot are pushing in the same way, and as
these two planes are below the center of weight, the vessel will
tip or heel more or less, and sometimes give her crew a very
uncomfortable sensation. Perhaps this sense of fear only comes
from a natural instinct, but to have a vessel broach to, or try to
broach to, can really be dangerous in a combing sea and, while
few boats have capsized in these conditions, in a severe heel or
knockdown, someone is apt to get hurt and most everything
below deck goes galley west.

This is all very different in a nice-shaped double-ender, for,
when running in a head sea, the stern lets the bow rise so easily
that the vessel will fill you with admiration for her seaworthi-

ness. The double-ender does not need the excessive flare forward that has been found necessary with the wide-sterned craft, for, as they say, she rides the waves like a stormy petrel. The sensations in a following sea are even more satisfying, for often in a moderate sea and wind, the double-ender will hold a course wind-on-the-quarter without any change of helm. To be sure, the double-ender will yaw slightly as the wave rises under her stern, but as the crest passes amidships, her head swings back on the course of its own accord. A vessel that will do this without rolling unduly is a joy and suitable for cruising.

All that I say here applies to kayaks, motorboats, sailboats, and the larger craft, but particularly powerboats that have been the worst offenders in being sharp forward and full aft. I must apologize for using so many words of praise in describing the actions of the double-ender, but since the later history of bows and sterns is principally the story of asymmetrical ends, I will try to tell the reason for them.

The Viking ships perhaps were the last of the pure double-enders, and their underwater shape has never been surpassed for beauty. Some of them were the first vessels to have a wineglass midsection, or hollow garboards, but as we are talking about ends, their bows and sterns were swept up for the purpose of decoration, and the lapstrake planking in this region was a difficult feat and had to be made of wider boards than now are available. The Nordics used high stems and sternposts for several centuries with their smaller rowing and paddling boats, but at the time of the Vikings, the sternpost often had a finial like the tail of a sea serpent, while the stem had a removable dragon's head mounted on it. These figureheads were carved to be as fierce and frightening as possible to scare or awe the enemy, and the sagas tell us that there was a law that required these ships to remove their figureheads before entering their home ports, for it was feared that they would scare the women and cattle. There is no doubt that the Viking ships were good sea boats, and it is said the later ones kept up a communication with Iceland most of the year. I doubt if the wide-sterned powerboat of today could do that, particularly if she were undecked as were the Viking ships.

Before and during the Viking Age, the larger of the Mediterranean craft were using a very heavy ram as beak ahead of the bow. Some of these were at water level and some below. The early ones were stones shaped like the head of an obelisk, but later ones were apparently bronze castings of great weight. This weight forward or beyond the bow necessitated a full, burdensome bow, and this full or round bow was to persist on most sailing vessels to the end of their use in the naval and merchant vessels of the world. It is interesting that the early rams had two rudders, or a rudder both sides, which would indicate that they had steering difficulties. The burdensome bows, however, made vessels of that model subject to being pooped in a following sea, so that later vessels were built both with a raised poop deck and great bulk above water at the stern. As time went on and vessels were too large to depend on oars for propulsion, it was found that the high-poop-deck vessels would lie head to the wind better when at anchor, and that ability was of great importance in those days, for many of the large vessels of the time could not make good to windward in a strong sea and wind, so often when embayed, they had to ride out a gale at anchor. Of course a vessel that will ride head to the wind instead of tacking back and forth is much easier on her whole ground tackle. Also, the windage of the great sterns helped them to lay to without much sail set.

The raised poop was also found to give improved vision for the officer conning the ship, and as the ships of that time fought in and practiced sailing in close formation, this was very important, because when the sailing master can see the whole ship before or under him, how she is swinging or making leeway, it is a great advantage. In the days when a ship tried to give broadsides first from one side then from the other quicker than the enemy could reload, or tried to get in a raking position where his guns were most effective while the enemy's guns were useless, the advantage is easy to understand. Few people realize today how beautifully maneuverable the old ships of the line and frigates were, but for them to be handled well, the crews had to have much training and the sailing master ever so much more skill than the skipper of later racing yachts. The ships of that time had very small rudders and were handled by a multiplicity of sails, which were let draw or brought aback in the proper sequence, all according to the orders of the sailing master, who had to have a very clear head, particularly in the melee of battle. Besides conning the ship, he usually had beside him a commanding officer who was both of high rank and a titled gentleman, confusing him with impossible requests, while several signalmen were repeating to him the fleet orders of the admiral in charge. Today in a yacht race some young man may acquire quite a lot of conceit by winning a race by seconds, yet in a fleet action between the old wooden sailing vessels, certain maneuvers meant the loss of life of hundreds, depending on who got the advantageous positions.

To give the modern reader an example of the maneuverability of a handy squarerigger, I will cite a case that happened in my boyhood about eight or nine miles from where I lived. After the frigate *Constellation*, which was the training ship at Newport, became old or too complicated for the officers of around 1900 to handle, it was decided to have a new, small squarerigger built for the training station. She was a beautiful little brig—I should say about 100 feet on deck—named *Boxer* and painted white. Well, soon after *Boxer* arrived at Newport, the commandant of the station wrote letters to the head of the Navy Department in Washington saying that there was something the matter with the design of *Boxer*, as she could not be maneuvered. The Department decided to send someone up to see what was the matter and picked out a fine old gentleman with the obsolete rank of Commodore who had served his time mostly under sail. Soon after his arrival at Newport, they took him out on *Boxer* to show him how bad she was, and after some backing and filling, they finally got her out in the bay. Then the old Commodore requested them to let him have a try at her. After half an hour or so, when he had tacked *Boxer* and had been wearing ship so that he got a feel of how she balanced and saw that the crew carried out orders promptly, he decided to give her a real test. Now there is a small island named Gould Island a couple of miles northwest of the training station, and this island has bold water close to shore. Well, the old Commodore sailed *Boxer* around Gould Island backward, or stern first, including the hitch to windward, and some of the time the island was very close aboard.

After the Commodore had brought her back to her moorings between two stone docks, it is reported that he pronounced *Boxer* a very handy vessel and took the train for Washington. Gentle Reader, I have only digressed from the subject a few lines to show you that there once were men who could almost make a squarerigger talk, and if it had not been so, our ships of the past could not have gotten in and out of small ports before the tugboat was invented. Also, I should like to note that *Boxer's* bow, and particularly her stern, must have been about right to sail backward around the island so handily. If the present-day model makers can get the *Boxer's* lines and sail plan, they can make a model worth looking at, but, alas, soon after this time, poor dear Art's health began to fail and she passed away without issue in the 1920s. These words apply to the handling of vessels as well as to the designing of them.

But to get back to sterns. Poops kept growing higher and higher in some sort of international competition until Spain finally capped them with finials of three great lanterns that were large enough for several men to get inside for cleaning purposes. Spain's great religious enemies, Holland and England, soon followed suit. Another reason that the great ships of the line had such gorgeous and sumptuous after quarters was that one after another they were built to be flagships. The Admiral of the Fleet often had conferences that included most of the higher-ranking gentlemen of the fleet. These flagships were also often sent on foreign missions to make diplomatic agreements, and at times important international councils were held aboard. Then, too, it was thought important to make an impression of the wealth, strength, and power befitting the flagship's nation.

Although poop decks were gradually reduced in size and height after around 1700, it was not until Lord Nelson's time that they were almost done away with. Nelson, besides being a great naval strategist, was something of a naval architect: he persuaded the Admiralty to remove the high after decks of his flagship *Victory* and make her into a so-called flush-decker. In this way, besides doing away with a lot of wind resistance and fire hazards, he saved enough weight and space to allow a few more guns farther aft. Even before *Victory's* time, frigates and other small craft were built without a poop deck, so this style of building or designing for a century or two was referred to as frigate-built, no matter what the vessel's size, rig, or number of guns. But I do not want to take away from the fame of Lord Nelson, for he was a genius in many ways and not, least of all, in composing short messages to the men of the fleet that were hoisted in code flags so that each man down to the powder monkeys thought he had a personal message from the beloved Admiral and fought like a demon so that Nelson's ships were often referred to as the "wooden walls of England," and were certainly the principal thing that stopped Napoleon.

As for bows—well, their shape remained quite similar from the time of the rams, perhaps between the years 1000 and 1800 AD. They resembled a canal boat as much as anything, but sometimes they were well rounded off in profile under water and that made them yaw less when running wind-on-the-quarter in a seaway. The bows of most ships were so covered over with trailboards and lattice work that their true shapes were veiled. Nevertheless, the principal part of early bows was the extension (sometimes called a false piece, gammon, knee, or head), or that part that supports the bowsprit. This part was strongly bolted to the stem, for often both the gammon ropes and bobstays, which held the bowsprit down, were fastened to it. This head of a ship was a favorite place for decoration, with the whole scheme worked out by a specialist in this sort of art. Some of the large ships had complicated figureheads composed of several figures, like Neptune followed by mermaids and dolphins, or Diana, strange to say, chased by a small deer and hounds. Some of the carving was beautifully sculptured, and when we consider that Grinling Gibbons started his career as a carver of ships' garnish, we can see what high quality it was. No doubt the Dutch and French bow decorations were just as good, for these countries were perhaps more artistic than England, and just as good at wood carving.

It was not until the clipper-ship era that the true clipper bow came into common use. There were, however, profiles of heads that resembled the stem of a clipper before this, but the older ships usually had a rabbet line that was either straight or convex above the waterline. With the true clipper bow, the rabbet line somewhat followed the shape of the face of the stem, and all the space that had been occupied by the complicated ribbands and braces to the trailboards was filled in by the ship's planking. It is probable that with the speed of the clippers, all this forward complication would have been washed or swept away when the clipper dove into a sea. Also in this era, ships began to use flaring bows, and the clipper bow is the natural termination of flaring sections, as powerboats and the larger high-speed steamers are finding out. In other words, it is hard to plank up or plate a bow that suddenly changes from flaring sections to a plumb stem because the planks or plates have to take a sharp twist.

Some of the clipper ships had very handsome bows, and it has been said that G. L. Watson copied the last of the Scotch clippers in his fine steam yachts, but as he even excelled the best of the clippers' bows, it should be said that he "improved" them rather than "copied" them. Mr. Watson took great pains in developing his bows and had a fair-size mock-up of the bow built on which he made the final adjustments of the size of the figurehead, curve of the stem, sweep of the bow scroll, etc., until all parts blended together in a chaste harmony that has never been excelled. The clipper bow took the place of all other bows around 1880 with the larger yachts, for from the time England gave up her tonnage rule for rating, she too was using the clipper bow.

As for overhanging ends on yachts—why, the English cutters around 1850 began to use long overhanging sterns, for one of the measurements for calculating their tonnage was the length between perpendiculars, or, in other words, the length between stem and rudder post, and the stern beyond that point was not measured, or went free. However, overhangs on craft other than yachts were very ancient, and the earliest types of Egyptian craft had very long overhangs at both ends, said to facilitate landing on river banks. It was soon found out that the over-hanging sterns of the cutters lengthened their lines and allowed them to go faster so, when the tonnage rules for rating were given up, the English cutters also adopted the clipper bow to lengthen the lines forward above water. This, of course, made the cutters drier and better boats.

It was not until 1891 that the true overhanging spoon bow came out on the 46-foot rating sloop *Gloriana*. All the other yachts of her class had clipper bows, but *Gloriana* beat them quite easily, principally because this sort of bow allows a shorter waterline with much longer sailing lines when the yacht was heeled. This type of bow was quite an innovation in yachting and was given different names. We, at the time, called it the Gloriana bow; the Scandinavians called it the pram bow (as a Nordic rowboat of that name had a flat overhanging bow). In England it was sometimes called the swim bow, as some of the Thames barges had used a bow that somewhat resembled it, but as time went on, it was simply called an overhanging bow.

The first of the fin-keelers came out that same year, 1891, and in them the spoon bow was fully developed. At that time, both here and in England, the principal measurements for rating were waterline length and sail area, and as the fin-keelers could carry a large sail area on a short waterline, they became the principal winners in the next few years until they were barred from racing. However, the fin-keelers had shown how, with the long sailing lines of overhanging ends and the stability of a deep keel, a fast boat could be built with a short waterline, so during the next few years, 'most everything—from two- and three-masted schooners down to catboats—was built with overhanging spoon bows. The Gentle Reader must keep in mind that by shortening the waterline you were allowed more sail by the rules of that time, so the problem of gaining stability to carry sail made the yachts very wide. The larger ones also had deep keels, while the smaller ones used centerboards and depended on the weight of crew to keep them on their feet. These were the true skimming dishes or scows that needed a skillful crew to get the best speed. They were very slow in light weather and in fact had slow average speed, but when there was breeze enough to get them up on their long leeward side, they did very well both to windward and reaching, while in running before it, some of them were a better shape for planing than anything we now have. Nevertheless, by about 1903 they were as miserable in hull form as our present yachts are in sail plan. Some of them were twice as long overall as on the waterline, while our present yachts usually carry an actual sail area of more than twice their measured sail area.

The most extreme of the skimming dishes was *Outlook*, designed by Starling Burgess. Some of her dimensions were: LOA, 51' 5"; LWL, 21'; beam, 16'; draft of hull, 9"; sail area, 1,800 sq. ft. While our later rules, both here and abroad, have controlled or partly brought these overhanging ends back to normal, all racing yachts are still too short on their waterline for good average speed, so that a model like *The Rudder*'s how-to-build design *Rozinante* can beat the racers of her general size or sail area boat-to-boat because she has the proper length of waterline for her displacement. If the present-day auxiliaries were longer on the waterline, they would be faster under both power and sail, and in most cases would be all-around better yachts.

5. **The Advantages and Disadvantages of Different Rigs.** There is no doubt that a high, narrow rig has more driving power for its

Outlook. (The Common Sense of Yacht Design, *by L. Francis Herreshoff. Caravan-Maritime Books*)

area than a low, long one, no matter how many sections the low one may be divided into. Thus you might think a catboat with a high, narrow mainsail would be fastest, but a catboat has steering troubles, for her single sail revolves around, or tries to revolve around, one center, so as the catboat gains speed, she will try to head up in the wind so strongly that most catboats require very big rudders. Now, if a tall rig is put on a catboat, when she heels, the driving power is so far out to leeward that she will come up in the wind even with a large rudder at a good angle, so a tall-rigged catboat is not practical. The catboat also has mast-staying disadvantages, and if you don't believe these things, just try to sail a cat-rigged model yacht.

The sloop rig seems to be the fastest in every size from the largest down to the sailing canoe and toy boat. For many years the yacht clubs have kept records of the speeds of various rigs and varied the percentage that a sloop had to allow a schooner, yawl, and ketch, so these comparisons of the speeds of the various rigs must be correct. Some of the reasons a sloop is fastest are:

1. She does not have excessive steering troubles because her two, three, or four sails try to revolve around different

centers and she can vary the trim and size of her headsails; thus, the sloop can have a high rig.

2. A sloop can have a high, light rig because she has little
   mast-staying difficulties.
3. A sloop's rig has the least wind resistance of any rig, due
   to the fact that her headstay or headstays are at the
   forward edge of the sails and thus have no wind resistance.

A sloop is not a good cruising rig, or as safe and easy to
handle as a ketch. It is impossible to make a sloop lay-to in a
strong breeze and sea; in fact, you can't even make her jog along
under a trysail without having a man at the helm. As soon as
you shorten sail on a sloop, you will usually get her so out of
balance that she will steer wildly. With a sloop it is nearly impossible to make her steer herself on any course but close-
hauled, though the sloop and several other rigs can be made to
hold other courses with an automatic steering gear or some
arrangement like twin spinnakers, etc. If this were not so, sloop-
rigged model yachts would not be much fun. A sloop cannot be
made to lay head to the wind reliably during the procedure of
hoisting sail and getting the anchor. All that is said of the sloop
was true of the cutter rig that has long gone out of existence in
this country.

With the ketch, which is the best cruising rig at present, all
these things are quite different. A ketch can lay-to better than
any other rig. She can be made to steer herself on several
courses. A properly proportioned ketch can be shortened down
or reefed in something like thirteen balanced combinations of
sail, as I have shown in *The Common Sense of Yacht Design*. A
ketch with the mizzen set will lay at anchor head to the wind
all day if you want her to.

The ketch rig received rather a bad name in the old long-gaff
days because there was difficulty in supporting or staying the
mizzenmast on its forward side, but since the leg-o'-mutton sail
has come into vogue and a spring stay allowed between the
mastheads, the ketch rig has become par excellence for cruising
and for safe and comfortable afternoon sailing.

The yawl rig is about halfway between a sloop and a ketch in
usefulness, but its mizzen is too small to lay-to within a seaway.
The mizzen is too small to help much in steering or for use in
holding her head to the wind at anchor. However, as a yawl sets

light sails, and a spinnaker nearly as large as a sloop, the rig still has its advocates, though at present the rig is being looked on as a rule cheater, and it is the favorite rig of the so-called "out-of-sight racers" and "last-boat-wins" craft. Up until the early 1960s there were several yawls measured in with only 85 percent of the foretriangle measured, for, while they carry a mizzen staysail, that sail was not measured or went free. So they did win most races while coming in last boat, and what sails they carry when out of sight behind or at night it would be hard to guess, for they are sailed by men whose profession is making either yacht sails or yacht sales; or, again, making yacht sails for yachts that do not have measured sails to make more yacht sales. I am afraid I do not understand modern business, but one thing is certain, and that is that the nonprofessional owner no longer has a chance in out-of-sight racing.

At present the schooner rig is going out of use, for yachts are now too small to be rigged that way. The schooner also has the disadvantages of too much tophamper, too much weight aloft, too much wind resistance, and too much cost. I must have had quite a little experience with schooners and either worked on the design or sailed on the yachts *Westward* and *Elena*, 96 feet LWL; the fishing schooners *Mayflower, Puritan*, and *Columbia*, about 104 feet LWL. I designed the sail plan of the staysail-rigged schooner *Pleione*, which has won the Astor Cup several times. I designed the schooner *Mistral*, which many consider the last good-looking schooner, but still I do not like schooners in the small size that present economy makes necessary. Of course, in racing, the schooners are slow because they cannot well set as large running and reaching sails as the sloop, yawl, and ketch rigs. I realize the schooner is considered one of our national rigs and have always liked the looks of them, but it was a quite different thing in the great schooner days, the 1860s, when the schooners were about 100 feet on the waterline and had hearty crews and no dangerous rule-cheating sails. One of the large schooners could carry full sail in a breeze that would overpower a thirty- or forty-footer, and if you don't believe it, just try to sail a model schooner that has the same scale depth and sail area as the prototype. You will find that the model will be knocked on her beam ends in a ten-mile wind, while the 100-foot WL schooner will carry full sail in a thirty-mile wind if her spars and rigging are strong enough.

Sail plan, Mistral.

The large older schooners usually had three or four headsails, a foresail and foretopsail, a mainsail and main topsail, so their area was broken up into eight parts. Before the big mainsails came in, a large schooner was a handy vessel. The large schooners, like the Gloucestermen, could be made to partly lay-to or jog. This was done under the foresail and forestaysail, the latter sail being aback or sheeted to weather. The rudder blade also was swung to weather or, as is said, the helm was put nearly hard down, for up until something like 1900, the Gloucester fisherman used wheels whose upper spokes moved in the same direction a tiller would. Under this set of sails, when the vessel forged ahead, the lee helm would swing her toward the wind when the foresail would lose drive and the vessel slow down enough for the rudder to be less effective. The forestaysail, being aback, could then swing her off again. Under these conditions, the vessel made a series of moon-shaped courses, and it would be hard to tell without much experience where she would be in the morning. It is said that even in heavy weather, the Gloucester schooners were very comfortable when jogging, and seldom swung off enough to get in the trough, or came up enough for the foresail to flog much. It must also be mentioned that some of the Gloucester captains had a sense of direction, or homing instinct, equal to the fishes they caught, and I think the last of the cherubs who are on high to look out for Poor Jack must have had an eye on the Gloucester schooners. For anyone who loves the looks of a schooner as I do, my advice is to buy a fine painting of one and let it go at that.

6. The Pros and Cons of Gaff and Leg-o'-Mutton Sails. Many people today think the leg-o'-mutton sail is a new thing and call it a Marconi sail, a Bermuda sail, or a jibheaded sail, but as far as I know, the leg-o'-mutton or trysail far antedates the gaff sail. After all, the lateen sail is only an elongated leg-o'-mutton set on a yard at an angle, and in appearance it is quite similar to a leg-o'-mutton set on a mast at great rake. It is presumed that the Dutch developed the first true fore-and-aft sails that were set aft of the mast. Their early ones of before 1630 had a very short gaff or headboard at the head, and in old prints resembled a leg of lamb perhaps more than any later sails. This is the type of sail our Block Islanders had. True leg-o'-mutton sails were tried in the cutter racing in England about 1840, but it was found that with unlimited sail areas or large sails, the true cutter rig, with its topsail, housing topmast, and reefing bowsprit was best for reducing the area quickly, so the cutter reigned supreme for some sixty years, and the leg-o'-mutton sail seems to have persisted all these years at Bermuda. I don't think anyone knows just when such sail was first used in the Chesapeake bugeyes and log canoes, or the Connecticut River sharpies, but my guess is that it was before 1830.

The long gaffs were developed along with topsails for the revenue craft of France, Holland, and England, about 1750. As these countries were so close together, they all probably kept abreast of one another in the development. It was not until about 1850 that boats without topsails used long gaffs, but from that time on, gaffs grew in length, until about 1900 most gaffs throughout the world were approximately the same length as the hoist or luff of the sail.

During these fifty years, the gaff-rigged boats so outnumbered the leg-o'-mutton craft in racing that the latter were almost forgotten, so when some of the Nordic countries, and particularly Sweden, began using leg-o'-mutton sails for racing around 1912, it was looked upon as a new development. The other yachting nations soon followed suit, for by that time, the racing rules required enough displacement in the yachts that they could carry full sail in strong breezes. About this time, Sweden started the first of her sail area classes, and it was soon found that the leg-o'-mutton gave the most driving power for its area, and that tall, narrow ones were best. While it is true that many European racing yachts had roller-reefing gear, still, if you reef sail under a sail area rule, you lose some of your allowed potential. The leg-o'-mutton sail under different names in different countries has taken the place of all other sails in racing. Some of the advantages and disadvantages of the two rigs are about as follows:

The mast of a leg-o'-mutton sail can be very light for, as the sail is hoisted on a track at the after side of the mast, shrouds and spreaders can be attached wherever desired, and several sets of spreaders can be used on the larger yacht. Almost any section of mast can be used, and I developed the box section of mast in 1923 for the following reasons:

1. This section resists buckling the most of any.
2. The flat surfaces of a rectangular spar make an ideal way to attach shroud gangs and spreader attachments.
3. With a box section mast, the fore and aft and sideways dimensions can be varied as desired.

A streamlined section mast is one of the worst shapes to resist buckling, and as the wind in the forward part of a plane or sail is moving forward, their streamlining is all for nothing.

One of the best things about the leg-o'-mutton sail is its great simplicity, for it requires only one halyard and can get along without any lazy jacks quite well. So we must speak about the simplest of all rigs. This is the so-called dory rig, where the leg-o'-mutton sail is permanently seized to the mast and there are no halyards or stays.

To hoist or lower the sail, the procedure is as follows: the rig is stowed, or sail furled, by swinging the boom up parallel with the mast and wrapping the sail around the mast and boom together with the sheet. Then a turn of the sheet is taken around the whole bundle at the last turn of the sail, when the sheet is fastened with a half bowknot or other slip knot. To ship the rig, the mast is stepped through the mast hole into its step; the slip knot is pulled when the sheet and sail usually unwrap themselves gradually, and the boom comes down in place. In unshipping the rig, the mast is lifted out of its hole and let down aft. This is sometimes hard to do in a cranky boat if there is a breeze, so I must mention the old procedure that used to be practiced if caught in a squall with this rig. You simply swung the boat off dead before it and let the sheet out, until the sail and boom were straight ahead when, of course, the boat could stand any amount of wind.

The dory rig used old-fashioned boom jaws necessary both for scudding this way and for furling in the above-mentioned style, as well as for what the sailor calls "tacking down," or tightening the luff of a sail that is made fast at the peak. Yes, the dory rig is beautifully simple—just the sail, spars, sheet, and some seizing; no hardware whatever. If your home was near where you kept your boat, you threw the whole rig over your shoulder and put it in a shed or garage. On several of these rigs that I have had, I have left the sail on the spars furled as usual all winter, and the sail was only stripped off when the spars needed revarnishing. The old dory rig generally had a sail that was triangular, or the foot and luff were the same length, but they began to look old-fashioned fifty years ago. For the last of these rigs, I used a mast 19 feet long and a boom 9½ feet long. I think the whole rig weighed about forty pounds, and that is about the limit for the dory rig. Even then you have to have a mast hole with a hasp or ratchet arrangement on the after side of the mast partners so you can put the foot of the mast on the step and upend the rig as you would a ladder. The dory rig was also much used in sailing canoes, where the mast was stepped from a float or stepped before launching.

One of the great troubles with the early leg-o'-mutton sails was that some of the slides often caught and the sail could not be lowered away, and that for a long time made the cruising man dislike the rig. But that trouble has been almost altogether done away with now, because the tracks and slides are made of more suitable metals and because at the joint of the sections of the track, the burr is filed off or the track rounded off, and great care is taken to hold the ends in line at the joint. On small craft this is usually done by having one of the screw fastenings right at the juncture, so if the ends were in line when the hole was drilled, they have to remain so after the screw is driven.

Another great difficulty still remains, and that is the danger of getting paint or varnish on the side of the track toward the mast. While this trouble can be obviated on a new mast by not attaching the track until the last coat of paint or varnish is dry, still, in repainting the mast later on, it often happens that some paint, gummed up with sandpaper dust, clogs the track. Hence some yacht yards have special tools to fit the track that will scrape off hardened paint or varnish. These scrapers, and sometimes file arrangements, are hauled up along the track with the peak halyards and brought down by a downhaul. By far the greatest trouble with the leg-o'-mutton sail in the larger sizes is that it is apt to give out at the head or near the headboard. You see, almost all the strains that come on a sail are concentrated at that point, and the rule makers foolishly have required two small headboards. However, sailmakers have made great improvement in reinforcing the head of triangular sails during the last thirty years, and while I believe you now can get a mainsail of a thousand square feet or so that would carry you across the Pacific without mending, there still are experienced long-distance sailors who will not use leg-o'-mutton sails. Remember, the head of a good-sized leg-o'-mutton sail cannot be mended at sea, for it is definitely a sail-loft job. Sometimes I argue with them by saying, "Well, you use a trysail in heavy weather, why not use a triangular sail in fair weather?" But they are smart enough to reply, "Trysails usually have a short gaff or large headboard," in which case they are dead right. Of course, no cruiser or other sensible person likes the excessively long masts that are now used with leg-o'-mutton sails. They have too much wind resistance when anchored in a gale or in beating to windward with a trysail set, and few people will be able to stand the beating they will get if they have to go aloft on one when at sea.

The gaff sail still has some advantages, and not the least of them is that on the larger yachts you can set a topsail over them. This great advantage cannot be fully appreciated unless you have cruised and sailed on a topsail-rigged vessel. But the topsailed yachts of my youth could stand any usual summer weather with the topsail down, and it was a great relief to lower away and stow the topsail at night. Since the auxiliary has come into use, however, this shortening of sail is less important, for in the case of a squall, you can let everything down on the run and keep on your course under power. The gaff rig has the great advantage that the principal strains on the sail are distributed over the whole length of the gaff so the sail will last much longer. Also, most any sailmaker can cut a reasonably good gaff sail. One of the reasons for this is that the draft of a gaff sail can be changed or adjusted by peaking up or lowering the gaff somewhat. All the vital parts of a gaff sail are nearer the deck, and a sailor man can go or run aloft on gaff-rigged craft safely, quickly, and easily because they have mast hoops. With the sail set and the vessel heeled, if he grasped one mast hoop after another, and stuck one foot after the other on a hoop between the luff and the mast all the time, he would be quite safe.

It is my impression that the gaff-rigged yacht is not as much slower than a leg-o'-mutton one as is generally supposed, particularly for cruising, where you spend less time close-hauled than in racing. Also, when new things are tried on the water, it often happens that the new thing is on a new yacht with new sails, and the vessel is an all-around better model, with perhaps a higher percentage of ballast and light rig. Of course, the crew that is trying the new thing are right on their toes, while the poor old gaff-rigger, which was sold cheaply to an inferior sailor, probably had old dead sails, a foul bottom, and a crew who thought they were beaten before they started.

Some of the yacht clubs have records of the times of the yachts over various courses before World War I. The speeds for the waterline length compare very favorably with present-day craft, although our present-day craft have ever so much larger and better light sails for running and reaching. It is interesting to note that the Buzzards Bay 12½-footers, a one-design class, came out with gaff sails in 1913, but somewhere around 1925, many of them used the leg-o'-mutton rig. There was so little difference between the speeds of the two rigs, and because the Buzzards Bay people liked the gaff rig better, most of the later ones for the Bay were ordered from the original builders with the gaff rig, and you will see many of them with that rig sailing there now.

For several years I have thought some sort of a compromise between the two rigs could be arranged, and hoped that some of the good features of each could be combined, so, when designing the *Meadow Lark* class, I specified high, narrow sails with short gaffs. These little ships proved faster than ever expected. They have sails made by various makers that all seem excellent.

As for bowsprits, they are seldom necessary on yachts less than forty feet long, for our modern high rigs are ever so much shorter than they used to be. However, a clipper bow does not look right without a bowsprit, and as a bowsprit and its shrouds and bobstay make a protection for the figurehead or fiddle head, it is a temptation to use one. Most everyone who has inherited a love of the sea feels that the clipper bow is a befitting finial to a sailing vessel, as a beautiful head of hair is to a woman. Perhaps neither the long hair nor the bowsprit is necessary, but when either is removed, there is a loss of character that is hard to replace. The three principal things that make bowsprits necessary or unnecessary are:

1. The length of the overhang forward.
2. The rig of the vessel. The schooner rig is the longest on the base, the ketch next, then the yawl and sloop. So the schooner is most in need of a bowsprit.
3. The size of the vessel.

The larger vessel has more sail area than the small one, for the two following reasons: first, the velocity of the wind as compared to the length of the vessel (which has been spoken of before); and second, sail plans only increase in area in accordance with the law of squares, while displacement and stability increase according to the law of cubes. So we see that a large schooner would require quite a bowsprit, while a small sloop with a long overhang forward might have her forestay well inboard.

A Few Comparisons of *Puritan* and *Mayflower*

The new fishing schooner *Puritan* is very similar in model to *Mayflower*. When in the water, the *Puritan* may look quite different to the average eye, but this will only be on account of the stern of the *Puritan* being carried out and the transom given a graceful rake after the accustomed manner. This old-fashioned stern has the disadvantages of being a little harder to build, very much heavier, and a continual nuisance, as the sterns of the dories catch under it. Its only advantage is in appearance. The public demanded this overhanging stern; accordingly, Mr. Burgess had to put it on.

The *Puritan* has a fuller and slightly deeper forefoot, a decided advantage in going to windward, as it allows the ballast to be stowed somewhat lower. This should help considerably, as one of the principal troubles of all fishing schooners is lack of stability when heeled at any considerable angle.

The *Puritan*'s keel is shorter than the *Mayflower*'s, thus cutting down the wetted surface so that the *Puritan* should be better, for this reason, in light weather.

The *Puritan* has not quite as fine lines aft and not quite such a straight run from her midship section to rudder post, so that the *Mayflower* probably will be the fastest before the wind and reaching in a breeze. I think it is safe to say that the *Mayflower* will be a very hard boat for any sailing vessel to beat in a stiff breeze, with wind on the quarter.

The *Puritan*, although a bit shorter, has more beam than the

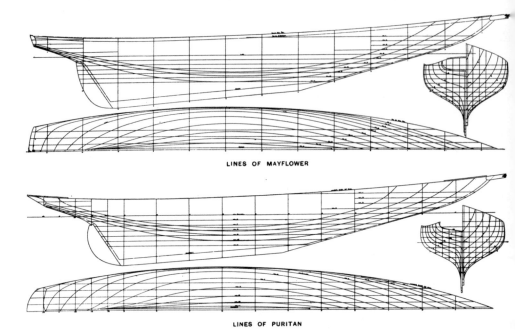

LINES OF MAYFLOWER

LINES OF PURITAN

(The Yachting Monthly, *May 1930*)

Mayflower, a point on which it is hard to say which is the more advantageous, but my opinion is that in boats with inside ballast, the beam is an advantage when on the wind.

These differences in models seem to forecast that the *Puritan* will be fastest to windward and the *Mayflower* best off the wind. Nevertheless, it may not turn out so, for there are many other very important things besides the model to consider. The most important of these probably is the sails. Now I do not mean by this the newness or the cost of the sails, but that the lucky schooner that has the sails of quite the right amount of draft in the right place will win. The curve of the sails is quite as important as the model under water; one is driving ahead and the other holding back.

Next in importance probably is the way the schooners are handled, of course considering that they are both handled moderately well. The things that count are the proper setting and trimming of sails, and the careful judgment of distances, knowing just when to tack ship to get advantage of tide, never overstanding the mark, etc.

Next comes the spars and rigging, which, if they carry away, are the most important of all, and right here is the point where the real science comes in; for the saving of every ounce of weight aloft is most important, so the perfect proportioning of every piece of rigging, spar, shackle, and forging becomes a very important work and can only be done by a man who has had experience at sea and a scientific training. Now the *Mayflower's* rigging was laid off by the naval architect so that it was in proportion to the rest of the vessel. She went through several severe gales last fall and everything stood the strain, although she could be greatly improved upon in the detail of masthead fittings, etc. The workmanship on the rigging of the *Mayflower* was very nearly perfect, and we hope that the spars, rigging, and fittings on the *Puritan* will be as good. This may play a very important part next year [1922], for in a hard beat to windward in a race where everything is driven to the limit, if anything gives out, it is all off.

Now as far as the seagoing qualities of the two boats are concerned, there will be nothing to choose between the two, except the name of their hailing port. And I would like to say right here that both of these fine, new schooners, built by Mr. James, are much stronger and in all probability will have a much longer life than any of the man traps now sailing out of Gloucester.

What a shame it is that in the years gone by so little paint was used on the frames and inside the planking of Gloucester schooners as they were being built! A few years ago, I saw one of them that was being replanked, and the frames were so rotten that new ones had to be put in to hold the planking fastenings. What a sin it was that so few fastenings were used in their construction! How pitiful that so little galvanizing was done on their iron work!

Now they are rotten in the bilge and are the nightmares of the insurance companies, who know that if they touch bottom but once, their whole keel will fall out, as most of them are only held together with Portland cement. No wonder the average age of the fishing schooner is only seven years! No wonder there are so many widows in Gloucester and no wonder it is hard to get people to put their money into such death traps!

Did you ever stop to think what the results would have been if one or two thousand more dollars had been spent in paint, fastenings, and the careful designing of all the details of these

Mayflower, *built 1921. (Nicholas S. Potter)*

On deck, Mayflower.

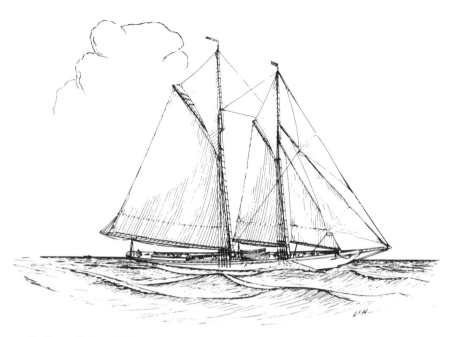

Puritan, *built 1922. This sketch was prepared by L. Francis Herreshoff to* *enable owners to visualize the schooner.*

Designer Starling Burgess aboard the Puritan.

schooners? Do you realize that it would be possible to nearly double the life of these schooners by scientific construction? Do you realize that they could all have been made much better sea boats, considerably faster and so perfectly balanced that there would have been no need for an auxiliary motor if a trained naval architect had been hired to make their complete design. As it is, most of the proud fishing fleet of Gloucester have been built by the rule of the thumb from a few simple lines of some second-class designer, who had been paid only about enough to put a week's work into them. Do you realize that most of the fishing schooners are so poorly balanced and clumsy that they can't be steered or swung off the wind without their auxiliary motors going?

Even in the case of auxiliaries—which of course have some advantages—there could have been a saving in cost of fuel of several times the architect's commission. If the models were carefully developed, the propeller, rudder, struts, etc., properly designed, they would have gone faster, and possibly the machinery would have taken up much less room.

It certainly is a pity that so little pride is taken in the Gloucester schooners of today by their crews. It wasn't so many years ago that some of the schooners were kept up almost like yachts and had all-American crews. Those were the days when the many famous poems and songs were written about Gloucester vessels. But, alas! What inducement is there for a young American to go to sea in the crates there now? So here is hoping that there are some fine vessels built in the next few years, for there are still many able captains in Gloucester who are natural navigators and should be masters of vessels worthy of them.

TO THE KNOCKERS OF THE SCHOONER *MAYFLOWER*

Oh ye sons of motorboat-driving land lubbers! There are many of ye and ye swarm upon the surface of muddy rivers, like flies on the cork of a rum bottle.

Know ye that the public sentiment of your horde has brought everlasting disgrace to an unchampioned nation.

Ye have said that the *Mayflower* was a yacht, and ye have said she had a dolphin striker, and ye have said many foolish things. But if any of ye had ever been down to the sea in vessels propelled by the wind, ye would have known better. If any of ye ever venture as far out into the sea as the head of some pier, where deep water vessels lay, ye can ask any old rigger what a dolphin striker is, and he will tell you the *Mayflower* has no dolphin striker, but has a martingale. He will also tell you that all sailing vessels that have long bowsprits have martingales, since long before the days of the *Santa Maria,* and one has even been seen on the famous *Flying Dutchman,* and if he tells you not this, then you will know him as no true son of the sea.

Many of your motley gang, who have never seen or measured parts of the *Mayflower*, have said that her hold was too small, or that she had cost too much, or she was built too light. But know ye that the *Mayflower* actually has the largest carrying capacity of any American fishing schooner.

Know ye that she was builded by one of the oldest and most noted builders of fishing schooners in the same place, manner, and way that he and his father before him had done for many a year.

Ye have spoken with scorn of the fine materials used on the *Mayflower*—the plow steel rigging in particular ye have condemned. Know ye that ye are daily lifted to your offices in an elevator that uses wire of this sort, as it has been found that for safety and long life, it is far more efficient than the other sort of slightly lower first cost.

Now if there are any among you who deny my words, let him come forth with any known sort of measuring instrument, and if one dare not venture it alone, come ye all, for ye are a cowardly lot, who loveth not the truth, and if any of ye ventures into the hold of the *Mayflower*, ye will be seasick, although she be made fast to the pier, and when ye return home at high noon, your own mother will not let ye into the home, for ye will have salt on your coat and slime on your shoes and ye will not eat fish for a good six month.

W. Starling Burgess

All of us who are interested in the art of yacht design will be distressed to hear of the rather sudden death [1947] of Starling Burgess, the designer of our last three Cup defenders. Starling's principal ambition in life was to design as many Cup defenders as had his father, Edward Burgess (which he did do); but besides that, he accomplished several other remarkable feats.

He was one of the early fliers and among the very first designers and manufacturers of aeroplanes in this country. It is generally conceded that he designed the first American gasoline launch to attain thirty miles per hour—the *Mercedes U S A*—besides designing successful racing yachts for most of our classes, and the fastest Gloucester fisherman.

Starling saw service in three wars, for he enlisted in the Navy in the Spanish-American War and served aboard the *Yankee* in the Cuban campaign. During World War I he was enrolled in the Navy and worked on the design of lighter-than-air craft. During World War II he worked for the Navy on anti-submarine devices and other experimental work, and at times perhaps overworked and strained his constitution in the trials of some of these things, which most likely shortened his life.

Starling Burgess deserves much credit, for he was very much a self-made man in his profession, his father having died before Starling was old enough to study yacht design. Starling went to Milton Academy and majored in English at Harvard, with the intention of becoming a poet, but his father's calling proved the stronger urge, so that he went into yacht design almost without any training. He had some hard battles and won his victories at times under great difficulties.

Starling Burgess certainly deserves a seat in the Halls of Valhalla, and his name should be entered in the book of fame in letters nearly as large as those of his illustrious father.

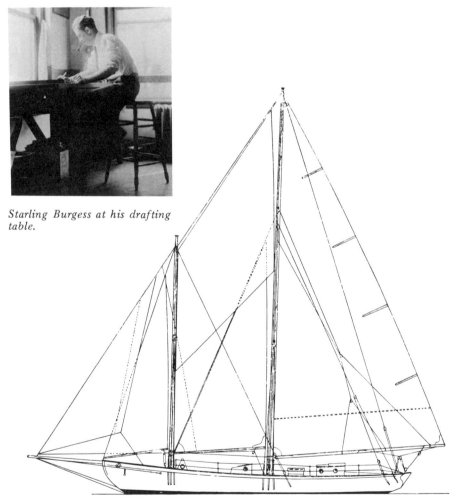

Starling Burgess at his drafting table.

Niña, a Burgess design. (Reproduced by kind permission of the Executors of Uffa Fox Deceased)

The Design of Fishing Vessels

I have been interested in following the discussions about the designs of fishing craft in the *Maine Coast Fisherman,* and having some opinions at variance with the points brought out by the several writers of these articles, I feel that I should say something about it.

In the first place all of the articles, excepting possibly the ones written by Mr. John T. Rowland, seem to intimate that the average design of fishing boats and vessels is basically wrong, bad, and old-fashioned, while I myself have always been amazed at what fine craft they have been, considering their cost. While I have never designed commercial craft, still, I did work for the firm of Burgess and Paine when they designed *Mayflower, Puritan,* and *Columbia,* and inspected these fishing schooners when under construction. I also made a cruise on a mackerel seiner years ago, so I do know something about the cost and profits under which a fishing vessel must operate.

I must say that some of the fishing schooners designed by McManus and built at Essex were very finely perfected vessels, and perhaps real engineering triumphs as far as cost is concerned. They apparently often cost less than one-third of a yacht of the same size, and while the last of the Essex-built sailers were not always built of well-seasoned wood, they had some fine material in them.

As for looks, which Mr. R. R. Steele, Jr., seems to ridicule, I will say that outside of the clipper ships, the Gloucester fishermen were the handsomest commercial vessels ever built, and while it is possible that some individuals do not appreciate beauty, it is an indisputable fact that nearly all highly developed and nicely perfected objects are beautiful.

It makes no difference whether it is a gun, violin, automobile, aeroplane, or a vessel; and I myself do not despise a beautiful woman. Nevertheless, while beauty in a fishing vessel may seem of quite secondary importance, it is a quality in a vessel that will always assure her of better care and will inspire her crew with a spurt of pride, which in the end will pay dividends.

There is such a very great difference in the types of vessels used for fishing that the French tunnyman, the Brixham trawler and the Gloucester fisherman were of quite different models, and I have no doubt that for their various localities and different types of fishing, each was best. And so it should be today with power—each type should be especially designed to best perform her peculiar duties or work out of a particular port. The best Block Island lobster boat would be of a different model and size than one, we will say, from Jonesport.

But when we go into the larger sizes where the type of fishing varies through the year—say, dragging in winter and seining in summer—the complications become greater. Perhaps it is not until we get to the big, expensive steel draggers owned by the large concerns that any very fixed type of craft can be standard.

That being the case, I, for one, think various types of rather small wooden fishermen that can be varied in design to best meet the local conditions will be the most satisfactory, and I believe the local builder can design or develop these craft much better than some so-called "naval architect," who has more conceit than actual knowledge of the conditions under which the boat will work.

As far as the small- and medium-size fishermen are concerned, if the local builder builds them altogether from what Mr. Steele calls "look," they will bring in much more money than if built with all the mathematics in the world. I think the Maine boat shops in the next few years will get the bulk of this business, for, as Mr. J. T. Rowland says, they have the materials close at hand, the knowhow, and low overhead cost. Take, for instance, the 27-foot launch designed and built by Hodgdon Brothers at East Boothbay; certainly no so-called N. A. can equal her for a clean-running, economical launch, and few present yacht designers could beat her at all.

Mr. Steele, in his long articles, told of many schemes that

would cost lots of money to try out, but he failed to mention any improvements in the fishing game that would not be expensive, and I will say that all fishing craft of all time would have been better if they had cost more.

The question is, would they have been more profitable, and could they have been built at all if the first cost was too much?

Perhaps when Mr. Steele gets a few more years on him, he will write a different article. Mr. H. I. Chapelle has the advantage of some years, and I certainly agree with much that he says, particularly the lines, "catching more fish at less cost is the self-evident goal of the majority of fishermen." This being the case, let every man play the complicated game as he thinks best, and if one is a genius at landing big catches with cheap gear, so much the better.

It is my guess, though, that the highliners of the next few years will be sailing on vessels that have the "look," and if you are a judge of character, these skippers will have the look of crafty men. You will find they know more about engines, models of fishing craft, and cost of operation than any N. A. you can turn up. They have credit with the banks and can get bigger craft, better gear, or nets if they thought it would pay, so what are you going to do about it?

In his letter, "Slow Speed vs. High Speed," W. C. Gould, marine sales manager of the Detroit Diesel engine division of General Motors, tells us that for the past 30 years a great many more millions of dollars have been spent on the research and development of the so-called high-speed, lightweight engine than has been spent by the entire marine industry in the past 50 years on the research and development of hulls and ship structure. While I would like to know where he got those exact figures, I would like also to point out to him that, while the business of manufacturing small diesel engines is a very young one, the science of naval architecture has been developing for the last 5,000 years, and when the end of the world comes and the final history of naval or marine achievement is written up, the contributions of the General Motors Corporation will be so infinitesimal that they probably will not be mentioned. I should like also to point out to him that most of the effectual spade work in developing the diesel was done in German, French, Italian, English, and Swedish ship yards in manufacturing diesel engines for submarines and early motor ships, which work, to a great extent, was no doubt done by naval architects or marine engineers.

As for the weight of marine engines on a fisherman, there is no doubt that weight is an advantage; not only does the weight itself absorb vibration and allow cylinder walls thick enough to permit cooling with salt water, but the heavier engine often is the very cheapest kind of ballast, for the heavy engine of the same horsepower is often the cheapest, and it must be admitted that most fishing vessels require ballast to make up for their heavy tophamper.

As for compactness, an engine to be used in the fishing business is very poor if it is so congested that its parts are not all accessible, and an engine for any marine use is very poor if its separate parts cannot be removed without dismantling the whole machine. Perhaps this accessibility is one of the hardest things to design, but we see in the engines built by the Lathrop Company (both gasoline and diesel) that this feature is always successfully carried out, and as this company's engines have been very popular with fishermen during the last 50 years, it is evident that said feature is appreciated by them.

As for the speed of engines, it seems to be possible at present to run the small ones 2,000 r.p.m., the medium-size ones 1,000 r.p.m., and the ones of, say, around 500 HP about 500 r.p.m., so it would seem that with the small fishing boat going ten miles an hour, a three-to-one reduction gear would be right, while with the medium-size engine of 150 HP, a two-to-one gear would do, while in the larger classes, no doubt direct drive will be popular for some time, but at present it is the custom to use propellers of higher speed than is the most efficient, particularly for towing or dragging. Of course, if an engine is speeded up, it gives more horsepower so is more efficient—in other words, about one-third of the heat or power passes out through the water jackets, but when a small engine is speeded up, while it gives more power, the cylinder surface has not increased, and while more cooling water is pumped through the engine, the overall economy in fuel consumption is much increased. I am afraid some salesmen are taking advantage of this and are selling smaller engines than are best, for of course a small engine speeded up will be cheaper to build than a large one that runs more slowly, while the larger engine may last so much longer and be free of expensive overhauls that it will be cheapest in the end.

One of the writers in the *Maine Coast Fisherman* has mentioned the gas turbines that are being developed, but so far as I know, they are about the least efficient power plants in use at present, as far as fuel consumption is concerned, and while they are compact and light for their power, I doubt if we shall see in the next 25 years anything as economical as the piston engine for small power plants. Nevertheless, the large gas turbines developed in Scotland and England may soon be used on naval vessels, and perhaps cargo carriers, where space and weight at times are more valuable than fuel consumption. So far all of the small gas turbines lose a lot of heat in a very large, hot exhaust, and until this is corrected, they will not be efficient, so it seems safe to forget the gas turbine as far as small fishing craft are concerned.

Several writers in the *Maine Coast Fisherman* have bewailed the fact that the Gloucester fisheries are less profitable than formerly, but this perhaps is because the fleet is manned with less skillful fishermen than the Yankees and Norwegians who used to man the Gloucester vessels, and if Rockland and Portland are landing much more fish than formerly, it may mean that the regions where there are some Yankees left who will go on the water will be the most prosperous, so hats off to the Maine coast fisherman.

Some of my readers will think that I have not given any more helpful criticism than Mr. Steele in his writings, but I can tell you a few things that will save you some cost of fuel without much expense, and we shall not have to apply to specialists or technicians, and they will not require any electronics.

At the speed most fishing craft move through the water, the surface resistance of the hull is about the same as the wave resistance; in faster-moving craft, the wave resistance is the greatest, and in slower craft, the surface resistance is the most. Now, if half of your fuel is being used up in surface resistance, it becomes most important to keep the whole wetted surface of the vessel as smooth, clean, and fair as possible. All rough seams should be worked down flush, and all splinters on the underside of keel and propeller aperture smoothed off. Of course the bottom should never be allowed to get foul or grow barnacles. All of this, you will say, is too much yacht fashion, but it will mean money in your pocket and allow faster speeds through the water, all at the slight expense of a little care and the use of high-grade anti-fouling paints.

Some marine engineers think the surface of the propeller nearly as important as the whole surface of the vessel and that the propeller should be kept very smooth indeed. If it is rough or pitted, it should be scoured down smooth with sandpaper, rubbing in the direction the blades will pass through the water. The entering edges of the blades should be kept fair and smooth, and if there are any dents or small twists in the entering edge, they should be brought into shape with a hammer and dressed down with a file, for if the entering edges of the blades make eddies in the water, the propeller's efficiency will be much reduced.

While it is true that a propeller sucks water toward it from many directions, it does shoot almost all of it astern in a rather condensed slip stream, and as this slip stream moves astern nearly one-third faster than the water around it, it becomes important to have the rudder, rudder post, or any parts in the slip stream nicely streamlined, or else it will cause considerable drag. While the parts in front of the propeller are not as important in some ways, still, if the water comes to the propeller in a boiling or agitated state, the angle of the blades is not correct to do the best work, and usually the propeller will set up vibrations that are often blamed on the engine.

As for model, it is my impression that most of the small fishing craft and lobster boats at present are much too wide aft, and if the stern had been made longer and brought up to a small transom, not submerged, a larger or longer launch could have been driven at the same speed with less fuel. The large stern requires a full flaring bow, and this combination makes a craft that jumps in a head sea, and steers poorly in a following sea. I believe it is a great mistake for fishing launches to copy the shapes of launches designed to go two or three times as fast, for these models are very hard to drive at the speeds that are economical for fishing craft.

For the larger craft my opinion is that the 70-foot dragger designed by Eldredge-McInnis for the Fisheries Division of the

New Brunswick Board of Industries is a remarkably fine craft in both model and construction. This vessel was shown on Page 17 of the *Maine Coast Fisherman* for November 1950, and proves that as far as design is concerned an existing naval architectural firm can produce a design that is beyond criticism, and I think it would be profitable for New England if she had several vessels like her. It is likely that the high cost of other foods will compel people to eat more fish in the next few years, and a vessel like this 70-footer would seem a good investment.

H. I. Chapelle intimates that streamlining is useless on trawlers, and while of course that would be so if the trawler always operated in a calm, still, when these vessels are working over a trawl at various low speeds, the action of side winds makes the work difficult, and as these vessels often work in wind velocities of 40 MPH, if there is not a sea running, the wind resistance is important and should be cut down by eliminating every useless appendage that the wind can take hold of. If the wind resistance is materially reduced, these vessels could be shallower, or perhaps of less displacement, but as it is, they have to be nearly as deep as a tug boat, which is another vessel affected by the wind when slowed down. Also at times, when the large trawlers are on their way home, they run into very heavy winds and if it is a head wind blowing 60 MPH and the trawler is going ahead 12 statute miles per hour, then the wind velocity is 72 MPH, and with cold winter winds, this can mean real heavy resistance and quite a different proposition from balmy summer breezes.

Speaking of the large steel trawlers, *Wave, White Cap,* and *Comber* were fine vessels that operated from the Boston Fish Pier before World War I, and I believe their design was based on Scottish-built trawlers. It was claimed that these vessels did not pay larger dividends than some of the smaller fry, and the reason for it was said to be that they required a large office and other operating headquarters, so it is possible that the medium-size independent fisherman is the best. No doubt the boat or vessel that is manned by a captain and crew who own shares in her will catch the most fish for the money.

It is interesting to note, when speaking about the cost of operation, that many young men along the New England coast start out with a dory and oars and a few pots they have made themselves. In a year or two they make money enough to buy a launch. Now their profits seem to be less, although they have set more than twice the number of pots, so they say, "Well, I'll get a larger motor and go faster and set still more pots," but this time they only about hold their own, and even make less profit than they did under oars, for the fuel bill and upkeep of their gear is taking a large part of the profit. So I advise the young fisherman to consider very carefully all things that increase his overhead, and bear in mind that it takes in the neighborhood of eight times the fuel to drive a certain boat twice as fast. Is it worth it?

Thoughts About Yachts Especially Designed for Ocean Racing

[Although L. Francis Herreshoff wrote the following thoughts about the ocean racing rating rules of the Cruising Club of America and of the Royal Ocean Racing Club thirty years ago, we feel confident that he would have expressed very similar ideas—perhaps even more strongly—about the current International Offshore Rule.]

Not long ago I had a very pleasant call from the editor of *Seacraft*, and it was a most interesting experience to talk with a yachtsman from the other side of the world. At the time that he called, he was standing by to sail on the *Myth of Malham* in the ocean race from Newport to Bermuda, so that our conversation naturally turned toward the types of yachts that our present [1948] ocean racing rules are developing. Perhaps in our talk I expressed rather strong feelings of dislike for the yachts the rules are producing. The editor asked me to write out some of these thoughts or sentiments, but now as I sit down to put some of these thoughts in black and white, I fully realize the complication of the matter, and while there is undoubtedly much to be said on the subject, it is hard to know how to begin. You know, in conversation one generally only speaks to one person, and as the talk goes along, he can correct certain mistakes he has made or amplify points not clearly understood by the listener. But when one writes out something to be read by thousands, he is something like a man stood up at the firing line to be executed, for, after he has said his little piece, he will be the target of most deadly ammunition.

Now I think that ocean racing is a noble and manly sport, but I object to rules that encourage or produce yachts that are too expensive for any but the very wealthy. I believe our present rules, both English and American, are much too complicated and involved to be clearly understood by the average yachtsman, and I believe that this fact is entirely unnecessary. My greatest objection to the ocean racers now being produced is that they are not comfortable seagoing craft suitable for cruising but are expensive racing freaks almost good for nothing after they are out-built or outmoded, whereas some of the cruising yachts of several nationalities have retained a good value in their old age because they were really good cruisers.

I believe the present ocean racing rules do not encourage or promote the type of yacht we used to consider a safe, comfortable cruiser, and, while there has been much written lately about the merits of the R.O.R.C. rule and the C.C.A. rule, still, the difference in ratings of an individual yacht under the two rules never would amount to the difference in speed between a good and bad crew; good and bad sails; poor and skillful navigation; or the difference between good and bad deck arrangement—well-placed winches, adjustable sail leads, etc.,—so there is little sense in comparing the two rules, for both allow and even encourage freaks.

Under the R.O.R.C. rule, a 30-square meter boat has done very well, proving that the rule does not penalize light displacement or high, narrow rigs enough to make up for the speed-giving qualities of these most undesirable proportions on a seagoing yacht. And now the *Myth of Malham*, with her deep draft, large stern, and big headsails, is doing well. You must understand that I am not criticizing the designs of the *Myth*: it is a rule that allows a yacht like the *Myth* that I criticize. Frankly, I believe the *Myth* is a very good design to fit the rule, but a very poor sort of craft for ocean sailing. She is too expensive, too deep, and requires a larger crew than she can comfortably accommodate.

You will find plenty of young enthusiasts who will say the *Myth* is a wonderful sea boat, but you will also find people who say that other very strange craft are good sea boats. In most cases, these individuals are either lacking in experience or

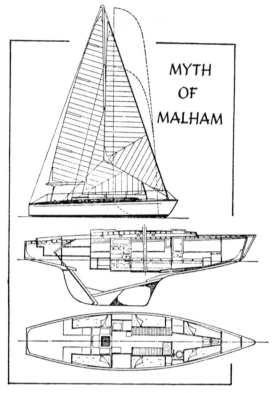

Sail plan, Myth of Malham. (The Sailing Yacht, *by Juan Baader. © 1965 Adlard Coles Ltd.)*

making false statements. The 30-square-meter boats were developed for class racing over courses of perhaps less than ten miles, and for that purpose, they are fairly good boats. I have designed seven of them and owned one for two years but could never think of them as safe, comfortable night sailers. Of course I admit that tough young men, as a lark, can drive them through rough water, but no experienced sailor would consider them a seagoing type. Comfortable sleeping and getting good meals is nearly impossible in such craft when at sea. Some older yachtsmen have prophesied that one of these days some of the present freaks will not return from one of the ocean races, and when that happens, ocean racing will get a setback.

Among the experienced sailors with whom I have talked, there are two principal models that are thought to be good sea boats. One has short overhangs and a deep, sharp bow, together with considerable bulk or displacement for the over-all length. While this model is most excellent for laying-to or jogging to windward, she is not good running before it in a wind and sea, for under these conditions she will roll considerably and steer hard; in fact, she will continually try to broach-to, for her deep forefoot gives her lateral resistance considerably forward of her center of weight.

Some experienced sailors think a model with the same displacement compared with her sail area, but longer over-all and a smaller midship section is an all-around good sea boat that can both be driven hard before the wind and lay-to with her head well up with the mizzen alone set.

A good measurement rule should allow this variation in model without encouraging or penalizing one or the other, so it probably is not good to use hull measurements in a rating formula, for this develops freak hulls. Instead, the rating should come from the sail area (or driving power) alone, and the proportion of both sail plan and hull should be controlled by limits not entering into the formula excepting as penalties.

Charles E. Nicholson

In the recent death [1954] of Mr. Charles E. Nicholson, the world has lost about the last of the great yacht designers. With the exception of our Clinton Crane, there are no others who have designed the larger sail and power yachts, as well as all of the types of smaller craft. Mr. Nicholson, or Mr. Charles, as he was fondly called, had practiced his profession for a little over sixty years, which almost exactly equals the long career of N. G. Herreshoff, but it is probable that Mr. Nicholson would have practiced longer if it had not been for the pressure of the two wars in which he was very active. In World War II Gosport and Portsmouth were frequently bombed and for years were never free from the threat of bombing, which of course made an unbearable strain on the manager of a shipyard.

Mr. Nicholson was of the third generation of Nicholsons who were both yacht designers and yacht builders, and of late years he and N. G. Herreshoff were the only ones who built their own yachts, which gave them a great advantage over others.

It is often said that yacht designing is a combination of art and science, and my estimate would be that Mr. Nicholson used art and science in nearly equal proportions, while some of the other great designers may have been rated as follows: Edward Burgess and the three Fifes were pure artists; George L. Watson, three quarters artist and one quarter engineer; N. G. Herreshoff, one quarter artist and three quarters engineer; Starling Burgess, one quarter artist and three quarters mathematician.

Sail plan, Patience, *a Nicholson design. (Reproduced by kind permission of the Executors of Uffa Fox Deceased)*

Charles E. Nicholson

Mr. Nicholson is best known in this country for designing the last four challengers for the America's Cup, but he probably designed the largest aggregate tonnage of yachts in late years and may only be surpassed by Watson in the past.

Mr. Nicholson was also a wonderful helmsman and as much at home in a sailing dinghy as at the wheel of a three-masted steel schooner. Perhaps his greatest service to yachting has been his many years of work on either the advisory board or the council of the Yacht Racing Association, where for well over thirty years he gave his valuable advice on technical matters.

Mr. Charles will always be remembered by his friends and acquaintances for his pleasant personality, for he was undoubtedly the most popular man in his profession. His opinions were unbiased and he had no petty jealousies, which has been unusual among yacht designers.

On the whole, Mr. Nicholson was perhaps the most important figure in yachting during the last quarter-century.

A Sail in the *Alerion*

The Editor of *The Rudder* now wants me to tell a story about a sail in a boat of the type and size of the H 28. It seems as if I never could suit him and, not being a writer, I doubt if I can succeed in spinning a yarn of any great interest for, after all, a sail is an everyday affair to many readers of *The Rudder*. The Editor is a queer fellow. He pays me more for a long yarn than a short one, Patient Reader, so if I take you around Robin Hood's barn a couple of times, you must blame him and not me.

The sail that I am going to tell of took place nearly a quarter of a century ago now. It was in the spring of 1920, April or May, and if the dates are hazy in my mind, some of the scenes are not.

As I remember the *Alerion*, she was about twenty-six feet on deck, maybe eight feet beam, only about two-and-one-half feet draft and, of course, a centerboarder. She was a gaff-rigged sloop and much the same model as the H 28, but with the rudder inboard two or three feet. The *Alerion* was designed by my father for his own use at Bermuda, where he had been in the habit of spending some of his winters, and named after that famous fin-keeler he owned in the gay nineties. She was as well built and fitted out a small yacht as it has been my lot to see.

Well, one year he decided to have *Alerion* shipped home (to Bristol, Rhode Island). She was to arrive on the deck of the Bermuda steamer at New York. So one day I got orders to go down and bring her up. In those days I used to travel light, so, wrapping an oilskin around a couple of charts, and thrusting a folded sou'wester in my starboard pocket, I took the train for New York, where in due course I arrived and taxied over to the Bermuda steamer dock. The steamer had not shown up yet, so, finding a small hotel in that region, I thought I would moor there for the night so as to be close to the scene in the morning. Well, when I approached the clerk to inquire for a room, he said, "Where is your bag?" So I said, "My things are rolled up in the charts under my arm." Then he said, "Well, I guess we can accommodate you, if you pay down first." That was easily arranged, so I deposited the charts and sou'wester in the room and went out to spend the evening with acquaintances.

In the morning the steamer had arrived, so, starting the complicated mechanism of going through the customs, we proceeded well. At that time we had prohibition in the land, so that though the revenue officer was quite satisfied, the prohibition agent had to examine every ditty box, sail bag, and what-not, which made me quite nervous, as the steam yacht *Corsair*'s port launch was standing by to tow us to City Island.

In the meantime the slings were rigged and the cargo boom swung over us. Seeing this, the prohibitionist left post haste, not relishing an aerial ascension at that moment. So the bo'sun blew his whistle and up into the ether we went, to the chorus of screeching winch engines and creaking cargo booms; then out and down into that brown, strange New York water sprinkled with dead cats, derby hats, and other North River flotsam. Well, the launch was well managed, and we were soon clear of our slings and cradle and on our way down the harbor, the launch man skillfully picking his way by the ferries, tugboats, and lighters till we reached Hell Gate, where with a fair tide, we soon shot into clearer water. Then, taking account of things with mop in hand, I concluded we had done quite well, not having shipped anything worse than a couple of old shoes and an orange crate. How good Execution Rock looked off to the eastward, as we entered the Sound! This seemed strange, for I had often considered it the last sentinel of decency, beyond which lay all the sordidness of the city. But now in the afternoon sun, its gray lighthouse took on more the aspect of the pearly gates to one who had just passed through Gotham and Hell Gate.

We swung into City Island harbor and moored alongside the steam yacht *Xarifa*, which that summer was to be tender for the *Vanitie*. Some of the afterguard of the *Vanitie* were on board, including my good friend Starling Burgess, who gave me a very pleasant evening, for his talks with me have always seemed more like poetry than plain conversation. In the morning the mate of the *Vanitie* (I don't remember now whether it was Baltic Jack or Coconut John) called some of the boys from the forecastle, saying, "Never mind about the cribbage board, ve gonto rig that Alegrion boat," so they swarmed on board. Now these were some boys who could lick their own weight in wildcats and knew the parts of a sailboat to boot, so the *Alerion* was rigged almost as rapidly as a gunner's mate would assemble a machine gun. The mast was stepped, standing rigging shackled, and running rigging rove, while some were bending sails, so that in about an hour, there she was, flag halliards rove and tiller lines crossed. They passed me down a bottle of water, some sardines, and a loaf of bread, and I shoved off with no fixed destination in view, only to get to the eastward.

That day was light with baffling winds, but about sunset we were off Greenwich, so we moored way up in the head of that narrow harbor, which the *Alerion*'s light draft allowed. The *Alerion* had no berths or mattresses or even cushions, as I remember it, but to me her little cabin seemed quite snug, and all I had to do to feel well fixed was to remember some nights I had spent in open boats in rainstorms. Well, I folded and refolded the canvas that had covered her on the steamer and made up something that looked like a mattress. Then I pounded over the storm jib in its bag so it made a pillow and, feeling all things quite shipshape below, I walked up to the town for a late supper. Then, thinking of an acquaintance who was a professor of art in a Connecticut college, I got him on the phone and invited him for a sail along the Connecticut coast. He accepted and, as Uffa Fox would say, came down like a shot, so that early next morning as I opened the cabin door, there he stood above me on the wharf, musette bag in one hand and a paint box in the other.

We were soon under way with a rattling northwester over our after port quarter. Now if there is anything pleasant, it is an all-day sail with an artist (when he is good natured). The changing lights and colors are to them as thrilling as a symphony, and much do they see that would have gone unnoticed, so that day, as the shafts of light and shadows ran out before us under the broken wind clouds, we enjoyed ourselves, unbuttoned our overcoats, and basked in the sun. It was pleasant under the lee of the weather coaming, for never does the sun feel so good as in those first false spring days. We had not yet had the May, or line, storm, so the warmth was unexpected. My friend was a landscape watercolorist of no mean ability, and as we talked of many things and took turns at the helm, he told me of the time he had studied under Maxfield Parrish and of his days abroad working with the late followers of the Barbizon school. But in our hurry to get started we had forgotten to bring along lunch. At first we thought we could feast ourselves through our eyes, but this worked out much better in theory than practice, so about four o'clock we began looking at the chart for snug and easily entered harbors. Now, after all these years, I can't seem to remember what harbor it was (for I have been into several of them along there at various times), but it may have been Southport. It was a small, shallow harbor. By the time we got everything snugged down, it had turned quite cold, as it often does after an all-day northwester, so we hurried ashore in the tender and inquired for an inn. Luckily for us there was one, though it was about two miles down the Old Post Road, so we started out half running and I thought I would perish of the cold before we got there. But if I can't remember the name of the port we were in, I can remember after all these years the steak smothered in onions and the steaming tea we had. Then of one accord we tumbled into bed and went sound asleep, although it was still quite light to the westward.

The next morning it was very cold for the season, but we were up bright and early and had some lunches put up while we were having our breakfast. After our walk to the harbor, we were warmed up, and as the wind had gone down some, it was quite pleasant, so we started at once. Out on the Sound everything was sparkling bright, and off to the so'thward quite a mirage. Stratford Shoal lighthouse stood up like a medieval castle, and the shore of Long Island loomed like the chalk cliffs of Dover. We could even see the seas breaking on Old Field Point and the Smithtown shore, although the Sound was nearly ten miles wide here. But this did not surprise me much, for a few years before, I had been on some of the high land of Block

Island on a clear November day when all the land to the eastward stood up like a topographical model. Cuttyhunk, Nasha-
wena, and Gay Head were gigantic headlands, and Buzzards Bay
and its environs were clearly visible, although they are many
miles over the horizon. It had been my experience that these
days of looming headlands foretold a storm of some severity
and, in fact, they now did, as we shall soon see. We made good
progress that day, so by midafternoon the Long Island coast
reappeared, and at sunset the high land on Orient Point was
abeam. The sun made a lee set in a dark cloudbank, which its
dying embers lit up like distant mountain ranges, and in the
twilight Plum Island reflected the last beams of the setting sun.
Soon the many lighthouses of this region came into being, one
after the other, and we told them off the chart to amuse ourselves. Right ahead was the lightship of Bartlett Reef; the powerful light on Little Gull Rock was on our forward starboard
beam, and off to the eastward were the lighthouses of Race
Rock, North Dumpling, and Seaflower Reef. We had a strong
head tide here and the wind was falling, so that by the time we
rounded Bartlett's Reef and stood up for New London, it was
pitch black but clear. How comforting it was to have the red
sector of New London light to guide us by the outlying reefs of
Goshen Point, for the cross tide and falling wind made me a bit
apprehensive, but as I had lived in New London a couple of
years, and with *Alerion*'s shoal draft, we took some short cuts
and soon entered the harbor, where we came to anchor off the
Scott Wrecking Company and a short way southwest of Powder
Island.

I think it was near ten at night, and we had been sailing some
fourteen hours and covered maybe sixty miles. I was dead tired
so, after putting my friend on the beach, I put my oilskin on
over my overcoat and turned in all standing with the jib for a
coverlet and the boat cover for a mattress, but I lost con-
sciousness almost instantly and, in fact, slept so soundly that,
although a bitter cold northeast storm broke that night, I was
entirely unaware of it until awakened in the morning by the
inner man grumbling with a certain rolling and rumbling, for we
had not had any supper the night before.

As I was already clad for the elements, it was a matter of
minutes to land on a small, sandy beach dead to leeward, where
I pulled the tender far above high-water mark and walked to the

city. There I hired a room and bath in a hotel where I was known. How good that hot tub felt, for there is nothing like a hot soaking to warm up one who has been chilled to the marrow. After donning a new suit of underclothes, which I had purchased on the way up, and eating a three-course breakfast, I felt like facing the world again. So, after buying a shave, I sallied forth to visit friends who judged people by other qualities than their clothes. One was a skilled watchmaker who was rebuilding an English chronometer: the other was a model maker making a fine model of Hendrik Hudson's *D-Halvemaen.*

Well, the northeaster blew for about three days, but I knew the *Alerion* was laying to a hand-forged Herreshoff anchor with a practically unused anchor warp. Now, Patient Reader, I have taken you around Robin Hood's barn a couple of times, and if you care to continue I will take you for a sail—and it was a sail.

Finally one morning it broke clear, with only a few fleecy clouds overhead such as you would see at Bermuda, and I hurriedly got under way. It must have been a lull near the storm center and the May storm at that. Well, I had only gone a few miles and was entering Fisher's Island Sound when, looking back over New London, I saw the sky was making up with some lead-colored clouds. Soon these clouds seemed to churn around and show movement. We were about abreast of Seaflower lighthouse with a fair tide carrying us to the eastward and a very light breeze. I doused all sail, took off the jib and replaced it with a small storm jib, and put the last reef in the mainsail (and the *Alerion* was very deep reefed for winter sailing in Bermuda). At first the wind came from the west, and only moderate, and I felt a fool for reefing so deeply, but it soon hardened to a whitecap breeze, so with the tide back of us, we rushed through the sound and soon were in the Narrows of Watch Hill, which is a fearful-looking stretch of water when a southeast swell is meeting an eastgoing tide. Well, we gritted our teeth and shot through and soon were breasting the easterly groundswell outside.

Now the flaws of wind, as they struck, had some power and bowled us along at a fine clip. The dark clouds were now overhead but were breaking up into sections, each succeeding puff seeming stronger than the last and making the *Alerion* quiver all over as they struck. This was one of those spring days when "horse manure blizzards" course down the city streets and the pedestrians pull the brims of their hats over their weather eye to

"Dark clouds were now overhead."

ward off the flying cinders and splinters. But out here it was quite different. One had a queer feeling of lonely recklessness— not a thing was in sight on the water, and only occasionally a gull could be seen having obvious trouble with his ailerons as he careened over one side, then the other. We were traveling along at a crazy rate, with the wind over our after quarter, and this long stretch of beach seemed to glide by in no time at all as the dark shadows of the clouds coursed on before us. The ground-swell was increasing as we worked to the eastward, and I began to be quite apprehensive about what it might be off Point Judy and determined to make for the breakwater there, but when we got there, there came a slight lull and I thought we could make it, so, keeping well offshore to avoid breaking seas, we rounded the tall light buoy. But Neptune was putting on a demonstration and shouldering up great, greenish gray hills, which fell in all directions as they met the eastgoing tide off the point. On shore I could see the men running between the lifesaving station and the boat shed, and I could well imagine their thoughts as they said, "What − − fool is out there today?"—and I was sorry for this, for old Captain Kenyon was a friend who since, alas, has passed over the bar where the lifeboats ne'er return.

Well, as we rounded up on our northeast course for Newport, a great gray-bearded comber appeared astern, and as it rose back of us, our tender, as if scared of this apparition, darted up abreast of us, so we went through the smother together. I then bent on her painter a line about fifteen fathoms long so she now trailed far astern and, in fact, was out of sight most of the time. Now this region is the rightful domain of the South West Wind, and he resented the intrusion that the northeaster had made and the northwester was now making. So, marshaling his legions, the sky to the so'thward took on an ominous look. About where Clay Head on Block Island would be, there appeared a luminous sector like a sundog or the colorless base of a rainbow. Now deploying his forces in formations of company straight into line, in a vast, unwavering front from Gay Head to Montauk, the South West Wind swept all before him. If one had been on a high cliff looking down, this battle of the elements would have been awe-inspiring indeed, but down here there was no hope for escape, and as the southwester rushed down on us, it was heralded first by a rustling noise, then a hissing like ten thousand pythons. As it struck us, the *Alerion* staggered and fell forward, but her backstays held and, raising her bow and shaking off the water forward, she started on a mad rush, throwing great wings of spray out before her. The helmsman, like one on a runaway horse, could guide but not control her. Onward we rushed toward the northeast, where all the universe seemed moving. As each succeeding swell rose under us and we reached its crest, the wind sang like the recurring strong music in *Erlkonig,* and as we settled down into the valleys, the higher notes in the rigging sounded like the child in his refrain seeing the Erlking.

The sun now brought his power to bear and pierced the clouds to the northward. A shaft of light came down out of the gloom. Whale Rock appeared as the seas hurled themselves half-way up its lighthouse. The send of each sea threw us onward and, as the combing crest rushed by, the centerboard and rudder hummed and chattered.

Now she yaws and the reefed boom end trails in the water. Now, with a crazy reel, she rights and the boom saws upward. How long can spar and sail stand this strain? There is no time to think of that, only hold her head to the northward. Steady now, keep your eyes always forward. I am beginning to tire with the strain and have long since thought the tender gone. How strange it seems to feel so indifferent—that beautiful tender I handled so carefully on the beach at New London. But all out to leeward now stretches that rockbound coast of Rhode Island, a seething cauldron of broken water. Onward we rush. The rocks come closer—Beaver Tail, Kettle Bottom Rock. I'm glad I am alone. If anything parts, we are goners.

Brenton's Reef Lightship now comes abeam. How different she looks than in the summer. But the seas are smaller! We head for Castle Hill. A miracle has happened—we rush on over smooth water, the groundswell has gone, the sun comes out. To the northwest, the legions of the West Wind are piled up in white columns. That stretch of water from Point Judy to Newport seemed minutes rather than the hour it probably was. But our troubles were not over. As we made the entrance opposite the Dumplings, a white-plumed knight with dark under-trappings, a venturesome vanguard of the North Wind, decided to make a last onslaught. Down he came, casting his dark shadow before him, making the bay feather-white in his fury. Fortunately for me, this was some distance ahead, but right in his path were a tug and three barges. The squall had somehow got them tangled, and the tug was making frantic signals with her whistle, short blasts of steam that could be seen but not heard. Now as they straightened out, they reached nearly across this narrow channel, for the shores are bold on both sides. To weather them we would have to tack, and to pass to leeward endangered a gybe. In this heavy wind I didn't want to do either, but reasoning that the leeward barge would soon pull ahead, I bore off as broadly as I dared and very slowly the barge did pull ahead, but as I gazed around her stern, the back wind threw the sails to windward so violently that the boom struck the weather backstay. Out again it went, and now we shifted our course to nearly north up the bay, so I had to turn around to haul in the mainsail.

Much to my surprise, there was the tender about a hundred feet astern, dancing on the end of her deadwood, with an expression like a terrier who has followed its master through all hell and high water. Ever since that moment, I have loved the tenders built from her model.

It was a close reach up the bay, and the sail was wet down to the gaff jaws. The flying spray from our weather quarter drumming a tune on the mainsail, we passed Sandy Point and headed for Hog Island light. There was some broken water here, but it seemed tame beside Point Judy. I was getting tired and numb, but the thought that not much more spray would thrum on my sou'wester cheered me on till we entered the harbor. The wind was still blowing great guns, so I reached well to the weather of the wharf, the home of *Alerion*, the young eagle. Then we luffed into the wind to lower the sail, for we were to make the last rush under bare poles.

As we shoot in the wind, the mainsail splits about one foot above the reef earing or cringle. Around we spin, with the halliards bowing to leeward. Now we round up under the lee of the stone wharf and shoot to windward. How good this shelter feels as we make fast to the spring line. As I climb up the ladder, I realize how dead tired I am, for we have sailed fifty-two nautical miles in a little over eight hours. There has been no time to eat, or a minute to light a pipe, and as I walk up the street, the land rocks and rolls on before me. How good it is to put on dry clothes and sit without bracing.

Often in life the pleasantest moments are in anticipation, but the recollections of that sail have always been a great pleasure. So the moral of this story, if any, is: Be careful how you put to sea in the springtime.

The Alerion is 26 feet overall, 21 feet 9 inches on the water, 7 feet 7 inches beam, 2 feet 5 inches draft. She was designed and built by the Herreshoff Manufacturing Company, and is now preserved at Mystic Seaport, Mystic, Connecticut.

The Dry Breakers

It is nearly twenty years ago now since I slept on the Dry Breakers, and like many another thing in past life, it all seems fantastic.

The Dry Breakers are two clumps of barren rocks situated about three and a half miles east of Marblehead Harbor, and although there are many small rocky islands about Marblehead, the Dry Breakers have seemed to me much the wildest and most desolate of them all. While most of the other ten or so islands or rocks are difficult to land on, I have visited most of them in a very strongly built double-paddle canoe, and several of them in all four seasons of the year. However, few people land on the Dry Breakers, simply because on the southeast side the sea is generally breaking, and on all the other sides the surrounding bottom is so strewn with boulders and ledges that, excepting to the lobstermen, they seem nearly unapproachable.

At a normal high tide the Dry Breakers are but a small clump of boulders, but at low tide their area (which is extremely irregular) would amount to several acres. This desolate clump of rock is called Dry Breakers because parts of them are usually some eight or ten feet above water. But in a winter storm, the waves course over them so freely that from the mainland this region looks like a fiercely boiling cauldron of white water three-quarters of a mile long by half a mile wide.

About half a mile east of here is another ledge of rocks, but under water, called Inner Breakers. Still farther east, about a mile distant from the Dry Breakers, are the Middle Breakers, which have a spindle on them and fairly deep surrounding water. From here to the southward lie the Outer Breakers, shoaling up to three feet at low water. If a very low tide should reveal the bottom of this region, it would appear like a veritable shark's mouth, with row upon row of rocky teeth. But perhaps the most remarkable rock formation is Half Way Rock. This pinnacle rock rises sheer from fairly level bottom one hundred feet below the surface and extends above the water perhaps fifty feet more, and I must say it seems much more than that when you are up on it. The sides of Half Way Rock go down very abruptly, so that vessels of considerable draft can approach it within a few yards.

One of the local traditions is that in old times a new vessel or fishing boat should pass close to this rock and toss up on its seamed surface a coin or two for good luck—a sort of toll, contribution, or votive offering to the aquatic gods of this region, which they have good reason to fear. I have been told by the local old timers that even English coins of colonial times had been found here, but this I doubt very much, for in a winter storm the seas mount to the very top of this rock and must scour it thoroughly. On my visit to the rock, not even a modern coin was seen, but perhaps I was so intent with holding on with all fours that I missed them. However, even today few Marblehead sailors will pass the rock without trying to cast a coin up on it.

On the east side of Half Way Rock is a steep ravine almost perpendicular, and when the waves of an easterly storm strike this concave wall, they spurt upward as much as two hundred feet, mostly in spray, which is an interesting spectacle even from the mainland, three and a half miles away. Another tradition of Half Way Rock told by old timers is that many years ago a hand liner (a lone man in a dory) who was fishing in that neighborhood lost one of his oars and was being blown out to sea near nightfall. By dint of hard paddling with the remaining oar, he made the rock and succeeded in clambering up its steep sides to the top, where he spent the night. This man, so the story goes, had jet-black hair the day before this experience, but the next day when he was taken off by a passing fisherman, his hair was snow-white, and when he got back to shore, some did not recognize him. But I suppose all rocks and small islands along our coast have their local traditions, so I will not bore the reader with any more of them.

Just why at the time I should have wanted to sleep on one of these rocky islands I can't quite remember, but it may have been that I was fed up with the town and wanted a change. To be sure, the town had its art club, but about the only art that they practiced was the art of handling the knife and fork, and the members' sole accomplishment seemed to be in pretending they were someone other than themselves. And while our historical society was in a fine old building, the dear old ladies who dominated it believed contradiction was the general object of conversation. But the principal interest of the town, among old and young alike, was the propagation of the genus Homo. Just why the townspeople's thoughts all radiated around this single matter I can't say, for the habits of this human animal, both in breeding and bartering, have not changed much in the last thousand years. Nevertheless, it so fascinated them that there was little time left over for other thought. The men couldn't tell one boat or yacht from another, and cared less. But if a couple, one male and one female, went out for a sail, the boat at once attracted attention. If a married man took someone else's wife out for a sail, then the boat or yacht would become notorious for several generations, while the poor boat in which the man and wife went sailing was lost in oblivion. It made no difference if the yacht had grace, quality, or ability. If she had not been manned by certain animals, she might as well never have existed. Don't think for a minute that the women of the town were much different, for from childhood to deathbed they too had this same wholly absorbing interest.

A neighbor of mine (a widow of about eighty summers) used to hurry through her housework so she could stand at the window all day to peer out to see who was going with whom. Most people have the curtains up when they want to look out, but not this one! She carefully drew the curtains all the way down, but by having one finger on the curtains at eye level, she arranged a peek hole, which certainly reported many strange incidences. Of course most of the neighborhood was well acquainted with her habits, but the curious lady received rather a shock one day when a young man of the town, who was somewhat of a blade and a wag, in passing her house and seeing the edge of the curtain flutter, turned around, faced the window, and took off his hat with a bow. It is said the edge of the curtain didn't flutter for two or three days after that, but firmly established habits are hard to break, and I am sure if you took a walk around the town today you would still see the edges of several curtains fluttering.

So you can well imagine I gave a sigh of relief as I shoved off from the shore on my way to visit regions where the breeding season was brief and where part of the year could be used for other purposes, and where there were species other than Homo sapiens. But there was one gauntlet I must run before being perfectly free. This was a public park by the edge of the harbor where there were benches for old codgers to sit for their all-day inspection of the bathing suits the girls were using that season. As only one cane was raised in derision as I passed, I could see that I was not distracting their attention much. However, although nearly an eighth of a mile away from the cane, I could well imagine the conversation of the cane's owner as he pointed at me and said to his neighbor, "You see him? He's atryin' to get drownded." For it never would have occurred to the owner of the cane that one might like to see the sun set from different surroundings, or be in places where the genus Homo could not be seen.

I had chosen for this lonely adventure a night near the full moon, and in the fall equinox, when the days and nights were about the same length. As I cleared the harbor and headed out to the eastward, I experienced the thrilling sensation of complete detachment, which to me and several other singlehanders seems a pleasant contrast to being continually under the restraint, necessary on shore, to appear normal. So I whistled, sang, and laughed as loudly as I could. This did not seem at all strange to the seagulls and tern, which were doing just the same thing. In fact, they seemed to come all the closer, and instead of saying, "This seems a strange fellow," they appeared to say, "We are glad to see one of you dumb creatures who can enter into the joy of living; one who can express his joy by screaming as loudly as the rest of us." On shore these expressions would be looked upon as heresy by the old women of both sexes, for to have expressed a joy in life after it had been created seemed to them quite sinful. Instead of being an exertion, the three-mile paddle was merely exhilarating.

One of the joys of these excursions was the extreme

L. Francis Herreshoff's double-paddle canoe.

simplicity of the equipment, for my conveyance consisted principally of two rather nicely shaped parts, one the canoe and the other the paddle, and experience has shown that neither would give trouble or break down if carefully handled. The paddle itself, we might say, was of one piece (or several pieces glued into one) and shaped so that every curve was for some well-thought-out reason, and thus it gave pleasure to handle. The canoe was of lapstrake construction, planked and framed, of nearly the same strength as a light yacht tender. Her model was that of an elongated lifeboat. She had watertight bulkheads at both ends and a white oak keel about one and one-half inches deep, shod with brass the full length. On each side of the keel were two chafing strips of lance wood, for this canoe had been planned for landing on these rocky islands even if there was some sea running.

As I approached the Dry Breakers, the groundswell was running in from the southeast, and this made it necessary to approach from the northwest, which brought me over a bottom with a strange but dreadful fascination for me, for one after another we would pass over submerged boulders, perhaps four or five feet below the surface, that looked for all the world like great aquatic monsters moving back and forth as the undertow with its motion carried the canoe about. Now and then a ribbon of kelp would surge up like a dorsal fin or a tentacle of the moving monster below me. Not only was I one of the most timorous souls that had ever ventured on the water, but for some years I had acquired the sailors' instinct to bear away suddenly at the appearance of any bottom. So as these brown-colored monsters appeared below the surface, it was hard for me not to call out "Hard alee" or "Helm up" as they appeared either to windward or leeward of my course, and my arms would take two or three strokes with the paddle to avoid them before my reason would bring us back on our proper course.

As I neared the shore, the rocks below made surface eddies, and now and then a slight breaker, but although the canoe was now in greater danger, it was apparent that we and not the bottom were moving back and forth. The sun was low in the westward and it was quite calm on the leeward side of the island, so the various rocks showed their positions plainly by the wave formations above them, and we threaded our way right to shore without grounding. In fact there is a pool of quite deep water at a certain place that makes landing easy at certain tides. I climbed out of the canoe sideways on a shelf of rocks and, having the painter in hand, had her high and dry before the groundswells had chafed her against the rocks.

Now I stripped the canoe of all her movable parts and para-phernalia, which to be sure were not much weight, and took them to the highest point of the rocks, which, as has been said before, was not much above high water. Then I dragged the canoe on her metal keel over the boulders to the same spot and blocked her firmly in place with driftwood, which is usually plentiful on these rocks. I suppose now the reader will wonder what I did for supper, for some people are quite panic-stricken if caught without a galley with six feet of headroom and enough pots and pans to make them a galley slave. But I can assure you that in this case a very good supper was had without washing a pan, for I had brought along a rather large cocktail shaker and the necessary things to put in it, which were some eggs, milk, malted milk, brown sugar, and, last but not least, some old New England rum. When these good things are properly proportioned and well shaken, they become an eggnog that not only restores one to vigor and happy thoughts almost at once, but is nearly as sustaining as a three-course meal, particularly if it is taken slowly while munching some hardtack.

I don't want the reader to think that I consider rum necessary with all meals, for I very seldom take it that way on shore. Nevertheless, I have found rum one of the most compact of all foods for a canoe trip and one that never spoils. However, I always measure it out most carefully, believing it to be as dangerous as gunpowder if two charges are taken when only one is called for.

By now the sun had set, but at that time of year there was nearly an hour of twilight, which I used in preparing my bunk in the canoe. This consisted chiefly in blowing up an air mattress, which not only covered most of her bottom but in the forward and after parts of the cockpit curled up nearly to her deck. (It was one of those tubular air mattresses that can lie on quite an uneven surface.) Needless to say, the mattress had to be laid out below the deck before inflation, but this was not difficult to do, as her cockpit extended to the after bulkhead. I then spread one small blanket over the air mattress, put the other blanket, folded lengthwise, at one side, while on the other side was my musette bag containing such comforts as a 44-caliber revolver, the bottle of rum, and several small knickknacks. The canoe had a nice-fitting canvas cover, which snapped down over several buttons outside the coaming, so that I now had a snug, warm, and watertight home to crawl into, which I soon did, for as I straightened up and looked around me, I was almost overcome by the dreary and mournful surroundings. Though I had spent many nights afloat singlehanded, I had never had such a sensation of loneliness before. In fact, I nearly became panic-stricken and considered launching the canoe and escaping from the dreadful place as soon as possible, but my better judgment made me realize that the attempt would now really be dangerous.

By this time the gulls, which no doubt I had kept from their favorite rookery, began settling around the rocks with a sad sort of croaking noise and an occasional strange squawk. The tide had risen quite high and the seas, as they broke on the rocks not a hundred feet away, sang a mournful dirge as they slowly surged in with a low moan and then receded with a gurgling noise, at times rolling a few stones along with them, which added to the uncanny noises of the desolate place. "My," thought I, "what a comfort it would be to have a dog with me," for it is only at such times that man appreciates his best friend. Then I thought of building a fire for its cheer, but knowing this might make people on Bakers Island think that someone was marooned on the Dry Breakers, and they might risk their lives or damage their boats, I reluctantly decided to go without a fire and instead shamefacedly crawled into the canoe and pulled the canvas cover over the cockpit, took a good stiff nightcap, and turned in.

But I could not sleep. The lonely surroundings were almost too much for me, and I began to think that it was nice to have Homo sapiens nearby in the nighttime, even if their number did seem overpowering on shore in the daylight. Then it occurred to me that I had been in the habit of spending my evenings reading, and this melancholy mood might be partly the result of discontinuing that habit, and I then wished I had brought something to read and had a light to see by. In fact, at that moment I was solely depressed, when it occurred to me that there was some reading matter on board for, strange to say, in my musette bag was a very small New Testament that in the past I had opened at times to read a few lines as I lay in the sunlight on these rocky islands. I cannot say I ever quite understood the meanings of its many short sentences, but somehow the construction of the sentences and the quaint words had had a soothing effect that made me more appreciative of my ' surroundings.

So I now opened the little book at random and, scratching a match on the underside of the deck, read this sentence, "Man shall not live by bread alone," and the match went out, leaving me again in the darkness. I began now to ponder on its meaning, and this thread of thought so absorbed my attention that the moaning of the sea and my lonely surroundings were nearly forgotten. Then I thought of the people on shore, all absorbed with the propagation of the species and stuffing themselves with bread. Surely this cannot be life in its full as the seagulls know it. Surely such an existence is futile. And to go through the process of dying without first truly living seemed unfair. What then can be the secret that makes the gulls so happy in the sunlight? Can they have a higher appreciation of beauty than we do? Perhaps. Or is it simply the contrast of the warmth of the sunlight after their gloomy night vigil on these drear rocks? For none are as appreciative of life as those who have recently nearly lost it. None, perhaps, can as truly appreciate the sunrise as he who has passed through dark hours.

With these thoughts, I raised the canvas cover and looked

around me. The moon had risen while I meditated, and the scene now had quite changed. The moon was almost white in color as it pierced the eastern haze, and in contrast, the rocks were black, the sea dark gray, excepting in the path to the moon, where it shimmered in white wavelets, the whole making a symphony in black and white whose cold beauty nearly overcame me. The wind had died out and the bell buoy to windward tinkled a languid tune, while off to the eastward the occasional groan of a whistling buoy could be heard. It is said that the full moon affects people's senses, disturbing some and calming others, but to me at that time, in those surroundings, it seemed delightfully intoxicating, and as I gazed at the moon, the spirit seemed to detach itself from the body and float off to dance on the white wavelets, defying space and time. I could see that some of the seagulls at the edge of the rocks were affected by the moon and were standing up balancing on one foot and then the other, while the wiser ones, with their heads set back into their feathers, looked like round gray rocks.

Seeing all quiet around me, I again slid back into my nest, but when I next looked out, the moon had nearly reached its zenith and seemed to be scudding through a fine mist that nearly obscured it. The foghorn on Bakers Island now brayed its mournful note and the clammy dampness soon drove me back under the blankets. How I now longed for morning, but I knew its welcome rays could not be expected for several hours. I must have dozed or slept some time, for when I next peered out, there seemed a pearly grayness in the air, and even as I looked, it grew a lighter gray. And now the rocks around me could be faintly seen. If in the moonlight we had had a symphony of black and white, now we had one of gray and lighter gray. Perched on a rock a hundred yards away was a lone cormorant whose quaint silhouette in black and gray gave token of the coming light.

Even as I looked, the eastern sky had turned from gray to pink, the mists were parting as though an outer curtain had been drawn to reveal the change of scene. A hallowed stillness seemed to fill the air. The seagulls softly winged away and left the rocks to grayness and to me. Now distance gradually appears, pink, yellow, gray, and now a golden beam. And in the east the ocean's rim is seen. In rapid sequence the colors change until the complete spectrum is filled. Now faint, now clear they seem, when from the eastern sea the sun appears and lights the heavens with his golden beams. The day is here! I bow in reverence to the newborn day, stand up and stretch myself, and seem to say, "Yes, I must live by other things than bread this day." I wash my face beside the rocks and feel the morning breeze, take the same repast I had the night before, pack up, launch, and leave that rocky shore.

The offshore breeze has rippled all the bay. I paddle on and on until I get my second wind and feel as if I could paddle to eternity. I know the seagulls' secret now, the contrast of the night and day, the changing scenes, the pleasant exercise that chases gloomy thoughts away and attunes the mind and body pleasantly. All that day I paddled heedlessly around and visited many a rock, cove, and rivulet. I stretched my legs on sandy beach and climbed Eagle Island's forbidding shores. Thus was the day spent with the crow, the seagull, and the tern. Yes, spent in a state of transcendentalism where the body seemed untiring and the spirit full of song. Many times during the day did I meditate on how useless it was to attempt to live by bread alone without variety, contrast, and pleasant exercise, and it occurred to me that perhaps nothing was more conducive to gaining this exalted condition than the double-paddle canoe.

But the time finally came when I had to return home. When I approached the town, to within about a mile, I noticed a peculiar odor, and on approaching closer realized that it was the town itself that stank. When I had been there before, I had not noticed it, but after breathing the fresh air of the islands for some twenty hours, it seemed quite noticeable, and I recollected that it is said the Indians can recognize a settlement many miles away by its scent. Perhaps this perfectly virgin air to breathe is one of the things besides bread that is necessary to really live, and perhaps nothing is better than the double-paddle canoe to breathe it from, for the large sailboat with its cabin and galley never quite gets clear of the town air, and the powerboat and the steamer (excepting the weather side in a breeze) are not much better than the town.

When I arrived home in the late afternoon, I got myself some tea, ate some crackers and cheese, and decided that after lying down for a short rest I would get up and cook a good supper. But, strange to relate, when I awoke again, another day had dawned and there I lay with my shoes and clothes on. This time when I arose it was decided that not only bread, but bacon and eggs were quite essential to proper living. But my visit to the Dry Breakers had made me a better man, and in some way has helped me to be happier ever since, perhaps only by contrast.

Frostbiting

You college chaps in derby hats,
  Dropping in for dinghy chats
    and selling bonds,
You, too, in sweatshirt on the float,
  Dressed as if you owned a boat,
    Your days are done.

Young yacht brokers everywhere,
  Telling all the lies they dare,
    And cutting throats.
Designers on the sidewalk, too,
  Putting all the blame on crew
    But not their boats.

You crews of thirty meter square,
  Just learning how to swear,
    Your boat is dead.
And you in dinghy over there
  That sculls the boat 'most everywhere.
    Enough is said.

You parents down to see fair play,
　　Scared your child won't win today,
　　　　Your feet are cold.
You wise guy with the tiller there
　　You won't finish anywhere,
　　　　Your tricks are old.

You girls who sit on icy rails,
　　With dresses on to match the sails,
　　　　You think you're swish.
But soon we know you'll have to bail
　　Or sit around with icey tail,
　　　　Then home you'll wish.

　You jovial soul with megaphone
　　Your body up with gas is blown
　　　　We think you great.
　The worst boat of the lot has won
　　Now there will be lots of fun
　　　　You'll call it Fate.

A Midsummer Night's Sail

ACT I

It has been hot on shore today—very, very hot—and the dry west wind from over the freight yard seemed stifling. The rattle of coupling freight cars, the pant of air pumps were continuous. The sun beat down relentlessly 'til the roofs shimmered in the heat waves. As one looked out on all this inferno, he was apt to question if life were worthwhile. But now this evening, after supper, a gentle breeze draws in from the ocean. The sun has passed well into its westing; the garden comes to life: the Canterbury bells and phlox nod their approval; the cosmos stretch their fronds for cooler breathing; again the heliotrope gives off its fragrance. What an evening for a sail with an understanding friend, or an equally pleasant companion!

As we launch the sailing dinghy from the float, she, too, bobs with animation. The sails are set, the rudder hung; quietly we glide beyond the harbor, leaving the harbor noises—that terrible anchored motor cruiser with its charger and loudspeaker, its drunken party all hoping another drink will make them insensible to their boredom. Slowly we sail. The wind is lighter. The setting sun with slanting shadows paints with inky brush the westward shoreline, edging it with copper background. Now the heat of day is passing and the sky and sea are changing, like an artist mixing colors, slowly changing—always grayer. Darkness comes, the quawks fly by us. Silently we move by magic.

Far away the harbor lights are—far away that human cosmic. Quiet darkness all around us, soothing, restful, cooling darkness. Overhead the vaulted heavens weave the pattern of the evening. First the evening stars appearing, scattered far, of gilded color. The weft now grows with living progress, whiter, lesser stars appearing, 'til the studded jeweled heaven stretches all the way above us. Larger ships with crews and engines try for many days to get here, try for months and years together, try in calm and windy weather, but they never will arrive, not until the sail's revived. Sailing, ghosting through the night, like a Triton, spirit light; sleeping sails our curvéd wings are, guided by the distant North Star. Coolly swirls our silent wake, liquid stars the phosphorus makes. Far behind the land we're leaving; listen! that's a porpoise breathing. Slow beneath us moves the sea, slowly breathing, steadily. Now the magic spell is changing— toward the east the light is ranging. Now the rippling bow waves make silver shadows in our wake. Oh, oh, look—the moon is rising! Look, it moves, its shape is changing! Now a flattened orange 'til it's moved beyond the ocean's sill. Now a planished golden ball lighting all the eastern wall. Moonbeams dance across the sea, twisting, moving merrily, 'til a golden path is made; crossways through this path we wade, making sails in silver sheen in the dewy evening gleam. Far to leeward shadows play, mock our sail plan as they may; darting, twisting crazily.

Helmsman speaking: "What an evening this is for the fairies to be out!"

Crew: "What do you mean, 'fairies,' now?"

Helmsman: "I mean what they always have meant; the fairies are ageless. W. Shakespeare knew them well; hardly a play he wrote without them. They're in the folklore of all the countries. I thought, as you do, that they were a myth until I saw them."

Crew: "I guess you saw them through the neck of some bottle or other."

Helmsman: "Not at all, but as for seeing fairies—'none are as blind as those who will not see'—for the fairies only show them- selves to those who want to see them."

Crew: "What do you mean, 'want to see them'?"

Helmsman: "Well, just this—if the fairies should become visible to the two trollops who are spending the night on the motor cruiser, they would think they were having the heebie- jeebies or the delirium tremens again. But when they show

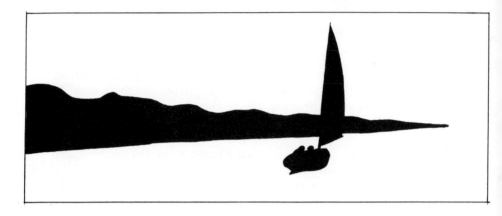

themselves to the poor little lame girl who lives back of the lighthouse (the one who had infantile paralysis), well, she just loves it and can hardly wait for evening to come so they will dance for her."

Crew: "How do you know about that?"

Helmsman: "Her mother showed me some drawings she had made of them dancing on the foot of the bed."

Crew: "Well—?"

Helmsman: "Yes, the drawings were quite well done. There was little Pear Blossom in her ballet dress; and Cobweb, too, that elfish fellow who in Shakespeare's time hung a pearl on each cowslip's ear. How should she know about them if she had not seen them?"

Crew: "Helmsman, you argue well for the fairies and this is passing strange, for I had always thought of you as a realist who dealt in cubic feet, pounds, and wind pressure. But methinks 'tis time to start for home. I thought I saw a flash of lightning toward the westward."

Helmsman: " 'Tis but some belated trolley car or city's gas retort. But I agree, 'tis time to fetch about; the wind seems going, the moon quite high."

ACT II
Scene: The same, but wind light over the port quarter.

The moon now shines with magic spell, reflected in each moving swell. The undulating golden light bathes all the sea this eerie night. The crew now nods, he stretches out, a mortal soul without a doubt. The helmsman then begins to feel the moon's attraction at his wheel; those reoccurring tides of thought that other moons and seas had taught. It moved him 'til, quite fancy free, he peopled all the deck and sea. Each moonbeam turned a fairy elf; in mystic thought he lost himself.

The wind has gone, the sea is calm; the helmsman dreams, no thought of harm. He does not see the darkening cloud the western sky does all enshroud. At last he sees a distant flash—to life he comes with instant dash. He wakes his crew with orders sharp—"Strike down the mast, get out the oar; we're headed for the nearest shore."

Why strike the mast, why hurry so?" A flash more livid lights the west; he obeys commands and thinks it best. They lower the sail, take down the mast; they stow away and make all fast.

Act III
Scene: Crew at oars; Helmsman facing him.

Crew: "How now, Helmsman?"

Helmsman: "Oh, all right, but we may have an exciting adventure ahead of us."

Crew: "Adventure, nothing! It's only a passing summer squall with heat lightning."

Helmsman: "You can never tell how they may turn out. I would hate to be blown offshore with a strong nor'wester, or driven on one of these rocky islands in the dark and smash the boat."

Crew: "How far are we from the harbor?"

Helmsman: "Maybe two miles."

Crew: "You don't expect me to row this —— boat all that way?"

Helmsman: "No, we will take turns at the oars. Come now, we must work under the lee or east side of one of these islands before the squall strikes."

Vivid flashes light the sky, dark clouds roll up a headland high; thunder echoes from the western shore. The moon's eclipsed; it lights no more. Now falling from the darkened night, a jagged light shows up the rocks to starboard on our right. But now the coming rain blots out the shore. They trust in God and in their good ash oar. A seething sound is heard and then, before some icy pellets fall, a flash—a roar. The squall has struck. The rushing wind and rain come all in one like spindrift scudding o'er the main. They crouch down low and cannot see; spin around and broach the coming sea. The weather quarter raises in the blast, the crew's oar tangles with the unshipped mast. The helmsman puts the helm alee and grabs the bail to keep her free.

The rain comes down in torrents now, blots out all sight beyond the bow; the swirling darkness all around vibrates with a roaring sound. The rushing wind and pelting rain make trust in ashen oar all vain, and all planned action quite insane. Instead, like leaf in millrace caught, broadside to leeward they were brought. A sea makes up, it's choppy now; with motion sharp it jerks her bow, and all along the weather rail the flying spindrift cuts like hail.

No word is passed between them now, to bail her out their only vow; so, braced against the midship thwart, their instincts move them without thought. All tangled with the mast and sail they struggle on without avail. She settles aft a little now, the waves lap o'er her weather bow. But now a blinding ball of light shatters the arrangement of the night. That awe-inspiring thunder clap balanced the static with one loud crack. The wind grows light and veers around, the falling rain the sea beats down; the lightning flashes far alee, the rain lets up, they bail her free. At first a lonely western star is all they see, but twinkling soon the heavens make a clearing in the storm clouds' wake. Oh, look, the moon! At first through moving silver veils she shone, but soon in calm and stately grace that cool Selenic face looked down. The billowing storm clouds, piling high, in silver paint the eastern sky. The sea is calm.

The Helmsman speaks, he stretches first, "My God, I'm cold," said he. The Crew, stripped down to his undershirt, is wringing his clothes in the sea. "Of all the stirring plays I've seen, of tragedies and farce, this night has changed its cast the most and I thought it was my last."

ACT IV
Scene: Under oars again in a flat calm.

Before the storm the moon had turned the sea to liquid gold, but rising higher in the night she shinéd down with a silvery light—a shimmering whiteness cold. The high cloudbank to leeward sank and, moving toward the lee, it left the sea and heavens now as still as they could be. The moon had sped to overhead and, facing square the sea, divided all the firmament in perfect symmetry.

Quite out of sight in this bright light the small stars seemed to be. But shining faintly on their right Orion's sword they see.

The Dipper now, o'er starboard bow, its rim they faintly make, so this would bring the pole star well to starboard in their wake. With this outline they soon did find a guiding star to make. They rowed a while toward this western star and never a thing did see, 'til a breeze sprung up from under the shore and they hailed it merrily.

The mast was stepped, the sail run up and now in the warmth of the lee, they sailéd on in a fragrant breeze that heeled them gentilee. This offshore breeze from rain swept trees and kelp along the shore—how good it smelt, for they had felt that they were still afar. Broad on their beam the breeze did seem and it sped them up the sound, 'til they could see the lighthouse top and all the islands 'round.

The bay was lit with silv'ry light, the moon o'erhung the town. The outer harbor rocks were strewn with streakéd silver brown. The lighthouse now is past the bow, the town is at their side, and through the shadows of the wharves they slowly seem to slide. They find the float and haul her out and finally step ashore; so, gentle reader, say—"Thank God there is no more."

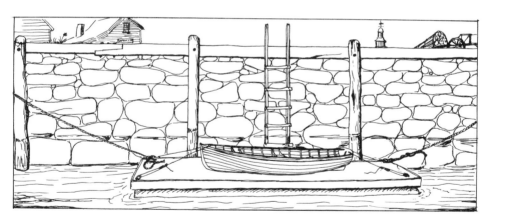

Index

FAMILY FARE OFF PEAK TRAINS

2 OR **1** Number of Pass Holders

5	4	3	2		No. of Passengers

OUT	IN

SOUTH SHORE	NORTH SHORE

**MASSACHUSETTS BAY
TRANSPORTATION AUTHORITY**

PASSENGER'S RECEIPT
NOT GOOD FOR PASSAGE EXCEPT FAMILY FARE

FORM A	Series 7

- CHILD
- SENIOR CITIZEN
- SPECIAL NEEDS
- STUDENT

BOSTON

	ZONE 1	☐	☐
	ZONE 2	☐	☐
	ZONE 3	☐	☐
	ZONE 4	☐	☐
	ZONE 5	☐	☐
	ZONE 6	☐	☐
	ZONE 7	☐	☐
	ZONE 8	☐	☐
	ZONE 9	☐	☐
	ZONE 10	☐	☐
	ZONE 11	☐	☐
	SPECIAL	☐	☐
	SURCHARGE	☐	

17	1	JAN
18	2	FEB
19	3	MAR
20	4	
21	5	APR
22	6	MAY
23	7	JUNE
24	8	JULY
25	9	AUG
26	10	
27	11	SEPT
28	12	OCT
29	13	
30	14	NOV
31	15	DEC
	16	

BOOK No.
000523
CHECK No.
4

SHOW FARE COLLECTED

$ Tens	1	2	3	4	5	6	7	8	9
Dollars	1	2	3	4	5	6	7	8	9
¢ Tens	1	2	3	4	5	6	7	8	9
Cents			0